TRADE, TAXES, AND TRANSNATIONALS

Kent Higgon Hughes

TRADE, TAXES, AND TRANSNATIONALS

International Economic Decision Making in Congress

PRAEGER

PRAEGER SPECIAL STUDIES • PRAEGER SCIENTIFIC

Library of Congress Cataloging in Publication Data

Hughes, Kent H
   Trade, taxes, and transnationals.

   Bibliography: p.
   Includes index.
   1. United States--Foreign economic relations.
2. United States--Commercial policy. 3. International economic relations. I. Title.
HF1455.H79   382.1'0973   79-13795
ISBN 0-03-051111-9

Published in 1979 by Praeger Publishers
A Division of Holt, Rinehart and Winston/CBS, Inc.
383 Madison Avenue, New York, New York 10017 U.S.A.

Printed in the United States of America

To my mother, Gwladys Higgon Hughes and the
memory of my father, John Kenneth Hughes

ACKNOWLEDGMENTS

The author is indebted to a considerable number of scholars who added thoughts and criticism to various drafts. Because International Economic Decision Making in Congress: Trade, Taxes, and the Transnationals builds on an earlier dissertation, the author owes a special debt of gratitude to his dissertation committee. Murray Weidenbaum, Professor of Economics at Washington University and director of the Center for the study of American Business urged the author to pursue his interest in an economist's view of international economic legislation. David Felix, Professor of Economics, Washington University, gave generously of his ideas and critical advice. Werner Hochwald, now Professor emeritus of economics, Washington University, also offered his support and pushed the author to keep consideration of international economic decision making in historical perspective.

Many colleagues and friends read various drafts of the book. Special thanks to Virginia Sammon of the General Accounting Office, Louis Krauthoff II of the Joint Economic Committee, Jane Gravelle of the Congressional Research Service, Warren Farb of the Department of Commerce and Henry Canaday of R. Shriver Associates. The reviewers are to be credited with many improvements in the text while the author retains responsibility for persisting in any errors that remain.

Keeping in mind that for want of good editorial assistance the book can be lost, the author extends his heartfelt thanks to Linda S. Kline of the Congressional Research Service and Patsy Ormond Thompson of the Joint Economic Committee.

In the course of research for this book, the author spoke to many individuals who were actively involved in the Congressional debate over foreign trade and investment. Although they remain anonymous throughout the text, the author is deeply in their debt.

CONTENTS

LIST OF TABLES

TRADE,
TAXES, AND
TRANSNATIONALS

CHAPTER 1

INTRODUCTION

Passage of the Trade Expansion Act of 1962 (TEA-62)[1] culminated almost 30 years of trade liberalizing legislation. This act received broad backing for organized labor, big business, major farm organizations, and consumer groups.[2] Less than a decade later the Congress was faced with a series of protectionist proposals that had strong political backing.

In no small measure the new pressures on Congress reflected the gradual decline of America's preeminence in the international economy, a decline that had been underway throughout the 1960s. The emergence of the European Economic Community, the European Free Trade Association, and a resurgent Japan had markedly shifted the balance of economic power. Chronic U.S. balance of payments deficits—the product of many political and economic forces—proved to be increasingly intractable. A fixed exchange rate and steadily rising export prices combined to erode the long-standing U.S. surplus in merchandise trade.

During this era a number of American industries experienced severe import competition. Not surprisingly, these industries were the labor intensive—shoes, textiles, consumer electronics—and the technologically stagnant—steel and autos. Suffering under existing trade policies, many of these industries sought some type of administrative or legislative relief. Voluntary curbs on cotton textiles[3] and steel[4] imports were partial victories, but many industries received no political protection from economic pressure.

As import competition continued to worsen, affected industries and unions increased their political activities. Although multilateral trade negotiating authority expired in 1967, trade-related pressures kept President Johnson from seeking anything but a very modest trade bill. His Trade Expansion Act of 1968 was not even reported out of the House Ways and Means Committee.[5]

1

President Nixon's Trade Act of 1969 was an equally modest proposal. [6] What emerged from the Ways and Means Committee, however, was a bill with potentially radical consequences for American trade policy. The demands of textile and shoe manufacturers were met with specific quota provisions. In addition, the bill promised tariff or quota relief for a wide range of goods depending upon the presence of economic injury and the degree of import penetration. [7]

Although the Trade Act of 1970 passed the House of Representatives, it never reached the president's desk. Long delayed in the Senate Finance Committee, it was eventually added to a series of amendments to the Social Security Act. Encumbered by controversial proposals for welfare reform and catastrophic health insurance, the entire measure died on the Senate floor at the close of the 91st Congress (1970).

The Kennedy and Johnson administrations were not unmindful of the growing problems in the foreign economic sphere, but they opted for small adjustments rather than pressing for any structural reform. Basically they grappled with the growing balance of payments deficit by seeking to reduce the outflow of U.S. capital. The interest equalization tax, the first voluntary and then mandatory foreign direct investment program, and the voluntary restraints on federal reserve banks became the principal vehicles. [8] It was the Nixon administration that brought major change.

On August 15, 1971, President Nixon simply closed the U.S. gold window. In addition to effectively devaluing the U.S. dollar, Nixon imposed an across-the-board 10 percent surtax on imports. In one day, Nixon had brought an end to the Bretton Woods agreements that had structured postwar international monetary relations.

Despite the promised benefits of Nixon's New Economic Policy, the protectionist pressures on Congress did not abate. In September 1971 Senator Vance Hartke (D-Ind.) and Congressman James Burke (D-Mass.) introduced the Foreign Trade and Investment Act of 1972. [9] Better known as the Burke-Hartke Bill, the Foreign Trade and Investment Act of 1972 was widely regarded as the protectionists' ultimate if not finest flower.

The bill presented a clear challenge to established U.S. foreign economic policy. Instead of granting the president new authority to negotiate further reductions in tariff levels, Burke-Hartke would have imposed mandatory quotas on all competitive imports. In place of general support for U.S. foreign direct investments, Burke-Hartke would have radically altered the tax treatment of foreign-source income. The tax changes were proposed with an eye to discouraging the continued outflow of U.S. capital for foreign direct investment and imposing a serious fiscal burden on existing U.S. direct investments abroad. In addition the president would have been empowered to act directly to stem the outflow of both U.S. capital and technology.

The particular interest of the economist, however, is not so much in the Draconian nature of the Burke-Hartke solutions as in the fact that the bill was extensively argued and considered on economic grounds. Proponents of Burke-Hartke quite explicitly contended that the rapid spread of technology, the existence of the multinational firm, and the emergence of large trading blocs had repealed the law of comparative advantage. And, for the first time, the U.S.-based multinational firm was put under legislative attack. Advocates of Burke-Hartke argued that the growth of direct foreign investment by the multinationals had reduced capital investment in the United States, cost Americans thousands of jobs, and threatened to erode the entire U.S. industrial base.

Strongly backed by the AFL-CIO, Burke-Hartke dominated the foreign trade and investment debate in Washington for the better part of two years. Multinational businesses, major business organizations, the national press, and other interest groups responded to the various economic arguments made in behalf of Burke-Hartke. Faced with strong and usually contradictory pressures from labor and business, individual congressmen were forced to deal with the issues raised by the Burke-Hartke Bill. Congressmen began to speak out on the bill, congressional committees conducted hearings, and business groups commissioned studies designed to rebut labor's contentions about the economic impact of existing foreign trade and investment policies.

The free trade alliance between labor and business had been eroding for many years. With the introduction of Burke-Hartke, labor moved into full combatant status with big (usually multinational) business over a broad range of international economic issues. The rift between business and labor has persisted throughout the 1970s. In part, labor's break with the free trade coalition was a product of economic circumstances. The very success of America's postwar reconstruction policies in Europe and Japan had created new economic rivals. As the dollar became progressively overvalued in the 1960s, both export-oriented and import-competing industries were put under greater pressure. By concentrating their export initiatives on particular products or industries, newer industrial powers forced more adjustment on the American economy than bilateral trade balances alone would suggest. In labor's view, the growing mobility of large American corporations threatened not only present and potential jobs but also the existing balance of power in collective bargaining.

The unsteady international economy of the 1970s has not been able to eliminate the pressures for restricting the free flow of goods or capital. It was hoped that the move toward a regime of flexible exchange rates would ease the problems of international economic adjustment and reduce international economic tensions. Flexible exchange rates have had their successes. The U.S. merchandise trade account moved from a deficit in 1971 and 1972 to a surplus in 1973, a turnaround in no small measure brought about by a devalued dollar. American exports became more competitive in international markets and Americans turned to domestic goods since it took more dollars to buy imports.

One of the difficulties with the Bretton-Woods system was that it put the burden of economic adjustment on the country with a deficit in its international payments. Flexible exchange rates have helped equalize that burden by threatening a surplus country with a virtually automatic loss of export markets unless the surplus country increased either its own imports or allowed more capital to flow overseas. From the perspective of 1979, it is hard to imagine how the Bretton Woods system of fixed exchange rates could have survived an era when domestic inflation rates and economic policies varied so widely among countries.

But despite admitted strengths, the flexible exchange rate system has not silenced the domestic critics of current American trade and investment policies. Why? Part of the answer lies in the fact that countries can and do intervene in foreign exchange markets to keep the value of their currency from rising or falling. The sharp fall in the value of the dollar in 1977 and 1978 was partly caused by Japanese purchases of dollars in 1976. If the Japanese had not intervened, the dollar would have declined earlier but more gradually. American goods would have become more competitive sooner, and the U.S. trade deficit would have been smaller.*

There have also been growing pressures for greater stability in the international value of the dollar from both our major trading partners and countries that have large dollar holdings. In late 1978 the Carter administration announced a massive intervention plan to stop what had become a precipitous drop in the international value of the dollar relative to the world's other major currencies. Domestic considerations were also involved in the Carter administration's decision to intervene, since dollar depreciation had gotten to the point where it imperiled the president's antiinflation program—particularly around a then-still-vague promise of a real wage insur-

---

*In January 1976 the signators of the International Monetary Fund (IMF) agreed on several amendments to the IMF Articles of Agreement. Among other changes, the IMF was given surveillance powers over exchange rate intervention. The hope was that the IMF could prevent the manipulation of an exchange rate for the unfair trade advantage of a particular country. It is still too soon to say if the IMF will be able to put more pressure for adjustment on surplus countries than they could under the old Bretton Woods system.

ance program. But the decision to support the value of the dollar despite large trade and current account deficits was also a clear recognition of the dollar's continued special role as the key international currency. However, to the extent America preaches flexible exchange rates, but still practices dollar stability by direct market intervention, it will slow international economic adjustment and add to domestic pressures to directly restrict trade and investment flows.

In any case, it would have been too much to expect exchange rates to shield the United States from the economic storms of the 1970s. The industrial world has not yet fully recovered from the decision of the Organization of Petroleum Exporting Countries (OPEC) to quadruple the world price of oil in 1973—a decision that added to the inflationary pressures still plaguing the United States and several other industrial powers, pushed energy-inefficient equipment into obsolescence, and contributed to the deepest recession in the post-World War II era.

Because some of the major oil producers had small populations and largely undeveloped economies, they generated huge merchandise trade and current account surpluses. Those surpluses meant a deficit for the rest of the world. And that deficit was passed around like a financial hot potato.

The industrial countries have been slow to recover from the 1974-75 recessions, and the United States has had the strongest and most protracted recovery of all the major industrial powers. For the past two years, the United States has grown consistently faster than most of its principal trading partners. Comparing 1977 growth rates for the United States, Canada, Japan, France, and Germany to the average growth rates achieved in the 1960-73 period, only the United States has exceeded (4.9 percent to 4.1 percent) its 1960-73 growth rate. The best performance in the remaining countries was less than half its 1960-73 average rate of growth. The slow growth abroad has been particularly troublesome for U.S. exports that are heavily concentrated in machine tools and other types of capital equipment.

The persistence of protectionist pressures to restrict the flow of goods and capital reflects far more than the limitations of flexible exchange rates and the slow recovery of the industrial world from the 1974-75 recession. The economic potential of the advanced developing countries has become an important source of apprehension for labor and a number of individual industries.* Several of the

---

*In Resolution No. 126 adopted at the 12th AFL-CIO Constitutional Convention in December 1977, the AFL-CIO called for repeal of the Generalized System of Preferences, which applies zero tariffs

developing countries are already active exporters to the American market[10] as well as important export markets for the United States.[11]

There is a growing consensus in the Congress and the country that the rest of the world does not play by the same set of economic rules. To many minds the failure of other countries to maintain an open trading system has been a major contributor to the record American trade deficits and the problems of adjustment in the international economic system as a whole. The result could be an increase in protectionist pressures.[12]

There has also been a gradual shift in the intellectual climate that makes restrictions on trade and investment more respectable than they were when labor first broke with the free trade coalition. A group of English economists has recently called for import controls as the best way to stabilize the British economy.[13] Leading American economists have suggested that an across-the-board surcharge or some other restriction on imports may be necessary to stabilize the international value of the dollar.[14] The controversy over Burke-Hartke and what became the Trade Act of 1974 stimulated a good deal of research on the labor view of international trade and investment. Some of that research has tended to support the labor view.[15]

The congressional debate over trade, taxes, and the transnationals provides a touchstone for the current conflict between major U.S. interest groups and is pregnant with implications for the future conduct of U.S. foreign policy. It also offers a rich opportunity to study congressional decision making at a crucial juncture in the design of foreign economic policy. More than most debates, it shows an important part of the public sector weighing the economic evidence and making up its public mind. And with the growing influence of Congress, its role in setting foreign economic policy warrants closer scrutiny by all observers.

Previous studies of economic decision making in Congress have generally stressed the strategies of group pressure, power relationships between competing factions, and the intricacies of congressional structure. Although this study will cover some of the same ground,

---

to exports of some goods from some developing countries. They also sought elimination of the Overseas Private Investment Corporation, which insures certain investments of multinational corporations in developing countries. See Statement of Rudy Oswald, Research Director, AFL-CIO, in the 1978 Economic Report of the President, Hearings before the Joint Economic Committee, Congress of the United States, 95 Cong. 2d sess., Part 2 (Washington, D.C.: U.S. Government Printing Office, 1978), pp. 386 and 387.

the emphasis is different. The principal focus will be on the economic impetus for major interest groups and the way in which the
economic arguments were presented to the Congress. A secondary
focus will be maintained on the manner in which Congress reacted
to the pressures of the interest groups, how Congress evaluated their
economic arguments, and what factors conditioned the final congressional decision. Throughout, there will be a heavy emphasis on
rational persuasion—on what the interest groups presented and how
Congress explored the different facets of the economic issues.

THE LITERATURE

There is an abundant and detailed economic literature that
seeks to explain the pattern of international trade and a not inconsider-
able literature that examines the matter of foreign direct investment.
Chapter 3 is devoted to a brief and selective survey of trade and
investment theory. Little of this material, however, focuses directly
on interest group behavior. There is Johnson's exploration of the
political economy of tariffs.[16] And Walter's attempt to explain the
origin of trade-related pressures.[17] In a historical context, Kindleberger suggested a link between English parliamentary reform and
subsequent repeal of the corn law.[18] More recently, Pincus has
sought to judge the effectiveness of industrial pressure groups in
determining the content of the Tariff Act of 1824.[19]

There is also a large and growing body of political science
literature on the role of groups in the congressional process.[20] At
least two of these have taken the making of foreign trade policy as
their subject. There is the early study of the Smoot-Hawley tariffs
done by Schattschneider[21] and the subsequent study of the Eisenhower
era reciprocal trade acts by Bauer, de Sola Pool, and Dexter (hereafter Bauer).[22] More recently, there has been a study of how the
large oil companies interacted with the congressional process.[23]

In many ways the Bauer book is the most direct precursor to
this effort. Explicitly eclectic in its theoretical approach, Bauer
saw Congress as a complex system of independent individuals who
were subject to a wide variety of interest group and other pressures.
But even here there is virtually no effort to place the interest group
behavior in the context of economic theory and only a limited attempt
to explore the nature and substance of the economic argumentation
involved.[24]

The general literature on Congress is quite extensive. Histor-
ians, political scientists, and journalists have all found the Congress
to be fertile and fascinating ground. In the past ten years, political
scientists have been particularly active in exploring the details of

the congressional process. Major pieces have been done on the House Appropriations Committee[25] and the House Ways and Means Committee.[26] Although Appropriations and Ways and Means make the bulk of the economic decisions in the House, neither of these studies paid any particular attention to the clash of major interest groups or to the economic issues involved. Rather, their principal concern was with power relationships and the social dynamics of small groups.

The more strictly economic literature on congressional behavior is extremely scant. Aside from Bailey's Congress Makes a Law, there is really very little.[27] Economists have done work on the overall decision-making process in the United States[28] and even have gone so far as to propose an economic theory of democracy.[29] The marginalist school of thought has invaded political science and applied itself to the logic of maximizing something other than profits. But none of these approaches has dealt with Congress as an institution or with decision making other than in the most abstract and general terms.[30]

The extensive literature on foreign trade and foreign direct investment theory does not focus on interest group behavior but does implicitly suggest a number of areas where labor and capital might be at economic odds. The actual clash of interests in the Congress and the economic deliberations of the Congress are a much more uncharted area. The voluminous literature on Congress contained much that was helpful but virtually nothing that suggested a model for studying the making of foreign economic policy in Congress. Faced with a similar mix of paucity amid apparent plethora, one current student of the congressional process likened the situation to that of "the man who has a large roll of dollars." The danger was that "we may deceive ourselves into thinking that the quantity of literature makes us rich, when in fact we are quite poor."[31]

THE STUDY

The study will follow the battle over trade, taxes, and the transnational corporations as a way of assessing the conduct of major interest groups and exploring the manner in which Congress reaches decisions in the area of international economic policy. Interest group behavior is frequently explained on a "shoe pinches" basis. Given the impact of domestic inflation, a fixed exchange rate, an emerging trade deficit, sharp increases in particular types of imports, and the marked growth in the direct foreign investments of U.S. firms, it is tempting to describe labor's foreign trade and investment position as a reaction to specific economic events. The study details many of these events and places them in the general context of the post-World War II Bretton Woods era.

The "shoe pinches" approach, however, need not be the only or necessarily the best guide to interest group behavior. The impact of foreign investment on the distribution of income between labor and capital provides an alternative and possibly a more enduring indicator of self-interest.

Foreign trade and foreign direct investment theory will be subjected to a brief and selective survey with an eye to its possible implications for interest group behavior. Most of the hypotheses derived from economic theory will be stated in terms of two factors of production—capital and labor. In evaluating the hypotheses, however, the major emphasis will be on the behavior of big labor (chiefly the AFL-CIO) and big business (especially the large multinational firms and the major business organizations) in the context of the foreign trade and investment debate. In predicting major interest group behavior, economic theory must be used with some particular caveats. The generally abstract nature of theory may make the leap to legislative affairs somewhat difficult. It is equally important to distinguish between the use of economic theory to explain the formulation of a position and its use to rationalize a position adopted for other, possibly more parochial, reasons.

Although an inviting and intriguing prospect, little attempt will be made to explore the inner workings of the interest groups. Questions about how the interest groups reached a particular decision or set their own house in order will be largely ignored. Rather, the focus will be on the economic impetus to interest group action, how the interest groups approached the Congress, what type of economic arguments they presented to the Congress, and what sort of analysis supported their stated economic views.

In addition to the emphasis on interest group behavior, there will be a secondary focus on the congressional assessment of the debate over foreign trade and investment. How did Congress weigh the economic evidence and evaluate the various economic arguments? Did the Congress act largely as a judge in an adversary proceeding or did Congress seek independent means to explore the positions of the major interest groups? None of this is to say that rational persuasion is the only or even the principal determinant of a legislative battle. Nor is it to suggest that the lobbyist's hand is never quicker than the researcher's eye.[32] It is enough to say that argumentation (not unlike money) does count.

The exploration of how Congress has wrestled with questions of foreign trade and investment is very much in the nature of an extended case study. And, like a case study, it is burdened with speculation and uncertainty. Both economic events and economy theory suggest certain hypotheses about major interest group behavior and this study will very definitely attempt to assess their validity. But even the economic hypotheses are a step into uncharted and possibly troubled waters. Overall, the study is much more a hypothesis-generating than a hypothesis-testing type of study. It is much more an "experiment of light" than an "experiment of proof."[33] Any conclusions are necessarily tentative. The author hopes as much to stimulate further research as to settle questions about the making of congressional foreign economic policy. In sum, the author hopes to add a footnote on how Congress makes a decision to an illustrious predecessor on how "Congress makes a law."[34]

The study will cover the eight-year period between 1970 and 1978. This period encompasses the early signs of labor's disaffection from the free trade coalition, the debate over Burke-Hartke, the passage of the Trade Act of 1974, and trade and investment issues in the 94th (1975-76) and 95th (1977-78) Congresses. Because the early 1970s were more focused on trade and investment issues, proportionately greater material is drawn from that period.

The study will be presented in the form of ten separate chapters (including the introduction). Chapter 2 will present the basic foreign trade and investment issues in their changing legislative garb. Because it still represents a major portion of the labor program on international economic issues, the provisions of the Burke-Hartke Bill will be spelled out in some detail. The chapter will attempt to look forward to the 96th (1979-80) Congress as well as covering the period 1970 to 1978. Chapter 3 will peruse foreign trade and investment theory for suggestions about the behavior of major interest groups in a foreign economic policy debate. The chapter will also provide a framework for the economic arguments of the different groups and a background and standard against which congressional deliberations can be assessed. Chapter 4 focuses on many of the economic pressures that help explain the breakup of the post-World War II free trade alliance. It places the foreign trade and investment debate in an appropriate historical context and details some past protectionist pressures.

Chapters 5 and 6 present the labor position and the business response to it. The economic arguments of both labor and business will be restated in terms of current foreign trade and investment theory.

Because of the congressional focus of the study, some attention must be paid to the nature of the congressional structure and the intricate play of congressional personalities and procedures. Chapter 7 presents this material in as brief a form as is practicable.

Chapter 8 details the interaction of big business and big labor with the Congress. The material not only provides a further instance of major interest group behavior but also focuses on the more formal deliberations of congressional committees. Much of the material in this chapter will be drawn from congressional hearings and congressionally commissioned studies.

The entire debate over Burke-Hartke was also greatly affected by the conduct of the Nixon administration. The eventual influence of the devaluation of the dollar and the ability of the administration to respond to particular problems in the foreign trade field had a considerable impact on the nature of the pressures that were brought to bear on the Congress.

In a similar fashion the Carter administration's response to specific cases brought under the Trade Act of 1974, the initiatives of Ambassador Strauss (the U.S. special trade representative), and the administration's general conduct of foreign economic policy have had a major influence on the course of the foreign trade debate in the last (95th) Congress. The impact of the administrative branch on congressional deliberations is explored in Chapter 9.

Finally, Chapter 10 presents a number of conclusions, speculations that merit further research, and some thoughts on what the foreign trade and investment debate foretells about the future conduct of U.S. foreign economic policy.

THE DATA

Data for the present study came from four main sources. The figures on direct foreign investment, repatriated profits, balance of payments, and balance of trade are almost entirely drawn from selected issues of the U.S. government's Survey of Current Business.

There is also the extensive public record. In fact, throughout the study the emphasis will be on public documents. The hearings, newspaper coverage, and public statements of the interest groups form most of the grist for this particular mill. The author does not attempt to downgrade the importance of informal contacts, preferred campaign contributions, or angry constituents in the congressional process, but the thrust of the entire study is on how the major interest groups made their case before the Congress and on how the congressional part of the public sector dealt with a series of international economic issues. For this approach to interest-group behavior and congressional decision making, the hearings and published statements of various interest groups are much more than the tips of ever-changing icebergs. It is unlikely that an interest group would make substantive economic arguments in private that do not find their way into the public record. And in the final analysis, most legislation takes a public form that is built upon an established record that involves considerable public scrutiny.

Although both economic events and economic theory did much to explain the activities of the major interest groups, there remained some apparent anomalies. In an effort to eliminate the unexplained factors, the author conducted a number of interviews with individuals who had been active in the foreign trade and investment debate. The interviews included a former member of the Nixon administration, staff members of congressional committees, and both research people and lobbyists from several major interest groups.

Finally, and perhaps principally, there is personal experience. From January 1972 through March 1973 the author worked as a legislative counsel and staff economist for Senator Vance Hartke (D-Ind.). Although responsible for all Finance Committee legislation (mercifully exempted from the intricacies of the social security law), the author was mainly concerned with foreign trade and investment issues. As a prime sponsor of the Burke-Hartke Bill, Senator Hartke was constantly subjected to solicitations from industry as well as pressures from the AFL-CIO. The author was exposed to most of these pressures as well. The author wrote speeches, drafted amendments, spoke to corporation presidents, and attended administration briefings. In other words, the author was a very close participant observer.

After leaving Senator Hartke, the author worked on international economic policy problems "across the street" at the Congressional Research Service. At the beginning of the 95th Congress the author joined the staff of the Joint Economic Committee as an international economist with special responsibility for questions of international trade and development. Needless to say, the analysis and conclusions that make up the study are entirely the responsibility of the author and do not necessarily reflect the views of his present or past employers or colleagues.

NOTES

1. For a discussion of the provisions of the Trade Expansion Act of 1962, see Stanley D. Metzger, Trade Agreements and the Kennedy Round (Fairfax, Va.: Coiner Publications, 1963). The law itself can be found at 76 Stat. 872.

2. A brief discussion of the congressional consideration of TEA-62 can be found in John W. Evans, The Kennedy Round in American Trade Policy: The Twilight of the GATT? (Cambridge, Mass.: Harvard University Press, 1971), Chapter 7. In fact, the bill had the "largest majority in the history of the trade agreements program. . . ." C. Fred Bergsten, "Crisis in U.S. Trade Policy," Foreign Affairs 49 (July 1971): 619.

3. The Long-Term Arrangement Regarding International Trade in Cotton Textiles was adopted in 1962. For a brief discussion of the arrangement, see Gerald M. Meier, Problems of Trade Policy (New York: Oxford University Press, 1973), pp. 96-102.

4. The first voluntary steel agreement was reached in January 1969 "after months of negotiations with the U.S. State Department, steel producers in Japan and in the European Economic Community. . . ." Richard S. Frank, "Trade Report/Consumer Movement Shifts Tactics, Not Goals in Legal Attack on Steel Quotas," National Journal, August 5, 1972, p. 1258.

5. For the text of the Trade Reform Act of 1968, see Hearings before the Committee on Ways and Means, U.S. House of Representatives, 90th Cong., 2d sess. on Tariff and Trade Proposal, Part 1 (Washington, D.C.: U.S. Government Printing Office, 1968), pp. 13-27.

6. The text of the Trade Act of 1969 can be found in Hearings before the Committee on Ways and Means of the House of Representatives, 91st Cong., 2d sess. on Tariff and Trade Proposals, Part 1, (Washington, D.C.: U.S. Government Printing Office, 1970), pp. 15-19.

7. A summary of the House-passed version of the bill can be found in Committee on Ways and Means, U.S. House of Representatives, 91st Cong., 2d sess., Press Release Summary of Provisions of H.R. 18970, "The Trade Act of 1970" (Washington, D.C.: U.S. Government Printing Office, 1970).

8. For a brief discussion of these programs and their possible impact, see Samuel Pizer, "Capital Restraint Programs" in Commission on International Trade and Investment Policy, United States International Economic Policy in an Interdependent World (Washington, D.C.: U.S. Government Printing Office, 1971), pp. 87-112.

9. The text of the Foreign Trade and Investment Act of 1972 can be found in Congressional Record, September 28, 1971, pp. S15142 et seq.

10. Jeffrey W. Lins, "U.S. Trade with the Developing Economies: The Growing Importance of Manufactured Goods," Staff Economic Report. Office of Economic Research, U.S. Department of Commerce, Washington, D.C., June 1975.

11. See, for instance, Helen B. Junz, "Adjustment Policies and Trade Relations with Developing Countries," paper presented at a session on "Prospects of an Economic Crisis in the 1980s," meetings of the American Economic Association, August 30, 1978, mimeographed.

12. A recent poll by Patrick Caddell, Cambridge Survey Research, suggests protectionist sentiment may well be on the rise. According to a report in The Economist, Caddell attributed the rise to dollar devaluation. "Protection could replace tax cuts as the big American political issue in 1979," The Economist, December 23, 1978, p. 77.

13. "Fiscal expansion accompanied by direct control of imports . . . is the only practical means by which the UK, and probably

several other industrial countries, can sustain expansion of national
output sufficient to restore full employment in the next decade."
Francis Cripps and Wynne Godley, "Control of Imports as a Means
to Full Employment and Expansion of World Trade: The UK's Case,"
Cambridge Journal of Economics 2 (1978):327. For an early and
critical response to the view of the Cambridge Economic Policy
Group, see Peter Jay, "The Radical Cambridge Alternative to Slow
Death by Export Starvation," The Times, March 29, 1976, p. 14.

14. In a July 12th statement before the Joint Economic Committee, Edward Bernstein, a widely respected authority on international monetary affairs, called for a 10 percent across-the-board
tariff on all imports except for foodstuffs and raw materials. In
subsequent communications with the Joint Economic Committee,
Bernstein spelled out his proposal in greater detail and tied it to his
view that the large U.S. trade deficit was "prejudicial to the economic
interests of the United States and destructive of the international
monetary system." Mid-Year Hearings, Joint Economic Committee
(Washington, D.C.: U.S. Government Printing Office, 1979).

Labor was quick to take note of the testimony. A subsequent
union newsletter quickly fitted the Bernstein position into the long-
standing labor view of trade and investment. See "Free Trader
Switches, Calls for Tariffs," Maritime Newsletter (Voice of the
AFL-CIO Maritime Trade Department), AFL-CIO, Washington, D.C.,
October 1978.

15. See, for instance, Robert H. Frank and Richard T. Free-
man, "The Distributional Consequences of Direct Foreign Invest-
ment" and Jack Baranson, "Technology Transfer: Effects on U.S.
Competitiveness and Employment," in The Impact of International
Trade and Investment on Employment, U.S. Department of Labor,
Bureau of International Labor Affairs (Washington, D.C.: U.S.
Government Printing Office, 1978).

16. Harry G. Johnson, "An Economic Theory of Protectionism, Tariff Bargaining and the Formation of Customs Unions,"
Journal of Political Economy 73, no. 3 (June 1965):256-83.

17. See Ingo Walter, "How Trade Policy is Made: A Politico-
Economic Decision System," in The United States and International
Markets: Commercial Policy Options in an Age of Controls, ed.
Robert G. Hawkins and Ingo Walter (Lexington, Mass.: D. C. Heath,
1972), pp. 17-38.

18. Charles P. Kindleberger, Foreign Trade and the National
Economy (New Haven, Conn.: Yale University Press, 1962).

19. J. J. Pincus, "Pressure Groups and the Pattern of
Tariffs," Journal of Political Economy 83, no. 4 (1975):757-78.

20. For a terse summary of the interest group literature in
political science, see Bruce Ian Oppenheimer, Oil and the Congres-

sional Process: The Limits of Symbolic Politics (Lexington, Mass.: D. C. Heath, 1974), pp. 2-5.

21. E. D. Schattschneider, Politics, Pressures and the Tariff (Englewood Cliffs, N.J.: Prentice-Hall, 1935).

22. Raymond A. Bauer, Ithiel de Sola Pool, and Lewis Anthony Dexter, American Business and Public Policy: The Politics of Foreign Trade (Chicago: Aldine Atherton Press, 1972).

23. Oppenheimer, op. cit.

24. See Bauer et al., op. cit., pp. 19-22.

25. Richard F. Fenno, The Power of the Purse: Appropriations Politics in Congress (Boston: Little Brown, 1966).

26. John F. Manley, The Politics of Finance: The House Committee on Ways and Means (Boston: Little Brown, 1970).

27. Stephen K. Bailey, Congress Makes a Law (New York: Columbia University Press, 1950).

28. R. A. Dahl and C. E. Lindblom, Politics, Economics and Welfare (New York: Harper, 1953).

29. Anthony Downs, An Economic Theory of Democracy (New York: Harper, 1957).

30. For a recent summary of possible models of congressional behavior, see John A. Ferejohn and Morris P. Fiorina, "Purposive Models Legislative Behavior," American Economic Review, Papers and Proceedings, May 1975, pp. 407-14.

31. Oppenheimer, op. cit., p. 5.

32. For instance, in 1975 a series of disclosures about the American Medical Association suggested that their actual lobbying activities ran counter to their testimony at congressional hearings. Stuart Auerback, "'Sore Throat' Gives AMA High Fever," Washington Post, July 13, 1975, pp. C1 and C5.

33. George Caspar Homans, Sentiments and Activities (New York: Macmillan, 1962), pp. 259-68 as quoted in Manley, op. cit., p. 4.

34. Bailey, op. cit.

CHAPTER 2

FOREIGN TRADE AND INVESTMENT LEGISLATION BEFORE THE CONGRESS: 1970–79

As the 1960s drew to a close, America's changing place in the world economy had begun to put pressure on both the international accounts and the domestic economy of the United States. Not surprisingly, the stress of international events found expression in a wide variety of legislative proposals.

This chapter is not designed to constitute a comprehensive list of all the trade and investment bills introduced into the Congress during the course of the 1970s. Rather, the focus is on the major proposals that trace labor's break with the free trade coalition and the growing pressures for change in international economic policy that emerged with the 95th (1977-78) Congress. Considerable emphasis is placed on the AFL-CIO-backed Burke-Hartke Bill, which was the legislative culmination of the sharp shift in labor's position on international trade and investment questions. The views of the world economy that led to Burke-Hartke continue to dominate labor thinking and the specific legislative proposals contained in Burke-Hartke still make up the heart of the AFL-CIO program on foreign economic policy.

In the four years since the passage of the Trade Act of 1974 (hereafter TA-74), the provisions of the act itself have set a good part of the trade agenda for the Ford and Carter administrations. First, there is the Tokyo Round of multilateral trade negotiations (1973-79). Under the authority created by TA-74, the United States has not only bargained over reciprocal tariff cuts but negotiated agreements[*] on such nontariff barriers as export subsidies and buy-

---

[*]The outlines of the tentative agreement and the notice of the president's intention to enter into an agreement were sent to the

national provisions. Second, by easing the standards for seeking import relief from both fair and unfair foreign competition, TA-74 has increased the number of trade decisions the president must make. For the most part the president has either rejected recommendations by the International Trade Commission (ITC) for import restrictions or provided an alternative import-restricting remedy.

Domestic problems have tended to dominate the consideration of economic policy in both the 94th (1975-76) and 95th (1977-78) Congresses. Recovery from the severe recession of 1974-75 and then the seemingly intractable problem of inflation have been at the top of the congressional economic agenda. Particularly in the 94th Congress, changes in international economic policy came principally in tax legislation designed to limit gains from overseas income, whether earned by foreign subsidiaries or by exports from the United States. Trade matters were not a matter of major concern to the Congress.

The 95th Congress also passed little trade or international tax legislation. But interest was beginning to shift again to the international sphere. Record trade deficits in 1977 and 1978 and the sharp fall in the international value of the dollar were very much the subject of congressional debate. The more active pace of the multilateral trade negotiations also quickened Congress's interest in trade matters. And presidential decisions to dilute or deny import relief recommended by the ITC often brought sharp congressional responses. A number of bills were introduced to protect individual American industries, to ease our balance of trade and payments problems, and to make the United States a more effective competitor for world markets.

LABOR CHANGES DIRECTION

The advent of the Burke-Hartke Bill marked the final defection of labor from what had been the dominant free trade alliance. Starting with the retreat from Smoot Hawley in 1934, labor had supported both the Reciprocal Trade Agreements Acts and the major Trade Expansion Act of 1962. No doubt labor's general support for free trade reflected a number of considerations: the strength of Franklin Roosevelt and the crusading spirit engendered by World War II,

---

speaker of the House and the president pro tem of the Senate on January 4, 1979. A copy of the president's letter and the attachment describing the tentative agreements in some detail can be found in Federal Register 44 (January 8, 1979): 1933-54.

which was perpetuated by the Cold War. It also reflected labor's
assessment of the international economy.

Labor kept its eye on the economic implications of trade for
its members. In supporting the Trade Expansion Act of 1962, George
Meany, president of the AFL-CIO, noted the clear economic gains
that accrued to union members from foreign trade. In particular
he compared the number of jobs created by trade to those lost to
imports. And trade came out a clear winner over protectionism.[1]
Meany also stressed the proposed adjustment assistance program
for workers displaced by imports. In 1962, then, labor's support
was principally grounded on both the jobs gained from trade and the
promises of help for those subject to any injury.

In 1968 President Johnson introduced the Trade Expansion Act
of 1968. The new trade bill would have extended the unused portion
of the tariff-cutting authority created by the Trade Expansion Act of
1962. The focus was not on initiating a new round of trade talks but
rather on giving the president flexibility to respond to particular
circumstances. For instance, if a domestic industry could demonstrate injury linked to an increase in imports that in turn was caused
by lowered tariffs, American duties on the product in question might
be raised. Under GATT (General Agreement on Tariffs and Trade)
rules, the United States is bound to offer compensation to its trading
partners in the form of lowered tariffs on other goods. Without the
extension of at least some tariff-cutting authority, the president
would be unable to fulfill America's obligations under GATT.

In addition, the Trade Expansion Act of 1968 would have eliminated the American Selling Price system of customs valuation. Under
the American Selling Price system certain imports—mainly benzoid
chemicals—were dutied on the basis of the current price in the United
States rather than the actual cost to the importer. As part of the
Kennedy Round of negotiations in Geneva, the United States had
agreed to eliminate the American Selling Price practice in return
for tariff and other concessions on American automobiles and tobacco.
The agreement, however, was subject to congressional approval,
which was never given.

Despite the extremely modest nature of the Trade Expansion
Act of 1968, the opposition to the bill was sufficient to prevent it
from leaving the Ways and Means Committee. When testifying on
the proposed trade bill, labor spoke critically of the adjustment
assistance program and raised a warning about increased imports.[2]
Although basically wedded to a free trade posture, the AFL-CIO had
started to focus on new forces in the international economy.

The changing world order was beginning to have a very definite
and rather sudden impact on the American labor movement. The

Bretton Woods system with its tilt toward reconstruction and fixed exchange rates surely played a part. The steady growth of U.S. foreign direct investment may also have helped close the technology gap and thereby change the nature of America's comparative advantage in trade.

As the balance of payments deficit began to be troublesome and the trade surplus began to decline, labor started to feel the pinch. The merchandise trade figures for specific commodity groupings hint at a possible source of economic difficulty. The persistent trade deficits in textiles, steel, autos, and consumer electronics spelled troubles for workers in the affected industries. Labor spokesmen pointed to the growing percentages of certain commodities that were accounted for by imports.

The AFL-CIO was equally strong in its criticisms of the protective mechanisms contained in then-current trade law. There was almost a sense of betrayal with regard to the once-touted adjustment assistance program. First introduced in the Trade Expansion Act of 1962, adjustment assistance was to be made available to both workers and firms under certain specified circumstances. Benefits for workers included unemployment compensation (up to 65 percent of the national average manufacturing wage) as well as retraining. The difficulties, however, stemmed less from the type of benefits than from a series of stringent requirements. To qualify for adjustment assistance, the loss of jobs had to be due in major part (larger than all other causes combined) to an increase in imports that in turn was due in major part to a reduction in tariffs. By rigorously applying these requirements, the U.S. Tariff Commission failed to grant any relief to a worker's petition until 1969. And then the change in policy resulted from a strained interpretation of statutory language, a new commissioner, and the president's frequent exercise of his tie-breaking authority.[3] Similarly restrictive standards were applied to the "escape clause" provision under which a whole industry could receive tariff protection as a bulwark against increased imports.

The AFL-CIO had also become increasingly concerned about the functioning of Item 807 (hereafter simply 807) of the Tariff Schedules of the United States. Under 807 a firm could manufacture parts in the United States, ship them abroad for assembly, import the completed product for sale in the American market, and pay a tariff only on the value that had been added abroad.[4] In most instances the foreign value consisted of assembly work by laborers paid well below the American scale. In part stimulated by the 807 program, assembly plants sprang up along the Mexican border and in several other countries.[5] The AFL-CIO sought repeal of 807 but with little success.[6]

The 807 program was frequently justified as an efficient division of capital- and labor-intensive functions along lines of rather obvious comparative advantage. Many companies contended that without 807 they would be forced to transfer whole operations abroad. Whatever the merits of this proposition, the AFL-CIO leadership contended that assembly and manufacturing operations were being transferred abroad at an increasing rate.

The AFL-CIO had already experienced the prospect of whole plants closing and moving. The previous shift of industry to the South had proved to be a boost to management's strength at the bargaining table. At least in some cases, the threat to move was clearly credible. The AFL-CIO had responded with Operation Dixie, an attempt to spread union membership and union standards throughout the South. The operation was far from a total success, but the unions could at least operate under the same law and the same basic political system throughout the nation.

The multinationals proved to be a more intractable kind of "runaway" plant. A single firm might operate in a dozen political or legal jurisdictions, none of which were easily accessible to the AFL-CIO. In many of the Third World countries there was not even a free trade union movement. The multinational was starting to emerge as a problem.

Another part of the story can be read in the deteriorating trade situation. Between 1967 and 1968 the U.S. trade surplus dropped from $3.8 billion to just over $624 million, a fall of well over $3 billion. And there was only a slight recovery in 1969 to $660 million. In fact, when AID-related and P.L. 480 exports were subtracted from the total, the United States had actually experienced its first trade deficit in 1968.

Aggregate unemployment rates for manufacturing workers remained low. But there was trade pressure on certain industries. The steady growth of import penetration in selected areas is highlighted in Table 7 (see Chapter 4), and AFL-CIO members in the steel, footwear, textile, electronics, and a number of other industries saw a growing percentage of the market for their goods supplied by imports.

No doubt other changes, both within and without the AFL-CIO, had an impact on what policy choices were finally made. Certainly the election of Richard Nixon over the union-backed Hubert Humphrey deepened labor's suspicions of the Executive Branch on foreign trade matters. The 1968 departure of the United Auto Workers removed a strong free trade force from the AFL-CIO. Some have suggested the 1965 ouster of the Steelworkers' president David J. McDonald by I. W. Abel was a pivotal event.[7] With more than 1.4 million members, the Steelworkers held a central position in the AFL-CIO's

Industrial Union Department, the traditional heart of the union. A full exploration of the internal workings of the AFL–CIO, however, is well beyond the scope of this particular study. Whatever the sum total of the various causes, the AFL–CIO had begun its retreat from its foreign trade policies of the past.

The first break came with the introduction of President Nixon's Trade Act of 1969. Quite similar to President Johnson's trade initiative, the Trade Act of 1969 included limited authority to cut tariffs and a provision to repeal the American Selling Price system. In testifying in trade hearings before the House Ways and Means Committee in 1970, Andrew J. Biemiller, chief lobbyist for the AFL–CIO, spelled out the new labor position. Calling for new policies for a new economic world, Biemiller detailed the changes that had altered the trade position of the United States. After mentioning resurgent foreign economies, the common external tariff of the Common Market, and the domestic boom, Biemiller turned to what he considered more fundamental matters:

> The basic causes are major changes in the world eco-
> nomic relationships during the past 25 years, which
> accelerated in the 1960s. Among these changes are
> the spread of government-managed national economies,
> the internationalization of technology, the skyrocketing
> rise of investments of U.S. companies in foreign sub-
> sidiaries and the mushrooming growth of U.S.-based
> multinational corporations. [8]

Aside from the role of managed economies—Biemiller referred to the government policies of our principal trading partners and not to nonmarket economies—the blame for present foreign trade problems is laid squarely at the door of the multinationals. Biemiller went on to advocate a streamlining of existing administration machinery designed to deal with either unfair imports (principally goods sold at below foreign market value or subsidized exports) or the impact of sudden increases in imports (escape clause and trade adjustment assistance). Government policy was to be bent toward restricting the outflow of U.S. capital and technology. He also put the AFL–CIO squarely behind Congressman Burke's H.R. 9912, which would have provided for the "orderly marketing" of imports beyond a certain level of market penetration. [9]

What went in as President Nixon's Trade Act of 1969 came out as Chairman Mills' Trade Act of 1970. Although containing a limited repeal of the American Selling Price, the Ways and Means Committee bill also contained explicit quotas for textiles (supported by the administration) and shoes (opposed by the administration) and a general

provision for quota or tariff relief that could be triggered by a combination of import penetration and a demonstration of economic
injury.[10] Although the Trade Act of 1970 eventually foundered in
the Senate—encumbered with welfare legislation and Senator Long's
particular answer to national health insurance—the bulk of the forces
behind the bill remained active. The position of the AFL-CIO in
particular continued to evolve.

The overall trade balance had improved somewhat in 1970,
but the import penetration of individual product lines continued.
Imports as a percent of new supply increased 6 percent in radio and
television receiving sets, 4 percent in rubber footwear, and 5 percent
in textile machinery and parts. For many workers the tide of increasing imports must have appeared irreversible. By 1970 imports
as a percent of domestic consumption accounted for 70 percent of
radios, 52 percent of black and white television sets, 30 percent of
nonrubber footwear, 15 percent of total steel production, and 12
percent of textiles.

At the same time the employment picture began to worsen.
The unemployment rate for all civilian employees went up 1.5 percentage points (from 3.5 percent in 1969 to 5.0 percent in 1970).
For blue-collar workers the increase was an even more marked
jump of 2.4 percentage points (from 3.9 percent in 1969 to 6.3 percent in 1970). Increases for workers in durable goods manufacturing
(2.8 percentage points) and for nondurable goods manufacturing (1.7
percentage points) were also sharp.

The rapid growth in direct foreign investment by U.S. multinational firms also weighed more heavily in the deliberations of the
AFL-CIO. The spectre of runaway firms had become increasingly
real. Foreign investment, the 807 program, the persistent growth
of imports, and the failure of administrative and legislative relief
all argued for a new foreign economic policy stance by the AFL-CIO.

By mid-1971 most of the thinking that was to find expression
in the Burke-Hartke Bill had taken a settled form. In a May 1971
statement by its Executive Council, the AFL-CIO spelled out its
latest position on foreign trade and the multinational corporation.[11]
In addition to the policies contained in the 1970 Biemiller testimony,
the AFL-CIO advocated a series of changes in the taxation of foreign-
source income as a means of bringing the U.S.-based multinational
corporation under some kind of national control. The general provision for orderly marketing had been replaced by a proposal for
quantitative restraints on all competitive imports based on the average
level of imports in the 1965-69 base period.

No doubt this all but final position reflected considerable negotiation within the AFL-CIO. The choice of base period presumably
reflected a compromise between unions already hurt and those who
were reacting more to impending injury.[12] Whatever the actual

reason, the inclusion of tax provisions opened up a possible alliance with various tax reform groups who might not be so sympathetic to the imposition of comprehensive import quotas. The stage was set for Burke-Hartke.

THE BURKE-HARTKE BILL

Emerging from big labor's increased concern with import penetration and the growth of the U.S.-based multinational firm, the Burke-Hartke Bill challenged much of existing U.S. foreign economic policy. [13] Among other things, Burke-Hartke was the first comprehensive trade bill to come before the Congress since the Trade Expansion Act of 1962. Instead of continuing the steady movement to expanded world trade represented by postwar U.S. policy, Burke-Hartke would have imposed quotas on virtually all imports that competed with U.S. production.

Pursuing the view that foreign direct investment and the multinational firm were a serious threat to labor's interest, Burke-Hartke proposed sweeping changes in the U.S. taxation of foreign source income. In case the change in tax rules proved inadequate to the task of discouraging U.S. foreign direct investment, Burke-Hartke empowered the president to directly limit the flow abroad of both capital and technology.

Although the proposed tax changes and the quotas were the heart of the bill and the debate, Burke-Hartke contained a series of provisions to speed the way in which U.S. industry and labor could react to foreign competition. The standards for obtaining escape-clause relief and trade adjustment assistance would be considerably eased. And the administration of the antidumping and countervailing duty laws would be noticeably tightened.

Because so much of the debate on foreign trade and investment policy in the 92nd and 93rd Congresses was in reaction to the proposals contained in Burke-Hartke, the specific provisions of the bill must be spelled out in some detail. Since the principal focus of the debate was on the tax and quota aspects of Burke-Hartke, the other provisions will receive a somewhat more cursory treatment.

The Taxation of Foreign-Source Income

In principal the United States claims the right to tax the income of any U.S. citizen regardless of the geographic location of the citizen's income. Income earned abroad and spent abroad is just as much subject to the long arm of the Treasury as is income earned and spent in the United States. In practice, however, the United

States has limited its taxing powers in a number of ways. In line with general international practice, the United States recognizes the right of the country of source (the country where the income is actually produced) to tax income produced within its borders.[14] In addition, the foreign-source income of a U.S. corporation is treated in ways quite different from domestic income. The principal differences lie in the existence of a foreign tax credit and a deferral of tax liability on some foreign-source income.

Under existing law, income taxes paid to a foreign government may be credited against U.S. taxes on foreign-source income. Burke-Hartke would have eliminated the credit altogether.[15] Instead, a corporation would be allowed to deduct taxes paid to foreign governments, just as a domestic corporation is permitted to deduct income taxes paid to the states before determining its federal taxable income. The difference, of course, is in the level of the income tax rates. State income taxes are generally quite low, while most developed countries have income tax rates that are similar to the 46 percent tax rate levied on U.S. corporate income.

And the tax implications for an American firm in Europe could be substantial. For instance, assume that France imposes a 46 percent income tax rate. If an American firm earns $100 in France, $46 is paid to the French government. When the remaining $54 of profit is remitted to the United States, existing rules require that it first be "grossed up" by the amount of income taxes paid to France.[16] The resulting $100 ($46 + $54) is then subjected to the U.S. corporate rate of 46 percent, yielding a tax liability to the U.S. government of $46. However, the $46 in taxes already paid to France can be credited against this liability, effectively eliminating any payment of U.S. taxes.

What if this is replaced by a deduction? The same $100 in gross dividends would now be reduced by $46 or the amount of taxes paid to France to yield a taxable income of $54. Applying the U.S. corporate rate of 46 percent, the company would now have to pay close to $25 in U.S. taxes. In effect, the profitability of the foreign investment has been cut in two.

In addition to eliminating the foreign tax credit, the Burke-Hartke Bill would also have repealed altogether the deferral of U.S. taxes on foreign-source income.[17] The deferral privilege depends crucially on the form in which a U.S. direct foreign investment is made. Existing law makes a basic distinction between the foreign branch and the controlled foreign corporation.*

---

*In some cases a foreign government may require a firm to incorporate. The U.S. income tax laws will nonetheless allow the

If a firm chooses to establish a branch operation in, say, France, income earned by the branch in France is immediately subject to taxation by the United States. Although the foreign branch can still benefit from the foreign tax credit discussed above, it receives no deferral privilege. Because the branch operation offers no delay on U.S. tax liability, most U.S. firms have chosen to establish incorporated foreign subsidiaries. The major exception is in the field of mineral exploration and production. By electing to create foreign branches, major U.S. oil companies have been able to avail themselves of a number of domestic incentives. No such allowance would be available to a foreign subsidiary.

The bulk of U.S. foreign direct investment, particularly investment in manufacturing facilities, has taken the form of a controlled (basically ownership of more than 50 percent of the voting stock by U.S. nationals) foreign corporation.[18] "Based on the somewhat fictitious assumption that the foreign subsidiary is a truly separate entity," the general practice was not to tax the unrepatriated earnings of a controlled foreign corporation.[19]

The basic rule was quite clear: deferral for a corporation, no deferral for a branch. In recent years, however, the deferral privilege has come under increasing attack from a number of quarters. On the one hand, some critics argued that the deferral privilege violated the principal of tax neutrality.[20] Others suggested that tax deferral and the attendant incentive to foreign direct investment was running counter to the national interest. The growing use of tax havens for "base company" income was also widely criticized. The result was a modest breach in the general rule on deferral.

Adopted in 1962, the new rules mandated that the income of a controlled foreign corporation would, under certain limited circumstances, be subject to U.S. taxation.[21] The new approach arose out of the following kind of business arrangement. For a variety of reasons, company A decides to establish a manufacturing subsidiary (company D) in Denmark. Under rules prevailing both before and after the Revenue Act of 1962, the income of company D is entitled to the deferral privilege. Prior to 1962, however, company A could further reduce its total tax liability by establishing a "base company" (company F) in the low-tax West Indies. By channeling insurance and services to company D through company F and by allowing company F to handle many of company D's sales abroad, the parent

---

U.S. firm to file a consolidated return with its foreign affiliate. In most cases firms following this procedure are in the field of mineral exploration and production. In essence they elect to be taxed as if they had a foreign branch operation.

company A could shift income from high-tax Denmark to the low-tax West Indies. In effect, company A was able to both avoid taxes in Denmark and yet defer taxes in the United States.

The Revenue Act of 1962 changed all that. Subject to a number of exceptions, income of base or tax-haven corporations would now be taxed when earned. The definition of what constitutes immediately taxable or Subpart F income (after the relevant section of the U.S. tax code) is narrow. There is as yet no indication that the existence of Subpart F either has restricted the flow of investment abroad or has had a major impact on Treasury revenues. It is probable, however, that the complexities introduced by Subpart F have bought some additional tax neutrality at considerable administrative expense.[22]

In addition to eliminating the deferral privilege and the foreign tax credit, Burke-Hartke would have repealed the exemption for personnel stationed abroad, changed the rules for the treatment of the transfer of patents, and forced firms to calculate their foreign depreciation costs on the basis of the straight-line method.[23] Throughout, Burke-Hartke reflected labor's concern with foreign direct investment. They saw it as draining needed capital from the United States, altering the established pattern of collective bargaining, and acting as a major conduit for the spread of U.S. technology. At times the changes Burke-Hartke contained appeared all but punitive. Certainly the proposed change in depreciation rules fit into this category.[24]

Under present rules, a U.S. corporation is free to use a variety of different depreciation methods in calculating its foreign-source income. Burke-Hartke would have required that all foreign-source profits be calculated on the basis of a straight-line method. Coupled with the other provisions in the Burke-Hartke tax package, the straight-line rule could have had a sizable impact on calculated profits and therefore tax liabilities.

Even if the foreign tax credit were maintained, straight-line depreciation could have a significant effect. Foreign taxes and therefore credits generally reflect an attempt to minimize foreign tax liability. A recalculation of foreign profits using a straight-line method might well leave a considerable gap between the foreign view and the U.S. view of the size of a foreign-source profit. That gap would not have been taxed abroad and therefore would bring with it no tax credit that could be used to offset U.S. tax liability.

The other two proposed changes focused more directly on the export of U.S. technology. Certainly the proponents of Burke-Hartke were concerned that U.S. patents and technical know-how were being distributed worldwide to the detriment of both the United States and the American working man. Current law on the recognition of gain from the transfer of such intangible assets is relatively lenient.[25]

Burke-Hartke would have tightened existing rules by taxing all such transfers, including those made between a parent and a subsidiary.[26]

In a similar vein, Burke-Hartke partisans contended that the export of technology had often been facilitated by placing specially trained Americans abroad to smooth the transfer of an industrial process or patented invention. In 1971 the law arguably provided a mild inducement to this process by granting a limited exemption to income earned abroad by U.S. citizens.* Burke-Hartke would have eliminated the exemption.[27] Although this repeal would not have had a major revenue effect, it might well have discouraged firms from locating Americans overseas.[28] In addition, there were political dividends to be made. Senator Hartke was fond of asking why the good people of Evansville (Indiana) should pay their full share of taxes only to subsidize the Parisian playboys of the multinational firms.

Comprehensive Import Quotas

The Burke-Hartke Bill was designed to join two rather different strands of thought about the international economy. On the one hand, proponents of Burke-Hartke wanted to bring the multinational corporation under government control. They argued that the continued flow of U.S. capital abroad would have an adverse impact on domestic investment, the gross national product, and labor's share of national income. The focus of these arguments was principally on the role of technology in determining the rate of economic growth, the changing nature of U.S. comparative advantage, and the long-range terms of trade. To accomplish these ends, Burke-Hartke incorporated a variety of administrative controls and tax changes. The proposed tax changes raised a host of intriguing economic questions that are still the subject of considerable controversy.[29] What is more, the tax provisions, particularly the proposal to eliminate the deferral privilege, attracted considerable academic support.[30] On the other hand, Burke-Hartke was designed to protect and preserve the existing pattern of U.S. industry. Without a doubt, the Burke-Hartke Bill contained the most protective proposals presented to the U.S. Congress since the much-criticized Smoot-Hawley tariff of 1930.

---

*The provisions for the exclusion of earned income were severely tightened by the Tax Reform Act of 1976. The implementation of the act was twice delayed and a liberalized treatment for the overseas earned income of U.S. citizens was restored by the Foreign Earned Income Act of 1978.

This is not to say that the United States had refused to use import quotas and voluntary export restraints in a variety of cases. At the time Burke-Hartke was introduced there were quotas on the importation of sugar, oil, and a number of dairy products. In addition, steel, cotton, and man-made textiles and certain categories of meat were the subject of "voluntary" quotas.

The original sugar quota dated to the middle of the Great Depression.[31] Renewed in the Sugar Act of 1948, it had been a vital prop for the domestic sugar beet industry throughout most of the postwar period. Although the Sugar Act makes a bow toward national security, apparently the principal purpose of the quota has been to assure reasonable profits to the domestic sugar industry coupled with stable (albeit higher than world) prices for consumers. The evidence suggests that the program had achieved these particular goals.*

With the emergence of the OPEC oil cartel as a major force in determining oil prices, it is easy to forget that at the time Burke-Hartke was introduced oil import quotas were an important and costly source of higher domestic oil prices. Controls on oil imports started as voluntary quotas in 1955. Within four years they had become mandatory, based on the Trade Agreements Extension Act of 1955 "and later acts authorizing restrictions on imports which would impair the national security."[32]

Mandatory restrictions on dairy products commenced in 1953.† Originally viewed as the necessary corollary of a domestic price support program, the existing dairy quotas have become increasingly costly over time.

---

*The 93rd Congress, however, failed to renew the Sugar Act. In 1975 the president set the rate of duty and quota for imported sugar under the existing authority of the Trade Act of 1974 [Sec. 201(a)(2)]. Since that time the overall quota has been reduced slightly and the rate of duty has been raised several times. In 1977 sugar producers sought to restrict sugar imports by filing for an escape-clause action under Section 22 of the Agricultural Adjustment Act of 1956. Shortly thereafter, producer interests sought escape-clause relief under the Trade Act of 1974. In both cases the ITC recommended import relief. Although the president accepted the ITC recommendation to adjust import fees quarterly in the first case, he denied relief under the Trade Act of 1974. The president cited ongoing negotiations over the International Sugar Agreement as the basis for his action.

†The control of agricultural products is generally based on Section 22 of the Agricultural Adjustment Act of 1933.

Mandatory quotas may have been the policy of choice for agricultural commodities (and oil), but they posed serious problems for manufactured goods. Both the general thrust of U.S. commercial policy and the existing pattern of international agreements made mandatory quotas less attractive in the industrial sphere. What emerged for the "endangered" industrial product was the voluntary quota. In the case of cotton and man-made textiles, these have been government-to-government agreements. In the case of steel, the U.S. State Department dealt directly with private producers.

Voluntary quotas on cotton textiles go as far back as 1937. Caught between the complaints of the depression-pressured textile industry and a firm commitment to expanding world trade, the Roosevelt administration relied on a purely private agreement negotiated by the Cotton Textile Institute in New York and the Japan Cotton Spinners' Association.[33]

Increased Japanese exports of cotton textiles in the early 1950s led to renewed pressures for some controls on Japanese exports. The eventual result was the Long Term Agreement (LTA) on the export of cotton textiles that covered the bulk of cotton textile importers and exporters. With the switch to man-made and other noncotton fabrics, the textile industry again sought import protection. After considerable maneuvering by both the Nixon administration and the Congress, the Japanese and other major noncotton textile exporters agreed to a voluntary limit on exports to the United States.

A steady growth in steel imports had a similar impact on the steel industry. In response to industry pressures, the State Department negotiated agreements with foreign producers in 1968 and again in 1971.[34]

Existing U.S. quotas vary widely in intent, in administration, and in overall impact on the consumer. Some of the quotas appear to have grown out of domestic support programs, others to serve some notion of national security, and still others to provide protection to specific activities. In no case, however, was the existence of quotas raised to the level of an overall national policy. For industry, administration after administration had offered only voluntary restraints for special cases. This does not mean that existing quotas did not impose a significant cost on both U.S. consumers and on the United States. Focusing only on the loss to the nation, Stephen McGee calculated the 1972 loss to the United States to be on the order of $3.6 billion.[35] The full cost to the consumer (or total user cost) would be much higher.

In calculating the cost of import quotas, the general practice is to distinguish between the total cost to consumers and the cost to the nation as a unit. The divergence exists because part of the consumers' loss may be a transfer of resources to domestic producers

or importers rather than a simple deadweight loss or a gain by
foreign exporters. The degree to which importers or exporters
gain from the existence of a quota depends crucially on how the quota
is actually administered. In cases where the government grants
import rights to domestic firms, the extra cost of imports will accrue
to the domestic producer (and thus not be lost to the nation). The
U.S. oil import program was essentially run along these lines. If
the government, however, chooses to grant rights to foreign exporters, foreign firms will reap the benefits (and impose a burden on
both the domestic consumer and the state). The U.S. sugar quota
has been administered in this manner. Voluntary quotas lead to a
similar result.[36] Although not currently used in the United States,
the government could always auction off the import quotas to domestic
importers. In this case the alleged advantages of a quota could be
obtained without sacrificing the revenue produced by a tariff.

Although focused on a relatively small number of products,
U.S. mandatory and voluntary quotas covered a substantial percentage of U.S. imports. For instance, in 1969 items subject to some
type of quota accounted for more than 20.7 percent of U.S. imports.[37]
In addition the United States still maintained an extensive tariff structure, subjected government purchases to a Buy American law, and
maintained a variety of other nontariff barriers to trade.[38] But
Burke-Hartke went far beyond any existing practices in restraint of
foreign trade. Instead of tariffs, quotas would have become the
central feature of U.S. foreign trade policy. Instead of a commitment to steadily expanding world trade, U.S. policy would have been
focused first and foremost on protecting the existing pattern of
industrial and agricultural production.

Under the Burke-Hartke approach quotas would be established
for virtually all imports that competed with U.S. production.[39] The
comprehensive quotas would be based on the average relation between
imports and domestic production over the period 1965 to 1969. For
many products this implied a serious roll back from then current
import levels. Estimates of the size of the roll back varied but were
generally substantial. One study suggested that compared with 1972
levels of imports, Title III would result in a reduction of "at least
30 percent" in U.S. imports.[40]

A proposed Foreign Trade and Investment Commission (FTIC)
would determine the amounts to be imported on a category-by-category
and a country-by-country basis.[41] As used in Burke-Hartke, category
refers to the five-digit and seven-digit item numbers of the Tariff
Schedule of the United States. Five- or seven-digit articles could
be grouped for the purpose of establishing a quota, but not at the
expense of the domestic production of any "item or component."[42]

An important feature of the quotas was their built-in flexibility. In most cases the annual quotas would be increased to maintain the same relation between imports and domestic production as existed in the base period (1965-69).[43] In effect Burke-Hartke mandated permanent market shares for current levels of technology, production, and trade. Proponents of Burke-Hartke were fond of referring to this adjustable feature of the quotas as an example of the "sliding" as opposed to the "closed" door.

The FTIC, however, would retain a certain flexibility in the application of the quotas. If imports were inhibiting "the production of any manufactured product" the FTIC could lower the quota below the level suggested by the 1965 to 1969 base period.[44] On the other hand, if a quota prevented sufficient importation of an intermediate good the FTIC could increase the quota.[45]

Nor was the ambit of the quotas quite as large as it might appear. First of all, the quotas would not have been applied so as to cause a "long-term disruption of United States markets."[46] This was generally interpreted as exempting "noncompetitive" imports from the quota provisions. Quotas imposed by other legislation and existing government-to-government agreements would take precedence over the quota formula.[47] Quotas on sugar, dairy products, oil, and the voluntary agreements on cotton and man-made textiles would be unaffected. However, the voluntary agreement between the private steel manufacturers and the State Department would no longer have had any effect. In addition, Burke-Hartke authorized the president to negotiate bilateral or multilateral agreements with foreign countries "regulating by category the quantities of articles" that may be imported into the United States.[48]

With at least a nominal bow to the possibilities of abuse, Burke-Hartke empowered the FTIC to reduce quota protection for an industry that used its assured market share to avoid the technological innovations necessary to remain "competitive with foreign producers."[49] The bill did not define what role profits, credit availability, or other factors might play in mitigating the requirement to make the required innovations. Nor did the bill explore the questions of why protection would be needed at all if the industry in fact remained competitive with foreign exporters.

The breadth of the Burke-Hartke quota proposals was virtually unprecedented in the history of U.S. foreign trade policy. Only the much criticized Smoot-Hawley Tariff Act of 1930 may have been as comprehensive in its effect—and even there the policy was to rely on tariffs. The static costs of Burke-Hartke to American consumers have been estimated in the billions of dollars.[50] In addition, there remain the dynamic costs to American industry and the possible loss of American exports through retaliation.

The quota section made virtually no attempt to relate a remedy to either a bilateral trade imbalance or actual injury to an industry. And the proposal was shot through with administrative complexities. In fact the quotas are such a radical departure from past practice that one wonders if they were not as much a sharp warning signal as they were a proposal for new legislation.

Technology and Capital Controls

Much of the Burke-Hartke Bill expresses big labor's concern with the flow abroad of U.S. technology and capital and the implications such a flow will have for U.S. employment. Not surprisingly, Burke-Hartke provided for some direct control of capital and technology flows. Under Burke-Hartke the president would have been empowered to prohibit any capital or technological transfer that would cause a net reduction in U.S. employment.[51]

Certainly these proposals were potentially significant. They would have allowed the federal government an extensive review of often-routine decisions by the multinational firms. The capital controls were so broad in scope that they extended to the transfer of capital from one foreign country to another as well as a transfer of domestic capital abroad. But the powers were to be put in the hands of a president generally felt to be hostile to big labor's concern with the multinational firm. And the technology controls covered only patents, not the myriad other forms of technology transfer that are so important. Taxes and quotas remained the heart of Burke-Hartke.

New Approaches to "Fair" and "Unfair" Import Competition

Although the focus was always on the multinational firm, proponents of Burke-Hartke also felt that existing methods of dealing with import competition had simply failed to function. Burke-Hartke advocates felt they were being victimized by the unfair trade practices of foreign exporters. They were particularly critical of the way in which the antidumping law and the countervailing duty act were being enforced. Originally enacted to prevent the sale in the United States by a foreign exporter of an item at less than its "fair value,"*

---

*In the ordinary course of events, fair value was determined by comparing the f.o.b. plant price of the exporter in its home or third-country markets to the price charged in the U.S. market.

the antidumping law had become the subject of considerable administrative delays. Burke-Hartke would have transferred the entire
antidumping procedure from the Treasury and Tariff Commission
to the proposed FTIC and imposed strict time limits on a final
decision.*

In April 1972, just six months after the introduction of Burke-
Hartke, the Treasury announced its intention to tighten up the rules
on defining fair value, to respond to complaints within 30 days, and
to make a dumping finding within six to nine months depending on the
complexity of the case.[52] Similar time constraints eventually found
their way into the Trade Act of 1974.[53] Burke-Hartke contained
roughly comparable provisions with regard to the Countervailing
Duty Law.[54] Designed to counteract the effect of a foreign government's export subsidies by applying additional or "countervailing"
duties, proponents of Burke-Hartke felt the Countervailing Duty Law
had simply fallen into slothful disuse.

The focus of a trade debate is so often on the general level of
tariffs or the existence of a pattern of import quotas that other methods
of dealing with import penetration are often ignored. Assuming the
imports in question are not the product of an unfair trade practice
(subsidized or dumped) nor controlled by either tariffs or quotas,
the domestic producer still has some additional remedies to slow

---

Adjustments were made for differences in the quantity sold and the
circumstances of the particular sale.

*Under the law in force at the time Burke-Hartke was intro-
duced, complaints of dumping were first filed with the Bureau of
Customs of the U.S. Treasury. Acting upon information gathered
by Customs, the Treasury Department then determined if sales were
being made at less than fair value. After the secretary of the Treasury found that goods had been sold at less than fair market value,
the secretary would advise the U.S. Tariff Commission (now the
International Trade Commission) of his findings. The Tariff Commission would then proceed to see if the sales below fair value had
caused injury to domestic industry.

Regulations in effect before 1972 allowed a lengthy process to
follow any complaint to the Treasury. Three months could pass
before a decision was made to investigate a complaint and two to
three years could go by before a fair-value decision was reached.
Tariff Commission findings would delay this process even further.
The FTIC, on the other hand, would be forced to make a decision
within four months after a complaint was filed. The proposed changes
in antidumping procedure can be found in H.R. 10914, 92nd Cong.,
1st sess., Title IV, Sec. 401.

the imports or adapt to them. At the time Burke-Hartke was introduced, a domestic industry facing severe import competition could
seek escape-clause relief. Under certain circumstances the affected
industry could receive additional tariff protection to relieve the pressure of imports. Alternatively, an industry, a firm, or a group of
affected employees could accept the increase in imports and seek
trade adjustment assistance.*

However, whether one sought protection or aid, the legal standards were extremely exacting. Increased imports had to be the
"major factor" in any injury to industry, firm, or worker. And the
increase in imports had to be the result "in major part" of a tariff
or trade concession.† In fact, the standards proved so restrictive
that neither the escape clause nor trade adjustment assistance provided any protection throughout the import-sensitive 1960s.[55]

Burke-Hartke contained a number of proposed changes in the
standards for both escape-clause relief and trade adjustment assistance.[56] Although injury would still be tied to an increase in imports,
the link to a past tariff reduction would be broken. Imports would
only have to "contribute substantially" to the injury rather than be
the "major factor" in causing it.[57] The definition of injury itself
would be expanded to include such items as underemployment, fringe
benefits, and decreased or stagnant wages.

Other Provisions

True to its overall "kitchen sink" spirit, Burke-Hartke contained a variety of other proposals. Although some had interesting

---

*Trade adjustment assistance was first introduced into the law
as part of the Trade Expansion Act of 1962. As originally enacted,
workers were to receive 65 percent of the average manufacturing
wage over a limited period of time and be offered retraining programs
under the auspices of the Department of Labor. Injured firms would
receive low-interest loans and technical assistance under the guidance
of the Department of Commerce and the Small Business Administration.

†Interestingly, TEA-62 actually tightened the requirements
for escape-clause relief. Under prior law the industry need only
have shown that the increase in imports "contributed substantially"
to any injury and that the increase in imports was caused "in whole
or in part" by a tariff or trade concession.

implications, only one ranked as a real priority for labor: the repeal of Item 807 (discussed above) of the Tariff Schedule of the United States.[58]

So much for the bill itself. Burke-Hartke was not one of those rare entries in the legislative race that pass smoothly from starting gate to winners' circle. But it did have its day before the Congress. Despite its often cumbersome appearance as a bill for all reasons, the tax and quota provisions of Burke-Hartke set off a lengthy debate between labor, business, and the Congress that has not yet been decided.

LEGISLATIVE ALTERNATIVES TO BURKE-HARTKE

The labor drive to restrict imports and control the flow of capital and technology also stimulated other legislative proposals. In fact, during the 92nd Congress most of what was introduced in the foreign trade and investment field was a clear response to Burke-Hartke.

Because the House limits the number of cosponsors, a number of bills were introduced that were identical to the Burke-Hartke Bill. This procedure allowed all the cosponsors to have their names on a piece of trade legislation. Some took the opportunity to introduce the bills themselves, giving them a clear "advertisement" that could be sent to interested constituents.

Two major alternatives to the Burke-Hartke Bill were introduced in the 92nd Congress, but neither received significant attention in the press or in the Congress itself. Congressman Boland (D-Mass.) and Senator Schweiker (R-Pa.) introduced similar bills that dealt with foreign trade.[59] The Boland-Schweiker approach centered around improvements in the antidumping law, the countervailing duty law, and the administration of trade adjustment assistance. Prior to introducing his own bill, Senator Schweiker had been one of three senators to cosponsor the Burke-Hartke Bill.

Congressmen Betts (R-Ohio) and Waggoner (D-La.) also introduced a foreign trade bill that was treated as something of a response to Burke-Hartke.[60] The Betts-Waggoner approach included a repeal of both the foreign tax credit and the deferral of tax liability on the income of the foreign subsidiaries of U.S.-based multinationals.*

---

*Another Ways and Means Committee member, Congressman Seiberling (D-Ohio), in H.R. 16326 also included a provision repealing the deferral privilege.

Although the bill would extend the bargaining authority of the president under the Trade Expansion Act of 1962, it also contemplated a possible increase in duties and carefully hedged the range in which further reductions could take place.

There was even less legislative response to Burke-Hartke on the Senate side. In part, this reflected a labor decision to concentrate its activities on the House, where any trade legislation would have to start. Senator Harris (D-Okla.), a Finance Committee member, and several other liberal senators did introduce a generally free trade proposal entitled the International Trade Act.[61] This act engendered virtually no comment. As an announced lame duck and an increasingly self-proclaimed maverick, Harris's proposals received little consideration by other Finance Committee members.

Senator Ribicoff (D-Conn.), chairman of the Finance Subcommittee on International Trade, focused his formal legislative efforts on hearings and the Economic Adjustment Organization Act (EAOA).[62] Under EAOA, adjustment and retraining programs would be centralized in the Department of Commerce. TEA-62 had already promised adjustment assistance to workers displaced in "major part" because of an increase in imports caused by a tariff concession. In addition the EAOA would have extended similar coverage to three broad categories of workers. The programs would apply to those who were unemployed or underemployed because of changes in federal programs or policy, an increase in competitive imports, or the relocation of a factory or firm overseas. In one act Ribicoff would have extended the compensation concept of TEA-62 to all federal actions. In addition he sought to extend the political logic of TEA-62 to individuals hurt by imports in general or by some of the private calculations of the multinational firm. Interestingly enough, Treasury Secretary Shultz took at least part of a page from the Ribicoff approach in piecing together his own trade strategy for the 93rd Congress. Arguing that unemployment in general was the problem—not just that induced by increased imports—Shultz advocated improved unemployment compensation programs in place of trade adjustment assistance. The Shultz approach was rejected by labor and neither the Ribicoff bill nor the Shultz proposal were seriously considered by the Congress.

Single industries or product lines have always elicited a sympathetic response from congressmen whose districts are affected. The 92nd Congress saw the usual bills designed to give import protection to a number of items. None of these bills was thought to be a major foreign trade matter.

The labor position on foreign trade and investment legislation did have a definite impact on the Trade Act of 1974. In some cases, particularly the provisions to ease access to relief from either fair or unfair import competition, the labor influence is quite clear. Burke-Hartke may also have contributed to the general congressional drive to assert greater control over foreign economic policy, including the conduct of the Tokyo Round of Trade Negotiations.

Burke-Hartke will almost surely never reappear as a single legislative package. It may have been a case where the sum of its separate legislative parts added up to too much change. But those separate parts are very much alive. When the AFL-CIO talks about trade, it draws heavily on the types of proposals contained in the Burke-Hartke Bill. [63]

TRADE AND INVESTMENT LEGISLATION IN THE LATE 1970s

Following passage of the Trade Act of 1974, the Congress was largely preoccupied with other matters. Even strictly economic debates were more often focused on the pace of economic recovery or the seemingly intractable problem of inflation.

The 94th Congress

Particularly in the 94th (1975-76) Congress, foreign trade and investment issues were treated in the context of much broader tax bills. The Congress enacted new limitations on the use of both deferral and the foreign tax credit.

Under the provisions of the Tax Reduction Act of 1975 (P.L. 94-12), the treatment of Subpart F (base company income) was tightened. In fact the Senate version of the bill went so far as to repeal deferral outright. The Tax Reduction Act of 1975 also changed the manner in which U.S.-based multinational oil companies can compute the foreign tax credit. A ceiling was placed on the percentage of income that could be claimed as a tax credit and the oil companies were required to use an overall method of computing the credit rather than the per-country method. In effect, the oil companies could no longer offset operational losses in a particular foreign country against domestic income.

The Tax Reform Act of 1976 (P.L. 94-445) placed two additional strictures on the use of foreign tax credits. First, the ban on use of the per-country method was extended to all investors. Second, income from investments in developing countries was placed on the same footing as income from developed countries. Prior to

1976, investment income from developing countries did not have to be grossed-up before figuring the foreign tax credit.[*]

Two other long-standing labor targets were affected by the Tax Reform Act of 1976: the Domestic International Sales Corporations (DISCs) and the taxation of income earned overseas by American citizens. The DISC statute had permitted a corporation to defer taxes on a portion of its income from export sales made through DISC.[64] Under the Tax Reform Act of 1976, the deferral privilege is limited to export income in excess of a certain base period. When added to the tax code in 1971, the DISC provisions had been justified as a stimulus to exports and a possible offset to the tax advantages deferral offered to foreign subsidiaries of U.S. corporations. From the start, DISC has been attacked by the AFL-CIO as more of a give-away to the multinationals than an export incentive.

Special treatment for income earned by Americans working overseas had been one of the many tax targets of the Burke-Hartke Bill. Prior to 1977, depending on the time spent working abroad, an American working overseas could exclude up to $25,000 of income from U.S. tax liability. Labor was convinced that the privilege of excluding income from U.S. taxation encouraged Americans to live overseas and helped U.S.-based multinationals to speed the transfer abroad of domestic technology. The Tax Reform Act of 1976 reduced the earned income exclusion from $25,000 to $15,000 and made several other changes in the law that would have the effect of boosting the tax liability of Americans working overseas.[65]

The 95th Congress

Domestic rather than international problems continued to dominate the 95th (1977-78) Congress. Concern that the lagging recovery would stop well short of full employment gradually gave way to a fear that inflationary pressures were getting beyond control. But the Congress had not, in fact could not, ignore the workings of the world economy. The record $9.3 billion trade deficit of 1976

---

[*]In tightening the treatment of Subpart F income, the Tax Reduction Act of 1975 also affected one of the incentives for investment in developing countries. Prior to the Tax Reduction Act of 1975, a company could exempt Subpart F (base company income) from taxation if it came from developing country corporations and was reinvested in developing countries. The reinvestment exception was ended on January 1, 1976.

had more than trebled in 1977. And 1977's record $31.1 billion trade deficit was likely to be followed by an even greater deficit in 1978. Severe dollar depreciation against other major international currencies added to a growing unease about America's economic strength in a changing world economy.

International Trade Commission recommendations for import relief and the accelerating pace of the Tokyo Round of trade negotiations also helped focus congressional attention on trade questions. In part, growing congressional involvement in trade matters had been mandated by the Trade Act of 1974. This act remains the principal legislative product of the congressional debate over foreign trade and investment policies in the 1970s, but it also contains several distinctive features that influenced the consideration of trade issues in the 95th Congress. They are likely to have an even greater impact in the 96th.

First, there is the sharp increase in congressional participation in the negotiating process. At the beginning of each Congress, five official advisers to the "United States delegations to international conferences, meetings, and negotiation sessions relating to trade agreements"[66] are selected from the House Ways and Means and the Senate Finance Committees. Second, administration agreements on nontariff barriers must be submitted for congressional approval.[67] Third, the Congress can reinstate the import relief recommended by the ITC, even when the president has found that a denial of import relief would be in the national interest.[68] The congressional representatives have been active participants in the negotiating process. When the president notified the Congress on January 4, 1979, of his intention to enter into a trade agreement, he set in motion a chain of procedures that will end with formal congressional approval or disapproval.

In the 95th Congress, major trade proposals were about equally split between measures that would protect import-competing industries and those that would improve America's export potential. After considering a variety of proposals, Congress failed to give additional protection to the domestic sugar industry. Favorable action was taken on the Meat Import Act of 1978 (H.R. 11545), but it was vetoed by the president. Both proposals should be back in the 96th (1979-80) Congress.

Congressional resolutions were introduced to override the president's decision to deny the recommendations of the ITC to grant import relief to the industrial fasteners (nuts and bolts) industry and to processors of high-carbon ferrochromium. In the case of industrial fasteners, the Trade Subcommittee of Ways and Means voted 7 to 6 to override, but the resolution failed in the full committee.

A variety of "Buy American" bills were introduced, in some cases with an eye to helping the domestic steel industry. The Buy American Amendments Act of 1977 (S. 2318) would have given domestic suppliers a greater advantage in securing federal contracts and state or local contracts where more than 50 percent of a local project was federally funded. [69]

In the context of record U.S. trade deficits and an unsteady dollar, the large bilateral trade deficit with Japan became a ready target for congressional concern. In April the House Ways and Means Committee appointed a special task force to study U.S.-Japan trade relations. As the bilateral trade deficit continued to widen, five members of the Ways and Means Subcommittee on Trade wrote President Carter, urging imposition of either a surcharge or temporary quotas on imports from Japan.* Senator Lloyd Bentsen (D-Texas), an important member of the Senate Finance Committee, also raised the possibility of a surtax on Japanese imports. [70]

Even the trade negotiations themselves have not been exempt from legislative attempts to restrict imports. Forty-six Senators joined Senator Ernest F. Hollings (D-S.C.) in seeking to prevent any tariff cuts on cotton, wool, or man-made textile or apparel items. Congressman James T. Broyhill (R-N.C.) and Congressman Ken Holland (D-S.C.) introduced a similar measure in the House. The Hollings Bill was added as an amendment to the Carson City Silver Dollar Act (H.R. 9937).† The bill passed with the Hollings amendment attached but was vetoed by the president. Bills exempting several other products were introduced but none reached the president's desk.

---

*Letter to the president, July 25, 1978, signed by Chairman Charles A. Vanik (D-Ohio), Dan Rostenkowski (D-Ill.), James R. Jones (D-Okla.), William A. Steiger (R-Wisc.), and Bill Frenzel (R-Minn.). The congressmen urged action under Section 122 of the Trade Act of 1974, which permits the president to impose an import surcharge of up to 15 percent or quotas for a period not to exceed 150 days. Although the surcharge or quotas would ordinarily be applied on a nondiscriminatory basis, if the president determines that the best course is "action against one or more countries having large or persistent balance-of-payments surpluses, he may exempt all other countries" from the surcharge or quotas. Sec. 112(d)(2), P.L. 93-618.

†The Carson City Silver Dollar Act would have authorized the disposal of $24 million worth of Carson City Silver dollars.

Sometimes congressional omissions are even more important than comissions, and this was certainly the case with the 95th Congress. Under the Trade Act of 1974, the secretary of the Treasury was granted the authority to waive the U.S. countervailing duty statute.[71] In effect, under certain circumstances foreign governments could subsidize their exports to the United States and not suffer any penalty. Largely enacted to give the administration added flexibility at the multilateral trade negotiations, the authority to waive countervailing duties expired on January 2, 1979. Although an extension of the countervailing duty waiver was attached to several bills,[*] it failed to reach the president's desk. Because an extension of the waiver provision was deemed essential to conclude the multilateral trade negotiations, the administration pushed hard for the waiver extension in the early days of the 96th Congress. This time they met with success.[†] It is widely felt that successful completion of the Multilateral Trade Negotiations will require quick enactment of the waiver provision.

None of the trade-restricting amendments had the sweep of labor's early proposals. None of them raised questions about the basic orientation of U.S. policy toward foreign trade and investment. What is particularly striking about the legislation introduced to protect import-competing industries was the united front presented by industry and labor. For instance, in testifying on the proposed Buy American Act Amendments of 1977, Bruce E. David, general counsel of Bethlehem Steel Corporation, referred to the amendments as "one of those refreshing issues where you have labor and management speaking together."[72] In moves to exempt textiles from the multilateral trade negotiations and to fight the extension of the countervailing duty waiver, textile companies and unions took very much the same approach.[73]

Trade expansion was also very much on the congressional mind. During the 95th Congress the Export-Import Bank was not only extended for another five years (until September 1983), but the loan authority was also increased from $25 to $40 billion.[74] Boosting agricultural exports was the basis for the Agricultural Trade Act of 1978.[75] The Congress also made an opening to the East with an eye on trade potential. Most-favored-nation (MFN) status (and

---

[*]The waiver was attached to the Sugar Stabilization Act (H.R. 13750) as well as the Trade Adjustment Assistance Bill (H.R. 11711).

[†]A bill extending the authority to waive the application of countervailing duties until September 30, 1979 was signed into law on April 3, 1979.

therefore lower tariff rates) was continued for Rumania without congressional objection and was extended to Hungary with congressional approval.* There were a variety of proposals to exempt the People's Republic of China from the freedom of immigration requirements for participation in Export-Import Bank financing. And the People's Republic was made eligible for three-year agricultural credits under the Agricultural Trade Act of 1978.

On the tax front the Congress said no to the presidential proposal to eliminate both deferral and DISC. After twice delaying the application of the Tax Reform Act of 1976 to the overseas earnings of American's living and working abroad, the Congress passed new legislation that largely vitiated the impact of the 1976 act. In citing reasons for the change, the House Ways and Means Committee included a finding that "the presence of U.S. citizens working abroad encourages the purchase of U.S., instead of foreign, goods and services. . . ."[76]

The Congress also displayed a great deal of interest in improving the conduct of U.S. export policy. Extensive congressional hearings on export policy were conducted in February and again after the president announced the first phase of his new export policy on September 26, 1978.[77]

Congress has remained active, though hardly focused, on trade issues in the four years since the passage of the Trade Act of 1974. Throughout this period, labor and the multinationals have continued to press their differing views of what American policy should be with regard to foreign trade and investment. The debate has encompassed everything from anecdotal horror stories to elegant academic studies. To put the debate in better perspective, Chapters

---

*Under the Jackson-Vanik amendment to the Trade Act of 1974 (P.L. 93-618, Title IV) neither MFN status nor financial credits could be extended to a country with a nonmarket economy that limited the right of its citizens to immigrate. Although the congressional debate had focused on immigration of Soviet Jewry, the ban on MFN and credits also applied to most East European economies and the People's Republic of China. The president, however, may waive the provisions of Jackson-Vanik [Sec. 402(c)(1)] if "he has determined that such waiver will substantially promote the objective of this section and he has received assurances that the emigration practices of that country will henceforth lead substantially to the achievement of the objectives" of Jackson-Vanik [Sec. 402(c)(1)(A) and (B)]. Through the end of 1978 the president had chosen to exercise his waiver authority with regard only to Rumania and Hungary.

3 and 4 will treat the economic theory behind differing views of big labor and multinational business and will place the debate in a historical context.

NOTES

1. See Statement of George Meany, president of AFL-CIO, Hearings before the Committee on Ways and Means of the U.S. House of Representatives, 87th Cong., 2d sess., on the Trade Expansion Act of 1962, Part 2, pp. 1148, 1150, and 1160.
No doubt, the existence of the arrangements on cotton textiles had reduced protectionist pressures on Meany from within the AFL-CIO. For an early exponent of that view, see Irwin Ross, "Labor's Big Push for Protectionism," Fortune, March 1973, p. 94.

2. See Statement of Andrew J. Biemiller, director, Department of Legislation, AFL-CIO, Accompanied by Nathaniel Goldfinger, director, Department of Research, Hearings before the Committee on Ways and Means of the U.S. House of Representatives on the Trade Expansion Act of 1968, Part 3, pp. 1091-1109.

3. For a brief resumé of a change in the Tariff Commission view, see Frank V. Fowlkes, "Economic Report/Administrative Escape Valves Relieve Pressures of Imports on Domestic Industries," National Journal, July 24, 1971, pp. 1544-50.

4. For background material on the 807 program, see U.S. Tariff Commission, "Economic Factors Affecting the Use of Items 807.00 and 806.30 of the Tariff Schedules of the United States: Report to the President on Investigation No. 332-61 Under Section 332 of the Tariff Act of 1930," TC Publication 339, Washington, D.C., 1970. A more recent treatment of the program can be found in Vladimir N. Pregelj, "Item 807.00 of the Tariff Schedules of the United States: Selected Facts and Comments," Congressional Research Service, Washington, D.C., 1976.

5. For an early study of the Mexican border industrialization program, see Donald W. Baerresen, The Border Industrialization Program of Mexico (Lexington, Mass.: D. C. Heath, 1971). The importance of the 807 provision is discussed in Chapter 5.

6. According to one AFL-CIO staff person, the search for relief from section 807 was the single most important influence leading to Burke-Hartke. The growing feeling that any administration would be unresponsive to AFL-CIO's trade problems suggested a legislative solution.

7. Ross, op. cit., p. 97.

8. Andrew J. Biemiller, Statement before the House Ways and Means Committee, Tariff and Trade Proposals, Hearings, Part

4, May 1970 (Washington, D.C.: U.S. Government Printing Office, 1970), p. 1001. Similar views were contained in the minority statement of I. W. Abel and Floyd E. Smith to the Report of the President's Commission on International Trade and Investment Policy (Williams Commission). See Commission on International Trade and Investment Policy, United States International Economic Policy in an Interdependent World (Washington, D.C.: U.S. Government Printing Office, 1971), pp. 338–42.

9. Ibid., p. 1010.

10. For a discussion of the Ways and Means Committee version of the Trade Act of 1970 and the so-called Byrnes basket, see Frank V. Fowlkes, "Business Report/House Turns to Protectionism Despite Arm-Twisting by Nixon Trade Experts," National Journal, August 8, 1970, pp. 1815–21.

11. AFL-CIO Executive Council, "The Critical Need for New International Trade and Investment Legislation," AFL-CIO (mimeo) Atlanta, May 12, 1971.

12. Two interviews with AFL-CIO staffers tended to confirm this view. The 1965–69 base period covered the time when most of the import penetration had taken place.

13. Burke-Hartke was first introduced as H.R. 10914, 92d Cong., 1st sess. The original Senate version was S. 2592, 92d Cong., 1st sess.

14. Richard A. Musgrave and Peggy B. Musgrave, Public Finance in Theory and Practice (New York: McGraw-Hill, 1973), p. 704.

15. H.R. 10914, 92d Cong., 1st sess., Title I, Sec. 103, pp. 15–18. The current foreign tax credit provisions can be found at 26 U.S.C. 901.

16. Until 1976 an exception to the gross-up rule was provided for Less Developed Country Corporations, 26 U.S.C. 902. Prior to 1962 the foreign tax credit was applied to the income of all controlled foreign subsidiaries following a Supreme Court decision in the American Chicle Co. v. U.S. case, 316 U.S. 450. The Revenue Act of 1962 imposed the gross-up provision but retained the exception for controlled subsidiaries in developing countries so as not to discourage U.S. direct foreign investment in the developing world. For further discussion, see Robert Hellawell, "The United States Income Taxation and Less Developed Countries: A Critical Appraisal," Columbia Law Review, December 1966, pp. 1393–1427.

17. H.R. 10914, 92d Cong., 1st sess., Title I, Sec. 102, pp. 3–15. Present treatment of the unrepatriated income of controlled foreign corporations can be found at 26 U.S.C. 951–64.

18. For a more detailed discussion of what constitutes a controlled foreign corporation, see Peggy B. Musgrave, United States

Taxation of Foreign Investment Income: Issues and Arguments, The
Law School of Harvard University, 1969, pp. 143, 148-51. For tax
purposes, the principal test for deferral is ownership of 10 percent
of the stock. See ibid., p. 149.

19. Musgrave and Musgrave, op. cit., p. 708.

20. See, for instance, Peggy Musgrave, op. cit., pp. 143-46.

21. The Revenue Act of 1962 was P.L. 87-834, 76 Stat. 960.
Extensive background information on the Revenue Act of 1962 can
be found in the Legislative History of H.R. 10650, 87th Congress,
The Revenue Act of 1962, Committee on Ways and Means, U.S.
House of Representatives, 90th Cong., 1st sess., Parts 1 to 4
(Washington, D.C.: U.S. Government Printing Office, 1967).

22. H.R. 10914, Title I, Sec. 104, 105, and 106. In Sec. 107
Burke-Hartke required the Treasury to submit a report on the administration of the U.S. tax code with regard to foreign source
income. The treasury would be specifically required to report on
any difficulties that were encountered in securing compliance with
the code.

23. See Peggy Musgrave, op. cit., p. 151.

24. H.R. 10914, Title I, Sec. 104. Burke-Hartke would have
amended the general rules for computing depreciation (26 U.S.C. 167)
and eliminated the exception for foreign subsidiaries from the restrictions on depreciation practice contained in 26 U.S.C. 312(m). The
latter section deals with the distribution of capital or earnings from
a corporations to its shareholders (in many cases another corporation).

25. Current law can be found at 26 U.S.C. 367.

26. H.R. 10914, Title I, Sec. 105.

27. H.R. 10914, Title I, Sec. 106.

28. Estimates for the tax loss from applying the pre-1976
tax laws to foreign-earned income of U.S. citizens was just under
$500 million. The changes made by the Tax Reform Act of 1976
would have pared this loss to about $180 million. In restoring liberal
treatment for foreign-earned income, committee reports emphasized
the impact the Tax Reform Act of 1976 changes would have on the
ability of U.S. firms to keep U.S. nationals overseas. See, for
instance, Foreign Earned Income Act of 1978. Report, 95-1463,
Committee on Ways and Means, U.S. House of Representatives, 95th
Cong., 2d sess. 1978.

29. For instance, see Peggy Musgrave's discussion of the
impact of capital flows on the domestic economy, op. cit., pp. 9-67.

30. The principal exponent remained Peggy Musgrave, a long-
time student of taxation of foreign source income. See Peggy B.
Musgrave, "Tax Preferences to Foreign Investment," in The Economics of Federal Subsidy Programs, Part 2, Joint Economic

Committee, 92d Congress, 2d sess. (Washington, D.C.: U.S. Government Printing Office, 1972).

31. Much of the factual material on existing U.S. quotas is drawn from Ilse Mintz, U.S. Import Quotas: Costs and Consequences (Washington, D.C.: American Enterprise Institute for Public Policy Research, 1973).

32. Ibid., p. 76. The provision was continued in Section 232 of the Trade Expansion Act of 1962. The current version can be found in Section 127 of the Trade Act of 1974.

33. Ibid., pp. 50-51. For materials on this and subsequent Japanese voluntary restrictions on cotton textile exports, see John Lynch, Toward an Orderly Market: An Intensive Study of Japan's Voluntary Quota in Cotton Textile Exports (Tokyo: Sophia University, 1968).

34. Mintz, op. cit., pp. 79-83.

35. Stephen P. McGee, "The Welfare Effects of Restrictions on U.S. Trade," Brookings Papers on Economic Activity, No. 3, 1972 (Washington, D.C.: Brookings Institution, pp. 669-74. His estimates for petroleum, textiles, and sugar are heavily influenced by Mintz.

36. In a rough calculation, McGee estimates the "Tariff-equivalent revenue lost to foreigners . . . is . . . $1.2 billion. . . ." Ibid., p. 673.

37. According to McGee, $7,456 million of U.S. imports were subject to quotas in 1969. Ibid., p. 669. The figures for total U.S. imports are from the Annual Report of the Council on International Economic Policy (Washington, D.C.: U.S. Government Printing Office). Presumably without the quotas, the covered items would have constituted an even larger share of U.S. imports.

38. Although extensive, the U.S. Tariff is not necessarily crippling. By distributing customs revenues for 1971 over all U.S. imports, McGee has found the "implied advalorem tariff rate" to be 6.1 percent. See McGee, op. cit., p. 664. Depending on the individual item, the nominal and the effective rate of tariff protection could, of course, be much higher. A catalog of what the Ways and Means Committee judged to be "alleged" U.S. nontariff barriers can be found in Briefing Materials Prepared for Use of the Committee on Ways and Means in Connection with Hearings on the Subject of Foreign Trade and Tariffs (Washington, D.C.: U.S. Government Printing Office, 1973), pp. 144-150. A brief description of current U.S. Buy American policies can be found in ibid., p. 145.

39. H.R. 10914, 92d Cong., 1st sess., Title III, pp. 24-30.

40. Terrence R. Colvin and Donald E. DeKieffer, "A Legal and Economic Analysis of the Quota Provisions of the Proposed Foreign Trade and Investment Act of 1972," International Lawyer 6, no. 4 (1972):777.

41. The provisions for the proposed Foreign Trade and Investment Commission can be found in H.R. 10914, 92d Cong., 1st sess., Title II, pp. 21-23.

42. H.R. 10914, 92d Cong., 1st sess., Title III, Sec. 303(e), p. 29.

43. H.R. 10914, 92d Cong., 1st sess., Title III, Sec. 301(b) (2)(A), pp. 24-25.

44. H.R. 10914, 92d Cong., 1st sess., Title III, Sec. 301(b) (2)(B), p. 25.

45. H.R. 10914, 92d Cong., 1st sess., Title III, Sec. 301(g), p. 27.

46. H.R. 10914, 92d Cong., 1st sess., Title III, Sec. 301(d) (3), p. 26.

47. H.R. 10914, 92d Cong., 1st sess., Title III, Sec. 301(d) (2), p. 26.

48. H.R. 10914, 92d Cong., 1st sess., Title III, Sec. 301(d) (1), p. 26. It was generally felt that the Canadian Automobile Agreement would have been exempted under this or the preceding [Sec. 301 (d)(2)] section. McGee, however, took the opposite view. See McGee, op. cit., note 60, p. 688.

49. H.R. 10914, 92d Cong., 1st sess., Title III, Sec. 301(d) (4), p. 26.

50. McGee estimated the first year net welfare costs to be $7.1 billion. See McGee, op. cit., p. 701.

51. H.R. 10914, Title VI, Secs. 601 and 602, pp. 41-42. The standard for technology flows was even more exacting. The prohibition would be justified if U.S. employment would be increased. Read in conjunction with the net employment test for capital flows, it appears that very little would be needed to trigger a restriction on the exporting of an individual patent.

52. Federal Register 37, no. 76 (April 19, 1972).

53. P.L. 93-618, Secs. 321(b)(1) and (2).

54. The Countervailing Duty amendments can be found in H.R. 10914, 92d Cong., 1st sess., Title IV, Sec. 402, pp. 32-34.

55. In fact, from 1962 to 1969, all of the 27 petitions for trade adjustment assistance were rejected by the Tariff Commission. See Carl H. Fulda, "Adjustment to Hardship Caused by Imports: The New Decisions of the Tariff Commission and the Need for Legislative Clarification," Michigan Law Review 70, no. 5 (April 1972): 795.

56. Amendments to the Trade Reform Act of 1962 can be found in H.R. 10914, 92d Cong., 1st sess., Title V, Secs. 501 and 520, pp. 34-41.

57. H.R. 10914, 92d Cong., 1st sess., Title V, Sec. 501(b), p. 35.

58. H.R. 10914, 92d Cong., 1st sess., Title VII, Secs. 703(a) (1) and (2), p. 44.

59. H.R. 15458 and S. 3708, respectively. These bills in essentially the same form were reintroduced in the 93rd Congress. For a brief summary of the 93rd Congress version of these two bills, see Vladimir Pregelj, "Burke-Hartke Bill and Other Major Trade Legislation in the 93rd Congress," Congressional Research Service, February 5, 1973.

60. H.R. 15472.

61. S. 384.

62. S. 3739.

63. See, for instance, Rudy Oswald, Statements and Reports Adopted by the AFL-CIO Executive Council, Bal Harbour, Florida, February 21-28, 1977, pp. 21-23.

64. For a particularly lucid summary of the DISC provisions, see Jane G. Gravelle and Donald W. Kiefer, "Deferral and DISC: Two Targets of Tax Reform" (Washington, D.C.: Congressional Research Service, Library of Congress, February 3, 1978), pp. 9-12.

65. For a brief discussion of how the Tax Reform Act of 1976 affected foreign earned income, see "Foreign Earned Income Act of 1978," Report 95-1463, Committee on Ways and Means, U.S. House of Representatives, 95th Cong., 2d sess., Washington, D.C., 1978.

66. P.L. 93-168, Sec. 161.

67. P.L. 93-618, Sec. 151.

68. P.L. 93-618, Sec. 152.

69. See The Buy American Act Amendments of 1977, Hearings before the Subcommittee on Federal Spending Practices and Open Government of the Committee on Governmental Affairs, U.S. Senate, 95th Cong., 2d sess. (Washington, D.C.: U.S. Government Printing Office, 1978).

70. "Congressional Critics Warn of Trouble for the Coming Freer-trade Pact," Wall Street Journal, December 15, 1978, p. 1.

71. Sec. 331, P.L. 93-618, also Sec. 303(d) of the Tariff Act of 1930 (19 U.S.C. sec. 1303).

72. Buy American Act Amendments of 1977, op. cit., p. 15.

73. See "Exemption of Certain Products from Tariff Reductions Negotiated in the Multilateral Trade Negotiations (MTN)," Hearing before the Subcommittee on Trade of the Committee on Ways and Means, House of Representatives, 95th Cong., 2d sess., Serial 95-102 (Washington, D.C.: 1978) and "Countervailing Duty Waiver Extension," Hearings before the Subcommittee on Trade of the Committee on Ways and Means, House of Representatives, Serial 95-107 (Washington, D.C.: 1978).

74. The Ex-Im provisions can be found in Title XIX of the Financial Institutions Regulatory and Interest Rate Control Act of 1978 (P.L. 95-630). As a sign that labor was active in this battle as well, one amendment to the Ex-Im Bank Act requires the bank's

directors to give full consideration to the impact of bank loans on domestic industries and employment.

75. P.L. 95-501.

76. "Foreign Earned Income Act of 1978," Report, op. cit., p. 7.

77. See Export Policy, Hearings before the Subcommittee on International Finance of the Committee on Banking, Housing and Urban Affairs, U.S. Senate, 95th Cong., 2d sess. (Washington, D.C.: U.S. Government Printing Office, 1978), National Export Program, Hearing before the Committee on Commerce, Science and Transportation, U.S. Senate, 95th Cong., 2d sess., September 28, 1978, Serial 95-113 (Washington, D.C.: U.S. Government Printing Office, 1978); Exports: Time for a National Policy, Hearings before the Subcommittee on International Economics of the Joint Economic Committee, U.S. Congress, 95th Cong., 2d sess., August 30 and September 29, 1978 (Washington, D.C.: U.S. Government Printing Office, 1978.

CHAPTER 3

TRADE AND INVESTMENT THEORY, INTEREST GROUP BEHAVIOR, AND CONGRESSIONAL DELIBERATION

TRADE THEORY

Few areas of economics are more extensively or elegantly developed than the pure theory of international trade. Although often kept within fairly narrow, theoretical grounds, the very proliferation of academic articles threatens to make any survey of the literature an encyclopedic task. In addition, a number of excellent surveys have already been made by Haberler,[1] Caves,[2] Bhagwati,[3] and Corden.[4] There is also an extensive and somewhat more technical three-part survey by Chipman.[5] More recently, Stern has provided an overview of developments in the theory of tariffs and other trade barriers.[6] Instead of attempting to provide yet another survey of the literature, the focus here will be on the main points of the different approaches to trade theory and their implications for interest group behavior.

In many ways the history of trade policy antedates any efforts to explain the pattern or nature of international trade. The sixteenth-century mercantilists sought to achieve an excess of exports over imports—focusing on increasing the store of liquid assets in the national treasury. Whether or not this policy could be justified by the difficulty of alternative means of filling the national coffers or the exigencies of financing national defense needs, it offered no general explanation of why trade existed at all.

An early theory of trade was contained in Adam Smith's The Wealth of Nations,[7] but a more general explanation was advanced by David Ricardo.[8] Drawing on the simple example of trade in cloth and wine between England and Portugal, Ricardo developed his well-known theory of comparative advantage. Ricardo used the notion of comparative advantage both to demonstrate the gains from trade and to explain the pattern of international commerce. Modern reconstructions of the Ricardian model generally assume a two-nation, two-commodity, one-factor, constant-cost world. Given these assumptions, the pretrade commodity price ratio will be solely a function of the different production functions in the two countries. The strong Ricardian proposition then states that differences in technology,* rather than variations in tastes or factor supplies, will determine the nature of international trade. To extend the Ricardian theory to more than two goods, however, requires the introduction of demand to determine exactly which goods will be traded. [9]

Despite the restrictive nature of the Ricardian model, it has generated a certain amount of empirical work. MacDougall pioneered in this area by comparing the ratio of U.S. and British labor productivities† to the ratio of their exports to third countries. [10] The initial work by MacDougall was followed up by Balassa, [11] Stern, [12] and some further work by MacDougall. [13] In general their results supported the Ricardian-type hypothesis.

Given its focus on one factor (almost always labor) in the production process, the Ricardian theory is relatively unproductive in terms of describing or predicting interest group behavior. With some modifications, however, it does provide an interesting focus on the potential impact of the international transmission of technology.

In discussing the impact of the English corn laws, Ricardo himself assumed diminishing returns to scale in agriculture and allowed for incomplete specialization. A number of recent attempts to formalize Ricardo's well known wine-cloth definition of comparative advantage adopt considerably more restrictive assumptions, and these allow a clearer focus on the role of technology.

For instance, the Caves-Jones version of the standard Ricardian model assumes that its one factor (labor) is totally homogeneous, perfectly mobile within a nation and completely immobile internationally. [14] Assuming different labor productivities and trade barriers, trade will take place and lead to complete specialization. The key difference in the two economies is the existence of different production functions brought about by the existence of different technologies.

---

*Technically, the variations in technology must be of a nonneutral nature to create the different commodity cost ratios that give rise to trade.

†Trade between the two countries was excluded so as to avoid the potentially distorting effect of tariff barriers. Presumably the United States and Britain faced generally similar trade barriers in third countries.

As technology flowed between the two countries, differences in their production functions would be eliminated and the Ricardian basis for trade would disappear. Presumably there would be no loss of welfare. However, either by dropping the assumption of labor homogeneity or introducing an adjustment period to the new technology, there might be real, albeit temporary, losers from the change. The impact of adding either more commodities or more trading partners would depend on whether or not they increased labor mobility.

The prospect of economic losses could well lead a portion of the affected factor (labor) to resist either the importation of new technology or the exportation of home technology (as happened in the Burke-Hartke Bill). This is not the only nor the most insightful explanation of the impact that international technology flows could have on interest group behavior. Like so much of the Ricardian theory, it is limited by the assumption of one homogeneous factor of production. But it does provide one possible framework in which trade in technology would have a substantial impact on both partners.

Although the Ricardian approach is very much a part of current thinking on trade flows, most recent work has been done within the framework of the Heckscher-Ohlin theory. Originally developed by Eli Heckscher,* but amplified by Bertil Ohlin,[15] the Heckscher-Ohlin theory makes several assumptions that differ from the traditional Ricardian theory.

The basic Heckscher-Ohlin (hereafter HO) model does maintain many similarities to the Ricardian world: two commodities, two countries, perfect competition, perfect internal and no external mobility of factors of production, and the presence of constant cost production functions. But two assumptions are fundamentally different: HO assumes that all trading partners (in the simple case only two) are possessed of identical technologies, and all trading partners have more than one (in the simple case capital and labor) factor of production.

The HO approach focuses on the factors of production as the key to an explanation of the pattern of international trade. According

---

*Ohlin was actually the first to introduce this portion of Heckscher's work to the English-speaking world. A full English translation of Heckscher's trade theories did not appear until several years after Ohlin started to publish his own work and many years after they originally appeared in Swedish. In addition to its seminal character, Heckscher's work lacked certain complicating embellishments that Ohlin had introduced. The whole episode is an interesting example of lags in the transmission of noncommercial information.

to the central proposition of the HO theory, a country will <u>trade the commodity that uses most intensively the factor of production that is relatively abundant</u>. The theory has an immediate appeal at even a common-sense level—after all, if capital is more abundant in one country than another one might expect that goods that use relatively more capital would be relatively less expensive. And such relative differences are the touchstone of comparative advantage.

The logical truth of the proposition, however, demands a number of other assumptions. First, one must decide on a clear definition of abundant. While most economists have adopted a physical definition of abundance (how many workers in each country), others have advocated the use of a price definition (comparing the ratio of wage rates to capital rentals). The physical definition has the advantage of allowing the testing of the theory in a world where trade is already taking place and it is the definition of choice here.

Given the physical definition of abundance, HO depends crucially on the existence of identical production functions, the lack of factor intensity reversals, and the tastes of the two trading partners in addition to the assumptions carried over from the Ricardian world. With identical production functions, factor abundance could have quite varying effects on commodity prices. The same can be said for community tastes. It is quite conceivable that the country with relatively abundant labor might intensely prefer the labor-intensive good. The result could be relative labor abundance and a comparative advantage in the capital-intensive good. The absence of factor intensity reversals is patently crucial to the HO approach. If not, there exists a persistent ambiguity as to which commodity uses the abundant factor.

The basic HO theory has precipitated a virtual flood of theoretical and empirical work in the postwar era. The work has followed three rather distinct paths. First, there have been attempts to spell out the implications of trade for the various factors of production. Second, considerable effort has been made to relax the various assumptions that are required by the simple version of the HO theory. Included in this group are attempts to generalize the HO theory to the n-commodity, n-country, n-factor case. Finally, there have been a number of empirical tests of both the theory and some of its basic underpinnings. Most important in this regard was the work stimulated by Leontief[16] and Minhas.[17]

Many of the possible implications of trade for factor incomes have been worked out within the framework of the HO model. Two are of particular interest for the study of interest group behavior. An early and much-refined aspect of the HO theory is the factor price

equalization theorem. Under certain specified conditions,* free trade
in commodities will lead to identical returns to the individual factors.
The implications for group behavior in a two-factor world are obvious.
In the capital-rich, relatively high-wage country, free trade will
tend to lead to a reduction in the real wages of labor. Under such
conditions one could expect the losing factor to allocate some of its
prefree trade income to resisting the creation or extension of free
trade.†

Just as rich in its implications for interest group behavior is
the Stolper-Samuelson theorem.[22] According to Stolper-Samuelson,
an increase in the price of a commodity increases the real income
of the factor used intensively in the manufacture of that commodity.
In other words, in a country where the imports are labor intensive,
a tariff can increase the absolute and relative income of domestic
labor. To the extent that the Stolper-Samuelson world represents
reality, it suggests a clear rationale for interest group conflict over
the existence or height of a tariff. If the tariff imposed is not pro-
hibitive, income is generated for the national treasury. In theory,
the income could be so distributed as to offset the effect of the tariff.
Given the imposition of an optimal tariff that increases national in-

---

*In addition to the usual assumptions made for the simple
Heckscher-Ohlin case, factor price equalization requires that neither
trading partner can specialize completely in one commodity. On the
other hand, the factor price equalization theorem may hold even in
cases where differing tastes have invalidated the HO theory itself.
See, for instance, Caves and Jones.[18] For a compilation of the
original and still complete set of conditions for the two-country,
two-commodity, two-factor case, see Bhagwati.[19] Bhagwati also
summarizes much of the work that has been done to extend the factor
price equalization theorem to the many goods-many factors situation.[20] Efforts to relax other assumptions have been less successful.
Bhagwati cites Laing's work to "underline the implications of Samuelson's analysis that constant returns to scale cannot be given up without invalidating the logical truth of the factor price equalization
theorem."[21]

†Given a world of complete certainty and the sole desire to
maximize factor income, the scarce factor might be willing to spend
all of the extra income it receives in pretrade as opposed to the free
trade situation. In the world of Washington lobbying, however, all
factors generally seek a number of goals, and in any case only a
limited portion of any factor's income is allocated to income protection.

come, both factors (labor and capital) could be better off. The presence of tariff-related income not only provides a further motive for interest group activity but fits in well with the log-rolling, everybody-gets-a-share view that is often attributed to the Congress.

In more recent times considerable effort has been made to expand the scope of the Stolper-Samuelson theorem.[23] None of these efforts, however, add much to the interest group insight of the simple two-commodity, two-factor case. Starting from the two-country, two-commodity, two-factor world with the usual assumptions about tastes, production functions, factor homogeneity and international immobility, growth and technological change, there is ample room for expansion. There is an extensive and still-growing literature on the various attempts to generalize the HO model. Of particular interest in the foreign trade and investment context are changes in technology, the introduction of factor heterogeneity, the possibility of international factor mobility, and the existence of oligopoly as an important market imperfection.

Most of the analysis of technological change has taken place within the context of a two-commodity world. Neutral or biased technological change is admitted in the production of one commodity and the analysis proceeds to spell out the implications for the production of both commodities. In terms of interest groups, the focus would be on both output (as an extremely rough proxy for jobs) and income. Although an admittedly abstract and restricted context, admitting technological change could provide some explanation for resistance to the importation of technology.

In the congressional battles over foreign trade and investment, however, the interest was in regulating the exportation of technology. Because the technology took so many forms—managerial know-how, skilled labor, organization, and advanced capital goods—it falls more nearly under the question of factor mobility. In any case the debate generally involved the introduction of market imperfections (the large, oligopolistic multinational firm) and often altogether non-HO type explanations of trade behavior.

Within the HO framework, Mundell broke new ground in allowing for international factor mobility.[24] Using a two-country, two-commodity, two-factor approach, Mundell demonstrated that factor mobility could substitute for trade in equalizing both commodity and factor prices. The introduction of transportation costs, however, destroyed this symmetry. Mundell went on to explore the implications of a discriminatory tariff in one country on national and factor income and factor flows. By positing the existence of sufficiently large economies of scale, the tariff-imposing country could increase the income of both factors. Somewhat surprisingly, little further work on factor flows has been built on Mundell's pioneering effort.

Perhaps it is because so much of the taxonomic work has been spelled out in the analysis of the differential growth of factor supplies.[25]

The two-factors-of-production assumption has proved a useful abstraction from reality for many purposes. There have, however, been a variety of attempts to move beyond the two-factor world. To some extent these efforts have been designed to seek the logical limits of a generalized HO approach. In other cases the focus has been on adapting the HO framework to a more complex reality. A relaxation of the two-factors assumption also played an important role in attempts to rationalize the Leontief paradox.

Caves's work in this area is particularly interesting.[26] By allowing the existence of oligopoly as well as sector specific capital, Caves provides an interesting insight into the pattern of direct foreign investment and the behavior of the multinational firm. Caves does, however, maintain the assumption of a homogeneous, internationally immobile labor stock.

From the standpoint of interest group behavior, heterogeneous labor supply and limited labor mobility take on considerable significance. A great deal of organized labor's concern has always focused on the difficulty and cost involved in moving from one job to another. A lost job may imply the loss of considerable human capital (training) that was specific to a narrow range of tasks. In addition the worker may lose pension, seniority, and other property rights. Generally this suggests that the less mobile a factor is the more likely it is to resist trade-induced or other adverse change. It is important to remember that the immobility may stem as much from geographic isolation as from skill specialization.

Market imperfections are also generally excluded from the HO framework. Competitive assumptions are crucial to the strict workings of the model and many of its derivative implications. But studying the behavior of large, generally oligopolistic American firms in the foreign trade and investment area demands a more flexible approach. Although labor and business are often at odds, they do frequently share the benefits of oligopoly power and profits. At some point shared benefits should reduce political conflict.

For much of the twentieth century the HO theory has occupied a central place both as an explanation of trade patterns and a guide to trade policy. In the preceding paragraphs there has been a brief discussion of some of the attempts to explore the logical basis for the HO theory and to expand its amplitude. There has also been considerable work seeking to empirically test the theory. In making an effort to test the HO theory, however, Leontief opened the theory to very serious attack.[27] Accepting the generally held view that the

United States was a relatively capital-abundant country,* Leontief examined the factor intensities of U.S. exports and U.S. import-competing industries. To his own and the professions' surprise he found that the U.S. import-competing industries were more capital intensive than were its export industries. Similar studies were made of several other countries with rather mixed results.[28]

A number of explanations were advanced to reconcile Leontief's findings with the HO theory. Leontief himself suggested that his calculations may not have accurately reflected the efficiency of U.S. labor. Without any clear basis, Leontief suggested that U.S. labor was on the order of three times as efficient as that found in its trading partners.[29] Given that view, the United States could be seen as a relatively labor-abundant country, thus bringing the Leontief approach in line with the HO theory. In a similar vein it was suggested that Leontief had failed to calculate the human capital involved in U.S. exports. Other explanations focused on the research intensity of U.S. exports or the possibility that more than simply two factors of production were involved.[30]

The Leontief paradox raises some very specific questions about the implications of both the factor price equalization theorem and the Stolper-Samuelson theorem for interest group behavior. If the Leontief paradox holds, it would suggest that capital owners not labor would be opposed to the creation of freer trade. The Leontief study was based on data from the early post-World War II period. It is possible that the rapid development of new technology and differential growth rates of labor and capital could have combined to change the nature of America's comparative advantage. Such a change might provide at least a partial explanation for labor's eventual break with the free trade alliance. With certain industries already protected by voluntary quotas, a change in the nature of the U.S. comparative advantage could also help to account for the widespread opposition to Burke-Hartke and other labor initiatives in the rest of the business community.

There is, however, no clear evidence that America's comparative advantage has undergone a basic change since World War II. A Bureau of Labor Statistics (BLS) study focused on the late 1960s does provide some indication of a reversal.[31] The BLS study sought to determine the number of jobs involved in producing American exports and the number of jobs that would be required to produce imports that competed with American industry. Comparing the years 1966

---

*Frequently the relative factor abundancies were never actually calculated.

and 1969, the BLS found a 200,000-job increase in export-related jobs and a 700,000 jump in the number of jobs required to produce competitive imports. The net difference of 500,000 was often cited by the AFL-CIO as a partial justification for the quota provisions contained in Burke-Hartke.

A relative decrease in the number of jobs needed to produce exports would at least be consistent with a shift in the nature of America's comparative advantage. The difficulty, however, is that the BLS study is not comparable to the Leontief study. First of all, only a portion of U.S. imports was included in the study. Second, the evidence suggests that the U.S. dollar was becoming increasingly overvalued during this period. As imports increased more rapidly than exports, one could expect that the number of jobs involved in exports would fall relative to those involved in imports regardless of the labor or capital intensities involved.

One is left with some lingering questions about the particular methods that Leontief used[32] and lingering doubts about the explanatory powers of the two-factor version of the HO theory. Nonetheless, the initial plausibility of the HO approach, the degree to which the theory has been developed, and the extent to which it has been applied have kept it in the forefront of international trade research. It also offers some insight into interest group behavior in the trade field. In addition, to the extent economics played an explicit role in congressional decisions, the HO theory would most likely be the "theory" of choice.

In recent years, however, a number of theories have been advanced that stand outside of or at least alongside of the HO approach. Many of these focus on technological change, scale economies, or the importance of natural resources. Linder distinguishes trade in primary products from trade in manufactures.[33] In explaining primary product trade, Linder stresses the relative endowments of natural resources, an approach well within the HO tradition. For manufactures, however, he suggests that the pattern of trade depends crucially on similarity in demand patterns of the trading countries. Given the existence of similar tastes and income distributions, similarity in demand boils down to similar levels of per capita income. Linder also mentions the importance of technological superiority, managerial skills, and economies of scale.

Kravis has suggested that the commodity composition of trade is controlled by the availability of different commodities.[34] "Availability" encompasses not only absolute unavailability (such as the lack of tin in the United States) but also situations in which additional output could be obtained only at a much higher cost. Kravis focuses on the difference between the relative elasticities of supply in domestic and foreign markets. In Kravis's view, the degree of technological innovation can play a crucial role in export industries.

Vernon also gives technology a central place in his product-cycle theory.[35] In the early stages of an innovation the emphasis is on the domestic market and the use of large amounts of skilled labor in the production process. As demand grows, capital and relatively unskilled labor take on an increasingly important role in production. Vernon's theory nicely incorporates the evident importance of technology, includes the probable importance of skilled labor in U.S. exports, and suggests a possible motivation for foreign direct investment as new production methods are developed and emulated.

This rather terse review of international trade theory has suggested some valuable hypotheses about the behavior of major interest groups in the formulation of foreign trade policy. The two-factor emphasis of the HO approach blends readily with the prominence of big business and big labor in the debate over Burke-Hartke and current trade policy. The factor price equalization theorem suggests that the relatively scarce factor could maintain pretrade gains by seeking to prevent a move to freer trade. In a similar fashion the Stolper-Samuelson theorem indicated that the relatively scarce factor could increase its real income by fighting for specific trade barriers. Either theorem could help to rationalize the behavior of big labor in the foreign trade debates.

Use of the HO theorem, however, must be made with some clear limitations in mind. First, there is the question of the Leontief paradox alluded to above. Second, there is the problem of describing the intricacies of interest group behavior with an admittedly abstract model. And finally, the two-factor HO approach lends itself to more than one theory of political behavior. The very emphasis on the antagonisms between labor and capital suggests the possibility of using a class-based, Marxist-type model to explain the behavior of business and labor groups.

Despite the possible fit between HO and a Marxist view of political reality, this study of congressional decisions in the foreign trade and investment field is very much a pluralistic approach adopted by such authors as Bauer. But if pluralism is the proper approach, where are the other groups? In part, different interests are contained within the large labor and business organizations. Differences are worked out within the organization before an approach to Congress is undertaken. Other interests, particularly in industry, were accommodated by the administration through the use of voluntary controls. That still leaves agriculture as a major interest that was simply not heard from on the Burke-Hartke Bill.*

---

*In an interview with a staff member at the U.S. Chamber of Commerce, the staff member mentioned that the Chamber had a siz-

Agriculture has a large and growing interest in the export market. In addition, certain agricultural commodities, notably meat and dairy products, have long been the subject of import competition. The major agricultural groups* were very active in support of the Trade Reform Act of 1973,[36] but they were virtually silent on the efforts of labor to control the flow of trade, technology, or capital. The explanation appears to be severalfold. Whether lumped in one package such as the Burke-Hartke Bill or considered separately, major agricultural interests saw Burke-Hartke as mainly a vehicle to attack the multinational firms. Agriculture is dominated by domestic firms and family farms. The largest and probably most conservative farm organization, the American Farm Bureau Federation, has taken no stand on the question of taxation of foreign-source income.† Even with regard to the battle over tax incentives for U.S. exports, agriculture is involved mainly as an accommodation to its business allies.‡ Burke-Hartke also left unaffected the agricultural groups that already had quota protection. Although the quota provisions of Burke-Hartke would have been substituted for existing voluntary quotas, any quotas mandated by U.S. law would have been allowed to stand. Furthermore, agricultural interest in foreign trade issues appears to have sharpened following the massive grain sale to the Soviet Union in 1973. Empty granaries and continuing world shortages of foodstuffs emphasized the export potential for American agriculture. In sum, agriculture was not as focused on foreign trade when labor broke with the free trade alliance and continues to feel that the labor drive was largely directed against the multinational firms. Since the passage of the Trade Act of 1974, agricultural interests have emphasized the importance of opening up foreign markets to American goods through the Tokyo Round of multilateral trade.[37]

The HO theory remains a useful and insightful approach to interest group behavior. Just as useful are the variety of theories

----

able number of individual members representing the agricultural sector.

*According to interviews conducted with agricultural and business organizations, agriculture was very active in lobbying for the Trade Reform Act of 1973. Both the American Farm Bureau Federation and the Grange were members of the Trade Action Co-ordinating Committee chaired by Ray Garcia of the Emergency Committee for American Trade.

†According to a June 1976 interview at the American Farm Bureau Federation.

‡According to a June 1976 interview at the Grange.

about technology and trade and the importance of various market imperfections. Starting with Ricardo, admitting the possibility of different production functions suggests the possibility of loss from the diffusion of technical knowledge. Certainly, big labor remains very concerned about the "export" of U.S. technology. The prominence of multinational firms in the foreign trade debate could be at least partially explained by the approach taken by Caves in stressing oligopoly, economies of scale, and the importance of technology.

Throughout most of the subsequent chapters, the ideas presented above play an implicit, sometimes even an explicit, role. They are at the very least a first point of departure in describing interest group behavior and suggesting the tools available for congressional deliberation in a foreign trade debate.

FOREIGN DIRECT INVESTMENT THEORY

During the interwar period, international capital flows were relatively moderate. It was trade and barriers to trade that were of principal concern. The Bretton Woods agreement reflected the concern for trade but did not foresee a marked change in the size or nature of international capital flows. In fact, the post–World War II era has been notable for the rapid increase in foreign investment, particularly foreign direct investment by U.S.-based multinational firms.

The advent of foreign direct investment as a major phenomenon in the international economy has presented a distinct challenge for trade and investment theory. In their standard formulations, neither Ricardo nor Heckscher-Ohlin admitted international mobility of factors. Within the HO framework, Mundell stands largely alone in his attempt to incorporate factor mobility.[38] As suggested above, some of the analytic implications of factor mobility were worked out from the standpoint of technological change or an increase in factor supplies.[39]

There has been, however, a certain amount of work done on the causes and effects of foreign investment. Much of this work does not specifically differentiate between direct and portfolio investments but is nonetheless relevant to the direct investment case. An increase in direct (or portfolio) investment may have the effect of driving down the rate of return on existing foreign investments, suggesting a difference between the social and the private marginal rates of return. Jasey[40] and Kemp[41] have both explored this point of view.

Foreign direct investment can also have an impact on the home (source of the investment) or the host (location of the investment) countries' terms of trade. In the case of raw materials, it may well be that the foreign direct investments of a raw-material-importing industrialized nation not only assure it of supply but also drive down the world price of similar materials.[42] For manufactured goods the impact may run the other way.*

Frankel has led the way in focusing on the possible externalities that may accompany a foreign direct investment.[43] Some emphasis is placed on the development of technology as a possible outgrowth of foreign direct investment. The added impetus to future growth from the development of new technology in the host country is per-force lost to the home country—a position that labor was to adopt in less explicit, less elegant terms.

More recently there has been some work done on the impact of foreign direct investment on the balance of payments. Following the earlier work of Bell,[44] Hufbauer and Adler[45] attempt to estimate "how many years are required before a single direct investment outflow . . . will produce a cumulative stream of balance of payments inflows equal to itself"[46]—or in their terminology, the recoupment period. The overall balance of payments impact in turn will reflect a variety of individual components. In addition to the direct impact on capital equipment and parts and components, Hufbauer and Adler include all exports associated with the investment. They also include the influence on imports, the possibility of displacing existing exports (of considerable concern to labor) and any multiplier effects.

Central to the Hufbauer and Adler approach were questions about whether or not foreign direct investment substituted for domes-tic investment in the host country or was supplementary to it. In a similar vein they asked whether or not foreign direct investment reduced investment in the home country. They distinguished four types of substitution that could take place and grouped these various possibilities in three different categories.

Two types of substitution may take place within the host country. First, there is the decision by the multinational firm to draw on home capital or to seek local debt or equity financing. Hufbauer and Adler refer to this as the financial mix choice. Second, there is host coun-try reliance on foreign capital or domestic resources. Hufbauer and

---

*Given the breadth of most industrialized countries' exports, it is unlikely that a particular investment would have a noticeable impact on the overall terms of trade. On the other hand, the breadth of U.S. foreign direct investment in the 1960s may have had some impact on the terms at which a large number of goods were traded. In many cases the result was actually to eliminate the United States from a number of export markets.

Adler refer to this as external substitution. The home country is also faced with two types of substitution. The multinational firm must decide whether particular investment funds are destined for a home or foreign locale. Hufbauer and Adler term this the capital budget choice. External home country substitution refers to "the tradeoff between home and foreign investment in the eyes of the nation."[47]

Hufbauer and Adler group various combinations of these substitution possibilities under three general categories: classical, reverse classical, and anticlassical substitution assumptions. In classical terms,[48] foreign direct investment completely supplements host country investment and completely replaces home country investment. In the reverse classical view foreign direct investment substitutes for host country investment that would otherwise have been made while it is in addition to investment in the home country. In other words, the level of investment in the home country is unaffected by foreign direct investment. The final category, anticlassical, assumes that foreign direct investment augments host country investment while leaving home country investment unaffected.

The classical and reverse classical approaches are particularly interesting because of their different implications for stabilization policy.[49] Reverse classical assumptions raise virtually no stabilization problems; the rate of investment in both the host and home countries is left unaffected. In the classical case, however, the home country may be faced with a very definite stabilization problem that in turn will have implications for future economic growth and income distribution.

Assume that a U.S.-based multinational firm has made a capital budget choice to make a foreign direct investment and they have furthermore decided to make that investment with U.S. funds. If the foreign direct investment is accomplished with U.S.-made goods, employment and gross national product levels would be unchanged with the major implications being for future growth. If, however, the foreign direct investment does not result in an equal amount of U.S. export, the government will be faced with a stabilization choice. In a sense the government will be able to decide whether or not the classical assumptions will hold for the home country.

If the government resists any new stabilization efforts, one would expect a reduction in employment, national income, and future economic growth. On the other hand, the government could use a variety of tools to compensate for the capital budget decision of the U.S. multinational. Some of these—such as a broad-based tax cut— appear to be relatively neutral in their implications. Others, however, could have a very direct impact on income distribution. For instance, use of the investment tax credit could well bias the distribution of

national income toward capital owners. Such a policy would give
capital owners a three-part increase in income: abroad if the return
on foreign investment is higher, at home because of an increase in
the relative scarcity of capital, and because of governmental tax
policy.

The various motives for foreign direct investment are also of
more than a little interest. "Broadly speaking, the recent theoretical
and empirical literature has emphasized market strategy rather than
short-run profit maximization as the key motivational force."[50] Certainly the recent work of Caves[51] and much of the testimony of business groups would support the market strategy view.

Labor put particular stress on the importance of low foreign
wages and the tax advantages of direct foreign investment. In particular, labor stressed the existence of the foreign tax credit and the
deferral of tax liability for foreign source income. Labor was not
alone in its focus on the tax question,[52] and it continues to be of
considerable interest to the Congress.[53]

By itself, the current analyses of foreign direct investment do
suggest both a convergence and divergence of interest among major
domestic interest groups. If foreign direct investment greatly reduces the net return on existing foreign direct investment, capital
and labor may find common cause in seeking some regulation of
capital flows. Capital loses directly and labor indirectly through
lost reinvestment of repatriated funds. Similarly, both labor and
capital may benefit by foreign direct investments in raw materials
that turn the terms of trade in favor of the home country.

The potential divergences, however, are ample. Classical
assumptions and a limited stabilization response would be a perfect
situation for labor and capital to find themselves in opposition. They
could be equally opposed in a classical situation where there was a
limited stabilization response centered on tax incentives to business.

Technology is another area where divergences are possible.
Following the Frankel approach, one would expect labor to favor
keeping any externalities at home because of their more limited international mobility. The export of technology in conjunction with capital
could also have a major effect through worsening the home country's
terms of trade or through actual export displacement. On the other
hand, labor and capital may share a certain common interest in technology exports. Certainly the product cycle theory suggests that
firms can improve the profitability of any technological development
through eventual licensing or investment abroad. Greater profitability
would presumably generate further investment in the development of
home technology with positive implications for both the home rate of
growth and level of employment.

In sum, both existing trade and foreign investment theories suggest that labor and capital may be persistent antagonists in any consideration of international economic policy. The implications of factor price equalization and of the Stolper-Samuelson technique for increasing real income provide clear grounds for differences between capital and labor. Relaxing the HO assumptions to allow for factor mobility and technological differences suggests further possibilities for labor-capital disagreement. The important externalities involved in technology, the applicability of classical substitution assumptions, and the choice of stabilization policy all delineate areas of conflict.

The legislative fight over Burke-Hartke involved a large number of economic issues. The preceding summary of foreign trade and investment theory suggests that, at least in part, business and labor may have been motivated by logical, internally consistent motives that could be deduced from economic theory. As noted above, the use of theory requires a necessarily large jump from a two-factor world to the intricate workings of large interest groups. It also involves a somewhat selective use of various qualifications of and deviations from the much-used HO approach. There remains a danger that the utility of theory for prediction will be confused with the use of theory for persuasion. It is quite possible that having adopted a particular position because of membership pressure, internal political difficulties, or simple misanalysis, either labor or business then proceeded to construct the best case possible for that position. Economists, like lawyers, would then be called in only well after the "crime" had been committed. In the following discussions of the positions taken by labor and business, the possibility of economics as rationalization will be considered.

With all these caveats, the preceding discussions of foreign trade and investment theory do provide both a possible description of major interest group conflict and an economic perspective from which congressional decisions can be assessed.

NOTES

1. Gottfried Haberler, A Survey of International Trade Theory, Special Papers in International Economics, No. 1, International Finance Section, Department of Economics, Princeton University, 1961.

2. Richard E. Caves, Trade and Economic Structure (Cambridge, Mass.: Harvard University Press, 1960).

3. Jagdish Bhagwati, "The Pure Theory of International Trade: A Survey," in Trade Tariffs and Growth, Jagdish Bhagwati

(Cambridge, Mass.: The MIT Press, 1969). The Survey first appeared in the Economic Journal in March 1964.

4. W. M. Corden, Recent Developments in the Theory of International Trade, Special Papers in International Economics No. 7, International Finance Section, Department of Economics, Princeton University, 1965.

5. John S. Chipman, "A Survey of the Theory of International Trade: Part 1: The Classical Theory," Econometrica 33, no. 3 (July 1965); ". . . Part 2, The Neo Classical Theory," Econometrica 33, no. 4 (October 1965); ". . . Part 3, The Modern Theory," Econometrica 34, no. 1 (January 1966).

6. R. M. Stern, "Tariffs and Other Measures of Trade Control: A Survey of Recent Developments," Journal of Economic Literature 11, no. 3 (September 1973).

7. Adam Smith, An Inquiry Into the Nature and Causes of the Wealth of Nations (Middlesex, England: Penguin Books, 1971), pp. 472-73.

8. David Ricardo, The Principles of Political Economy and Taxation (New York: Penguin Books, 1971), Chapter 7.

9. See, for instance, R. W. Jones, "Factor Proportions and the Heckscher-Ohlin Model," Review of Economic Studies 24 (1956-57).

10. G. D. A. MacDougall, "British and American Exports: A Study Suggested by the Theory of Comparative Costs, Part I," Economic Journal 61 (December 1951); ". . . Part II," Economic Journal 62 (September 1952).

11. Bela Balassa, "An Empirical Demonstration of Classical Comparative Cost Theory," Review of Economics and Statistics 45 (August 1963).

12. Robert Stern, "British and American Productivity and Comparative Costs in International Trade," Oxford Economic Papers 14 (October 1962).

13. G. D. A. MacDougall, M. Dowley, P. Fox, and S. Pugh, "British and American Productivity, Prices and Exports: An Addendum," Oxford Economic Papers 14 (October 1962).

14. See Richard E. Caves and Ronald W. Jones, World Trade and Payments: An Introduction (Boston: Little, Brown, 1973), pp. 119-37.

15. Bertil Ohlin, Interregional and International Trade, Harvard Economic Studies, Vol. 39 (Cambridge, Mass.: Harvard University Press, 1939).

16. Wassily Leontief, "Domestic Production and Foreign Trade: The American Capital Position Re-examined," Economica Internazionale 7 (1954).

17. B. S. Minhas, "The Homohypallagic Production Function, Factor Intensity Reversals, and the Heckscher-Ohlin Theorem," Journal of Political Economy 70 (April 1962).

18. Caves and Jones, op. cit., pp. 174-78.
19. Bhagwati, op. cit., p. 40.
20. Ibid., pp. 39-42.
21. Ibid. See N. Laing, "Factor Price Equalization in International Trade and Returns to Scale," Economic Record 37 (September 1961).
22. W. Stolper and Paul A. Samuelson, "Protection and Real Wages," Review of Economic Studies 9 (November 1941).
23. A recent survey is contained in the opening pages of Yasua Uekawa, "Generalization of the Stolper-Samuelson Theory," Econometrica 39 (March 1971), pp. 197-217.
24. R. A. Mundell, "International Trade and Factor Mobility," American Economic Review 47 (June 1957).
25. Much of this work is epitomized by Harry G. Johnson's, International Trade and Economic Growth (London: George Allen and Unwin, 1958).
26. Richard E. Caves, "International Corporations: The Industrial Economics of Foreign Investment," Economica 38 (February 1971), pp. 1-27. See also Richard E. Caves, International Trade, International Investment, and Imperfect Markets, Special Papers in International Economics, No. 10, International Finance Section, Department of Economics, Princeton University, 1974.
27. Leontief, op. cit.
28. Studies were made of Canada, East Germany, India, and Japan. East Germany fit closest the pattern predicted by the HO theory. A disaggregation of the Japanese data also yielded findings that were consistent with HO. Other results, however, were generally contradictory to the HO approach. See Bhagwati, op. cit., pp. 32-33.
29. There does not seem to be any empirical basis for the Leontief threefold superiority view. In a survey of multinational firms, Kreinin found that the effectiveness of the U.S. worker was more on the order 1.5 times his foreign counterpart rather than the 2 or 3 times suggested by Leontief. See Mordechai E. Kreinin, "Comparative Labor Effectiveness and the Leontief Scarce-Factor Paradox," American Economic Review, March 1965, pp. 131-40. Studies by Minhas also suggested some reservations about the Leontief view. In estimating Constant Elasticity of Substitution production functions for individual industries in different countries, Minhas found the only differences to lie in a uniform efficiency factor. The shape of isoquants remained the same—which suggests no special U.S. efficiency in labor. See Minhas, op. cit.
30. The emphasis on the skill composition of labor was part of the explanation. It also conforms to an expanded HO framework particularly useful for predicting interest group behavior. It was also suggested that the "affinity" of natural resources for capital

might explain the bias of U.S. import competing industries. See Caves and Jones, op. cit., p. 201.

31. Although the BLS study compared the years 1966 and 1969, the BLS relied upon a 1965 update of a 1958 input-output matrix for the United States. The results probably contained a number of biases. For instance, jobs involved in the unloading and transport of exports were included while those for imports were excluded. On the other hand, they did not correct the estimates for imports that contained components exported from the United States. The latter fact may have taken on added importance for the period in question because of the Canadian Automobile Pact signed in 1965. The pact substantially increased the number of automobiles imported from Canada, many of which contain U.S. components. For a summary of the study, see the testimony of then Secretary of Labor George Shultz, Tariff and Trade Proposals, Hearings before the Committee on Ways and Means, 91st Cong., 2d sess., Part 2 of 16 Parts (Washington, D.C.: U.S. Government Printing Office, 1970), pp. 608-13.

32. Bhagwati presents an excellent summary of these reservations in his 1964 survey. See Bhagwati, op. cit., pp. 27-33.

33. S. Linder, An Essay on Trade and Transformation (New York: John Wiley, 1961).

34. I. Kravis, "Availability and Other Influences on the Commodity Composition of Trade," Journal of Political Economy 64 (April 1956).

35. Raymond Vernon, "International Investment and International Trade in the Product Cycle," Quarterly Journal of Economics 80 (May 1966):190-207.

36. The Trade Reform Act of 1973 was introduced on April 10, 1973, by Congressman Wilbur Mills on behalf of the administration. The text of the bill can be found in Trade Reform, Hearings before the Committee on Ways and Means, U.S. House of Representatives, 93d Cong., 1st sess. on H.R. 6767, The Trade Reform Act of 1973, Part I (Washington, D.C.: U.S. Government Printing Office, 1973), pp. 4-100.

37. See, for example, European Community Restrictions on Imports of United States Specialty Agricultural Products, Hearing before the Subcommittee on Trade of the Committee on Ways and Means, U.S. House of Representatives, 95th Cong., 1st sess., Serial 95-34, September 12, 1977 (Washington, D.C.: U.S. Government Printing Office, 1977).

38. Mundell, op. cit.

39. Johnson, op. cit., Chapter 4.

40. A. E. Jasey, "The Social Choice Between Home and Overseas Investment," Economic Journal 70, no. 277 (March 1960): 105-13.

41. Murray Kemp, "Foreign Investment and the National Advantage," Economic Record, March 1962.

42. MacDougall is prominent among those who have focused on the host country. See G. D. A. MacDougall, "The Benefits and Costs of Private Investments from Abroad: A Theoretical Approach," Bulletin of the Oxford University Institute of Statistics, August 1960.

43. Marvin Frankel, "Home Versus Foreign Investment: A Case Against Capital Export," Kyklos 18, no. 3 (1965):411-33.

44. Philip W. Bell, "Private Capital Movements and the U.S. Balance of Payments Position," Joint Economic Committee, 87th Cong., 2d sess., Factors Affecting the United States Balance of Payments (Washington, D.C.: U.S. Government Printing Office, 1962).

45. G. C. Hufbauer and F. M. Adler, Overseas Manufacturing Investment and the Balance of Payments, Tax Policy Research Study No. 1 (Washington, D.C.: U.S. Treasury Department, 1968).

46. Ibid., p. 2.

47. Ibid., p. 6.

48. Hufbauer and Adler adopted the term "classical" because of a formal similarity to their assumption and the concern of classical economists over exactly how real goods followed a transfer of financial resources. For a brief summary of this debate, see ibid., pp. 2 and 3.

49. The approach taken in the following paragraphs is similar to that taken by Peggy Musgrave in her United States Taxation of Foreign Investment Income: Issues and Arguments, International Tax Program, Harvard Law School, Cambridge, Mass., 1969. See also Peggy Musgrave, Direct Investment Abroad and the Multinationals: Effects on the United States Economy, Subcommittee on Multinational Corporations, Committee on Foreign Relations, 94th Cong., 1st sess. (Washington, D.C.: U.S. Government Printing Office, 1975).

50. Hufbauer and Adler, op. cit., p. 2.

51. Richard E. Caves, "Multinational Firms, Competition, and Productivity in Host Country Markets," Economica 41 (1974). See also note 31.

52. See, for instance, P. B. Kenen, "Economic Aspects of Private Direct Investment," Taxation and Operations Abroad (Princeton, N.J.: Tax Institute of America, 1960).

53. Musgrave, Direct Investment, op. cit.

CHAPTER 4

FOREIGN ECONOMIC POLICY: THE DEMISE OF THE POST-WORLD WAR II ALLIANCE BETWEEN BUSINESS AND LABOR

Chapter 3 suggested a number of reasons why big labor and big business might differ over the conduct of foreign economic policy, but there was not always such a division. In fact, in the early post-World War II years, much of business and substantial portions of the labor movement joined in support of decreased world trade barriers, the Bretton Woods system, and America's role in worldwide economic reconstruction.

Although there were tensions between business and labor over foreign economic matters in the 1960s, the introduction of the Burke-Hartke Bill was labor's full call to legislative combat. To understand the origin of labor's changing view and the specific form it took, one must look at the economic circumstances in which it grew. For in many ways the new labor position on foreign economic policy was a product of both a changing world economic order and the limitations and inflexibility of the then prevailing system of international trade and monetary relations.

In 1970 and early 1971, when Burke-Hartke was being put into final legislative form, the United States was caught with a persistent balance of payments problem and an emerging trade deficit. The failure or inability of the United States to shield export prices from the impact of domestic inflation promised to put continuing pressure on the trade account.

Under the post-World War II Bretton Woods system of international financial practices, the principal responsibility for any adjustment was placed on the country experiencing a balance of payments deficit. The deficit country was expected to change its pattern of international expenditures or adopt a fiscal regime that would be sufficiently deflationary to restore balance to its payments account. Only where there was a "fundamental disequilibrium" could a country seek to devalue its currency. For the United States, however, the options appeared much narrower. Long-standing military and development assistance commitments made it difficult for the United States to reduce its official foreign expenditures. Deflation through fiscal austerity has always been a bitter economic pill for any nation to swallow. Even when tried in the early years of the Nixon administration, it failed to provide a short-term answer to steadily rising prices.

Although a number of other industrialized countries had devalued during the post-World War II era, most American policy makers felt that the dollar's role as the key currency in the Bretton Woods system made devaluation virtually unthinkable. In terms of the trade balance, the effects of devaluation could also be achieved by combining an across-the-board import surcharge with broad-gage export subsidies. The General Agreement on Tariffs and Trade, which embodied the postwar rules on international commercial practices, did allow a temporary surcharge, but for balance of payments not balance of trade purposes. Otherwise, most forms of export subsidies were banned under GATT.

The world economic order was also undergoing a steady change. The industrial recovery of Western Europe and Japan and the creation of major trading blocs began to rival the long-standing international economic preeminence of the United States. A customs union or other type of trading bloc, of course, may be either trade creating or trade diverting. Although we have maintained a slight trade surplus with the European Economic Community (EEC), the Community appears to have had a negative effect on U.S. exports (see discussion below). The EEC also became an attractive location for foreign direct investment by U.S.-based multinational firms. At one point the U.S. government did seek to limit the export of U.S. capital for balance of payments purposes. A series of both voluntary and mandatory controls appears to have had little impact on the growth of U.S. multinationals.

Japan presented yet another trade challenge to the United States. In 1955, when Japan acceded to GATT, many of the West European, industrialized powers elected to maintain a number of restrictions on Japanese exports. In line with a postwar policy of encouraging industrial reconstruction, the United States did not. In turning to the American market, Japan tended to concentrate its exports in certain specific product lines. The result was a sizable and highly visable penetration of the U.S. market by Japanese manufactures.

The proponents of Burke-Hartke felt that the existing framework of international trade and financial rules tilted against both the United States and the American working man. At the same time, the original drafters of Burke-Hartke observed the rapid growth of U.S.-based multinationals. They strongly felt that new foreign direct investment reduced capital investment in the United States, reduced domestic employment, and threatened to seriously alter the power balance at the collective bargaining table. Past government efforts to control capital flows had met with limited success and the Burke-Hartke backers did not expect a more ambitious effort by what they regarded as the probusiness Nixon administration. They sought their own solution.

To meet the problem of trade deficits, they suggested mandatory import quotas that would establish permanent market shares. To discourage capital outflows and the growth of U.S. business abroad, they proposed radical changes in the U.S. taxation of foreign source income. Rather than being a mere agglomeration of new tax, trade, and investment proposals, Burke-Hartke was very much a response to the postwar world.

THE INTERNATIONAL ACCOUNTS

Much of the story of America's foreign economic fortunes can be read in the changing pattern of the balance of payments statistics. Initial overall surpluses in the balance of payments figures[*] were replaced by small deficits. In fact, from 1950 on, the United States consistently ran a balance of payments deficit. At first manageable, later troublesome, the relatively moderate figures of the 1950s and 1960s eventually gave way to the massive deficits of the 1970s. By the time major trade legislation was before the Congress in 1971-74, these deficits had already become apparent.

Through almost all this period, however, the current account remained positive (see Table 1). Principally composed of merchandise trade, military transactions, net investment income, travel and transportation, and private remittances, the positive current account reflected the size of the merchandise trade surplus and investment income outweighing persistent deficits recorded by military transactions, travel and transportation, and remittances abroad.

Although the current account remained in rough balance or in modest surplus, the basic balance (see Table 2) was negative from 1960 on. Both the government and private industry contributed heavily

---

[*]As measured on a liquidity basis. The currently used Official Reserve Transactions (ORT) basis was introduced much later. Figures on the ORT basis have been computed only as far back as 1960. Because of the present regime of flexible exchange rates, the ORT is no longer published by the Commerce Department.

TABLE 1

U.S. Current Account, 1946-72
(millions of dollars)

Year or Quarter	Balance on Current Account	Year or Quarter	Balance on Current Account
1946	4,885	1960	1,801
1947	8,992	1961	3,069
1948	1,993	1962	2,456
1949	580	1963	3,199
		1964	5,783
1950	-2,125		
1951	302	1965	4,306
1952	-175	1966	2,320
1953	-1,949	1967	2,051
1954	-321	1968	-443
		1969	-1,050
1955	-345		
1956	1,722	1970	416
1957	3,556	1971	-2,790
1958	-5	1972	-8,353
1959	-2,138		

Source: Council of Economic Advisers, Economic Report of the President, 1974 (Washington, D.C.: U.S. Government Printing Office, 1974).

to the long-term capital outflows that tipped the basic balance into the red. And under the then current system of fixed exchange rates, the basic balance came to be touted as the best measure of an economy's fundamental strength in the international economy.

All these factors—overall balance of payments deficits, government programs, and private foreign investment—played important roles in the controversy over foreign trade and investment. But the central question revolved around foreign trade—or more specifically imports. For many years the United States ran a steady surplus in its merchandise balance of trade. As noted above, merchandise trade surpluses were one of the principal reasons the U.S. Current

TABLE 2

Current Account, Long-Term Capital Flows,
and the U.S. Basic Balance, 1960-72
(millions of current dollars)

| Year of Quarter | Current Account | Long-term Net Capital Flows | | Basic Balance |
		U.S. Govern-ment	Private	
1960	1,801	-889	-2,100	-1,188
1961	3,069	-901	-2,182	-15
1962	2,456	-892	-2,606	-1,042
1963	3,199	-1,150	-3,376	-1,328
1964	5,783	-1,348	-4,511	-76
1965	4,306	-1,532	-4,577	-1,804
1966	2,320	-1,469	-2,575	-1,724
1967	2,051	-2,423	-2,932	-3,304
1968	-443	-2,158	1,191	-1,411
1969	-1,050	-1,926	-70	-3,046
1970	416	-2,018	-1,429	-3,031
1971	-2,790	-2,359	-4,401	-9,550
1972	-8,353	-1,339	-152	-9,843

Source: Council of Economic Advisers, Economic Report of the President, 1974 (Washington, D.C.: U.S. Government Printing Office, 1974), Table C88, pp. 350 and 351.

Account was generally positive. Table 3 records the pattern of U.S. merchandise trade since 1946.

Despite the apparent surplus in merchandise trade, a portion of the Congress remained concerned about the impact of foreign trade on domestic industry and employment. In fact, the figures themselves became the subject of some controversy. As generally reported, the export figures in the balance of merchandise trade are reported on an f.a.s. (free alongside ship) basis. Although military grants and contract sales are excluded from exports, the figures do include some items that could not be considered commercial exports. Surplus

TABLE 3

U.S. Merchandise Trade, 1946–73
(millions of dollars)

Period	Exports[a][b]	Imports[b]	Balance (+ or -)
1946	11,707	5,073	6,634
1947	16,015	5,979	10,036
1948	13,193	7,563	5,630
1949	12,149	6,879	5,270
1950	10,117	9,108	1,009
1951	14,123	11,202	2,921
1952	13,319	10,838	2,481
1953	12,281	10,990	1,291
1954	12,799	10,354	2,445
1955	14,280	11,527	2,753
1956	17,379	12,804	4,575
1957	19,390	13,291	6.099
1958	16,264	12,952	3,312
1959	16,295	15,310	985
1960	19,650	14,744	4,906
1961	20,107	14,519	5,588
1962	20,779	16,218	4,561
1963	22,252	17,011	5,241
1964	25,478	18,647	6,831
1965	26,478	21,496	4,942
1966	29,390	25,463	3,927
1967	30,680	26,821	3,859
1968	33,588	32,964	624
1969	36,490	35,830	660
1970	41,980	39,870	2,110
1971	42,754	45,476	-2,722
1972	48,768	55,754	-6,986
1973	70,252	69,629	623

[a]Excludes transfers of goods and services under U.S. military grant programs as well as exports of goods under U.S. military agency sales contracts.

[b]Balance of payments basis (adjusted from Census figures for differences in coverage and timing).

Sources: Figures for 1946 through 1959 are from the Economic Indicators, prepared for the Joint Economic Committee by the Council of Economic Advisers, various years. Figures for 1960 through 1970 are from the June 1971 issue of the Survey of Current Business. Figures for 1971 through 1973 are from the June 1974 issue of the Survey of Current Business, Table I.

TABLE 4

U.S. Net Commercial Exports, 1960–73
(millions of dollars)

Period	Exports*	AID Loans and Grants	P.L. 480 Sales and Grants	P.L. 480 and AID Total	Net Commercial Exports
1960	19,650				
1961	20,107				
1962	20,779				
1963	22,252				
1964	25,478				
1965	26,478	1,140	1,323	2,464	24,014
1966	29,390	1,186	1,306	2,492	26,898
1967	30,680	1,300	1,229	2,529	28,151
1968	33,588	1,056	1,178	2,234	31,354
1969	36,490	993	1,021	2,014	34,476
1970	41,980	957	1,021	1,978	40,002
1971	42,754	915	982	1,897	40,857
1972	48,768	658	1,065	1,723	47,045
1973	70,252	657	750	1,407	68,845

*Excludes transfers of goods and services under U.S. military grant programs as well as exports of goods under U.S. military agency sales.

Sources: AID and P.L. 480 figures 1965 through 1973, U.S. Bureau of Census, Title, Highlights of U.S. Export and Import Trade (FT/990), December 1973 and December 1974 (Washington, D.C.: U.S. Government Printing Office, 1974 and 1975).

commodity sales under the Food for Peace (P.L. 480) program, as
well as exports financed by the foreign assistance program, count as
a plus in our merchandise trade account. In addition, exports financed
by the Export-Import Bank also appear in the merchandise trade
figures.

As early as 1968 the Executive Branch was pressed to present
export figures on a basis that would exclude the impact of various
government subsidies.[1] Table 4 details the difference between exports
inclusive and exclusive of federal subsidies. A similar controversy
erupted over the prevailing method of reporting import figures. The
United States, Canada, and a very few other countries report imports
on an f.a.s. basis, which roughly corresponds to the purchase price
of the goods in the port of exportation. Most of the rest of the world
and most of our principal trading partners follow the cost, insurance,
freight (c.i.f.) formula.[2] For some years a number of congressmen
have pressed for switching to a c.i.f. basis. Senator Russell Long
(D.-La.) chairman of the foreign-trade-controlling Senate Finance
Committee, became a strong advocate of the c.i.f. approach. But
not until January 1974 did the Department of Commerce begin publish-
ing c.i.f. import data.[3] Whatever the relative merits of reporting
imports on a c.i.f. as opposed to an f.a.s. or customs basis, the
c.i.f. figures tend to increase the value of imports. The greater
the cost of transportation and insurance with respect to imports the
more the total value of imports increases on a c.i.f. basis. The
impact of adjusting import values for the cost of insurance and freight
are shown in Table 5.

For those attempting to demonstrate the peril of the U.S. trade
position, it was the combined figures—those eliminating subsidized
exports and including the cost of insurance and freight in imports—
that told the true story. True or not, the adjusted figures did portray
a markedly different situation in the U.S. balance of merchandise
trade. Table 6 adjusts exports for AID-sponsored exports as well
as P.L. 480 sales of surplus agricultural commodities. Imports
are given on a c.i.f. basis as calculated in Table 3. The turnaround
in the figures is nothing short of dramatic. Strong surpluses in the
earlier years are significantly reduced, and the trade surpluses of
the late 1960s have turned into deficits.

None of the figures in Table 6 have suddenly come to light.
They were generally available throughout the Bretton Woods period,
but they were not the officially released figures. An official trade
surplus, however slight, did little to buttress opponents of then current
trade policies. To the extent that a trade deficit was a potential
trigger for policy change or congressional action, the fight over how
to report the figures takes on considerably more meaning.

TABLE 5

U.S. Imports C.I.F., 1960-73
(millions of dollars)

| Period | Imports* | | Insurance |
	F.A.S.	C.I.F.	and Freight
1960	15,073	16,323	1,250
1961	14,761	15,986	1,225
1962	16,464	17,831	1,367
1963	17,207	18,635	1,428
1964	18,749	20,305	1,556
1965	21,520	23,306	1,786
1966	25,618	27,744	2,126
1967	26,889	28,744	1,855
1968	33,226	35,319	2,093
1969	36,043	38,242	2,199
1970	39,952	42,429	2,477
1971	45,563	48,342	2,779
1972	55,583	58,862	3,279
1973	69,121	73,199	4,078

*Imports are on a census rather than a balance of payments basis.

Sources: U.S. Congress, Senate, Committee on Finance, U.S. Trade and Balance of Payments (Washington, D.C.: U.S. Government Printing Office, 1974), p. 4. Based on a 1966 Bureau of the Census study cited in U.S. Congress, Ibid., p. 1, c.i.f. imports have been set at 108.3 percent of f.o.b. imports.

The existence of an overall trade surplus or deficit has little to do with the concerns of any particular industry. The trade balances for specific industries varied widely from the overall figures. Some showed a persistent surplus, but others were in deficit from the early 1960s. In Table 7 the trade balance of a number of commodity groupings is spelled out in some detail. Even more striking was the growing degree of import penetration achieved by certain specific consumer goods (see Tables 8 and 9).

TABLE 6

Amended U.S. Balance of Merchandise Trade, 1960-73 (millions of dollars)

Period	Exports*	AID and P.L. 480 Exports	Net Commercial Exports	Imports c.i.f.	Amended U.S. Balance Merchandise Trade
1965	26,742	2,464	24,278	23,306	972
1966	29,490	2,492	26,998	27,744	-746
1967	31,030	2,529	28,501	28,744	-243
1968	34,063	2,234	31,829	35,319	-3,490
1969	37,332	2,014	35,318	38,242	-2,924
1970	42,659	1,978	40,711	42,429	-1,718
1971	42,549	1,897	40,652	48,342	-7,690
1972	49,219	1,723	47,496	58,862	-11,366
1973	70,798	1,407	69,391	73,199	-3,808

*Exports are on a census rather than a balance of payments basis so as to make them comparable to the import figures.

Source: Exports are from U.S. Congress, Senate Committee on Finance, U.S. Trade and Balance of Payments (Washington, D.C.: U.S. Government Printing Office, 1974), p. 4. AID and P.L. 480 exports are from Table 4 above. Imports c.i.f. are from Table 5 above.

TABLE 7

U.S. Trade Balance in Selected Commodities,[a] 1960–74 (millions of dollars)

	1960	1961	1962	1963	1964	1965	1966	1967
Aircraft and parts[c]	970	766	857	726	791	989	823	1,270
Computers and parts	44	105	128	177	214	219	280	412
Other nonelectric[d] machinery	2,576	2,775	2,986	3,002	3,409	3,504	3,508	3,474
Basic chemicals and compounds	52	141	155	329	521	589	556	644
Motor vehicles and parts[e]	643	803	850	955	1,063	934	537	237
Steel products	204	108	-2	-93	-51	-533	-646	-750
Textiles, clothing, and footwear	-396	-284	-540	-567	-548	-824	-978	-1,016
Consumer electronics	-53	-80	-109	-130	-164	-258	-374	-431

	1968	1969	1970	1971	1972	1973	1974[b]
Aircraft and parts[c]	2,016	2,139	2,382	3,049	2,508	3,556	4,851
Computers and parts	524	768	1,176	1,142	1,167	1,606	2,016

Other nonelectric[d] machinery	3,579	3,976	4,364	4,183	4,330	5,670	8,187
Basic chemicals and compounds	690	739	883	818	652	1,015	1,584
Motor vehicles and parts[c]	-588	-1,104	-1,823	-2,897	-3,492	-3,680	-3,905
Steel products	-1,380	-783	-764	-1,855	-1,945	-1,517	-1,505
Textiles, clothing, and footwear	-1,498	-1,819	-2,220	-2,823	-3,294	-3,306	-2,799
Consumer electronics	-632	-912	-1,123	-1,304	-1,736	-1,959	-1,902

[a]Exports are f.a.s. and imports are Customs values, generally the market value in the foreign country. Figures are given on a census rather than balance of payments basis.

[b]January-September at annual rates.

[c]Excludes engines.

[d]Excluding aircraft and auto engines and parts, and other office machinery.

Sources: Department of Commerce, Survey of Current Business, various issues. Table is taken from the International Economic Report of the President (Washington, D.C.: U.S. Government Printing Office, March 1975), p. 134.

TABLE 8

U.S. Ratio of Imports to Consumption, 1970

Product	Percent
Textiles (including apparel)	12[a]
Steel	15[b]
Flatware	22[a]
Footwear (nonrubber)	30[a]
Leather gloves	30[a]
Sewing machines	49[a]
Black and white televisions	52[b]
Amateur motion picture cameras	66[a]
Radios	70[b]
Calculating machines	75[b]
Hairworks, toupees and wigs	85[a]
Magnetic tape recorders	96[a]
35 mm still cameras	100[b]

[a]By value.
[b]By volume.
Source: Peter G. Peterson, The United States in the Changing World Economy, Vol. II: Background Material (Washington, D.C.: U.S. Government Printing Office, 1971), Chart 26.

Not surprisingly, many of the most ardent supporters of the Burke-Hartke approach were drawn from industries suffering from serious import competition. The textile and footwear industry, consumer electronics firms, and the domestic steel industry had all sought legislative and administrative action to reduce the flow of competitive imports. Usually the unions in the affected industries both supported and initiated drives for legislative remedies.

The balance of trade figures, then, largely reflected the changing fortunes of U.S. foreign economic policy with strong trade surpluses eventually changing to deficits. Although the trade account for specific industries may say little about how much import pressure is actually being experienced, the deficits appear to have traced a path of growing political resistance to imports by both labor and management in the affected industries.

TABLE 9

U.S. Imports as a Percent of New Supply (Output Plus Imports), Selected Products, 1965-71

Product Code	Title	1971	1970	1969	1968	1967	1966	1965
3141	Shoes (except rubber)	16	13	11	8	6	5	4
3021	Rubber footwear	34	29	25	23	18	14	15
3552	Textile machinery and parts	33	24	19	19	16	14	10
3651	Radio and television receiving sets	30	29	23	16	13	10	11
37111	Passenger cars and chassis	15	17	12	10	8	6	3
331 (part)	Blast furnace, steel mill, electrometallurgical products	10	8	7	8	6	5	5
3751	Motorcycles, bicycles, and parts	58	49	43	35	36	46	43
38613	Motion picture equipment	21	19	16	13	12	10	8
3872	Watchcases	21	16	12	10	12	9	9

Source: U.S. Commodity Exports and Imports as Related to Output: 1971 and 1970, U.S. Department of Commerce (Washington, D.C.: U.S. Government Printing Office, 1974).

TABLE 10

Unemployment Rates for Selected Categories of American Workers, 1960–75

	1960	1961	1962	1963	1964	1965	1966	1967
All civilian	5.5	6.7	5.6	5.6	5.2	4.5	3.8	3.8
Blue collar	7.8	9.2	7.4	7.2	6.3	5.2	4.2	4.5
White collar	2.7	3.3	2.8	2.9	2.6	2.3	2.0	2.2
Male	5.4	6.4	5.2	5.2	4.6	4.0	3.2	3.1
Married men	3.8	4.6	3.6	3.3	2.8	2.3	1.9	1.8
Wage and salary workers								
Agriculture	8.3	9.6	7.4	9.1	9.7	7.6	6.6	6.9
Construction	13.6	15.8	13.4	13.1	11.2	10.0	8.0	7.3
Private nonagriculture	6.2	7.5	6.1	6.1	5.4	4.6	3.8	3.9
All manufacturing	6.3	7.7	5.8	5.7	5.0	4.0	3.2	3.7
Durable manufacturing	6.5	8.5	5.7	5.5	4.7	3.5	2.7	3.4
Nondurable manufacturing	6.1	6.8	6.0	6.1	5.4	4.7	3.8	4.1

	1968	1969	1970	1971	1972	1973	1974	1975
All civilian	3.6	3.5	5.0	6.0	5.6	4.9	5.6	8.5
Blue collar	4.1	3.9	6.3	7.4	6.5	5.4	6.8	11.7
White collar	2.0	2.1	2.9	3.5	3.4	2.9	3.3	4.8
Male	2.9	2.8	4.4	5.3	4.9	4.1	4.8	7.9
Married men	1.6	1.5	2.6	3.2	2.8	2.3	2.7	5.2
Wage and salary workers								
Agriculture	6.2	6.0	7.6	7.9	7.7	7.0	7.3	10.4
Construction	6.7	6.0	10.1	10.3	10.3	8.8	10.8	18.4
Private nonagriculture	3.6	3.5	5.3	6.2	5.7	4.8	5.8	9.2
All manufacturing	3.3	3.3	5.6	6.8	5.6	4.3	5.8	11.0
Durable manufacturing	3.0	3.0	5.8	7.0	5.4	3.9	5.5	11.3
Nondurable manufacturing	3.7	3.7	5.5	6.5	5.7	4.9	6.3	10.4

Source: Bureau of Labor Statistics.

85

Overall unemployment rates also played their part in pushing labor to action on trade and investment issues. Much of the story can be read in Table 10. From the defense-fed boom of the late 1960s, the civilian unemployment rate started to move upward. The historically low rate of 3.5 percent in 1969 jumped to 5.0 percent in 1970 and jumped again in 1971 to 6.0 percent. Even more startling were the changes in durable manufacturing. From a low of 3.0 percent in 1969, the rate moved to 5.8 percent in 1970, and on to 7.0 percent in 1971. That type of change put pressure on both the union leadership and the Congress.

THE INSTITUTIONAL SETTING

What forces led to the persistent balance of payments deficits and the steady erosion of the U.S. trade surplus? No doubt the causes are many and varied. For the purposes of the 1970s debate on foreign trade and investment, however, several took on an added importance: the existing rules of international trade and finance, industrial recovery in Western Europe and Japan, the creation of major trading blocs, and the rapid growth of the U.S.-based multinational firm.

The makings of the institutional setting that helped to give rise to the labor push for restrictions on trade and the multinationals go back at least as far as the very early 1940s. Certainly, long before World War II was over, plans were being laid to reconstruct the world order. The onset of the depression, the Smoot-Hawley tariff and its aftermath, and the war itself had all seriously disrupted previous patterns of trade. As the economic and military leader of the allied powers, the United States took a strong hand in the early discussions on future international economic relations.

Although agreement had already been reached on the future world financial system (see discussion of the International Monetary Fund below) the United States did not submit a plan for the proposed International Trade Organization (ITO) until December 1945.[4] Parallel to consideration of a final charter for the ITO, the United States conducted a series of bilateral negotiations with its principal trading partners. The results of these negotiations and a preliminary understanding on trade rules were incorporated in GATT.[5] At first devised as an interim agreement, GATT adopted most of the commercial aspects of the ITO charter and in general "assumed the commercial policy role that had been assigned to the ITO."[6] With an eye to the eventual creation of the ITO, the GATT instrument is virtually devoid of institutional provisions. In fact, for some time the provisional secretariat of the never-to-be created ITO provided the institutional framework for GATT.

The American participation in the negotiations on both the ITO charter and GATT were colored by the twin preoccupations of postwar reconstruction and the restoration of relatively unfettered trade among nations. And the commercial policies contained in GATT reflect an occasionally uneasy compromise between these two goals. Some negotiators were apprehensive about an economic hegemony by the Americans. Others were fearful that too rapid a move toward free trade would disrupt rebuilding industries and limited foreign reserves. Many still-developing countries were anxious to shield budding industrialization programs behind protective tariffs and other devices. And to varying degrees, American negotiators were sympathetic to these needs. This is not to say that the effectiveness of GATT was negotiated away. Six rounds of tariff negotiations have already been held under the auspices of GATT and it has proved to be both pragmatic and resilient in the face of many problems. But the early compromises have left GATT with several practices that were to have some eventual bearing on the congressional consideration of foreign economic policy throughout the 1970s.

By taking only the commercial features of the ITO charter, GATT avoided the quagmire of attempting to coordinate domestic economic policies. The various contracting parties to GATT either entirely ignored the question of coordinating fiscal and monetary policies or left them to other international bodies.* The failure to provide for international coordination of macroeconomic policies did not loom so large in the early 1970s when the free trade coalition started to crumble. Since the severe recession of 1974-75, however, there has been a new awareness of the importance of international coordination, particularly among the industrial powers. The much more rapid pace of recovery in the United States than other industrialized countries has contributed to record American trade deficits of 1977 and 1978. These deficits played a leading role in the sharp dollar depreciation throughout this period, which in turn disrupted international markets for goods and money. Both before and after the November 1, 1978, decision to rescue the dollar, the Carter administration has emphasized the need for coordinated economic policy among the major industrial powers.

With regard to export subsidies, GATT did make one major venture into the tax field. Although generally hostile to export sub-

---

*The IMF and the OECD have had some role to play in this area. For member countries, the EEC has been active on the question of coordination. Economic summit meetings of the major industrial powers have, to some extent, acted as an ad-hoc mechanism that has sought to foster coordinated macroeconomic policies.

sidies, contracting parties were permitted to rebate indirect taxes
on exports and impose equivalent indirect taxes on imports.[7] Rebates
may not be given, however, for direct taxes. The distinction between
direct and indirect taxes rests both on past commercial practice[8]
and some traditional economic assumptions.[9] There is general agreement that for a profit-maximizing firm operating in a competitive
economy in the short run, the burden of a corporate tax will fall on
capital. In the long run, however, a portion of the tax may well be
shifted backward to labor. In the presence of imperfect markets,
some or possibly even all of the tax could also be shifted forward to
consumers in the form of higher prices. If the corporate tax is in
fact shifted forward to consumers, it acts very much like the direct
taxes exempted under GATT.[10] The question of exactly who bears
what portion of the burden of the corporate income tax is still the
subject debate among economists, but the problem of shifting has
now become a source of growing congressional concern.[11]

Although GATT sought to temper the use of quantitative restrictions and other nontariff barriers to trade, much remains to be done
in that area. Despite initial American pressure, a mix of balance
of payments considerations and industrialization goals have led many
countries to maintain an intricate structure of import constraints.
The use of explicit quotas on manufactured imports generally faded
in the industrial countries as they moved to fully convertible currencies. Quotas and an elaborate structure of other controls, however,
have continued to play a large role in developing countries. And
many other nontariff barriers continued to influence the pattern of
trade between the developed nations. Safety, environmental and
health legislation, buy-local provisions, and a host of other policies
continue to clog the channels of international trade.

GATT rules for the treatment of new members have also been
the subject of some controversy. Under GATT Article XXXV, any
contracting party may refuse to apply GATT rules to a new member.
"The most extensive use . . . of Article XXXV [was] against Japan
in 1955 by fourteen countries representing about 40 percent of the
foreign trade of GATT contracting parties."[12] In accord with its
interest in free trade and industrial reconstruction, the United States
was not among those that invoked Article XXXV. Faced with a relatively restricted market in Western Europe, Japanese export strategy
came to focus on the large American market. Certainly the widening
trade deficit between the United States and Japan was one of the many
forces that eventually led to proposals such as Burke-Hartke that
would strictly control the flow of imports into the United States.

While ambitious ideas were being distilled in the form of a
proposed International Trade Organization, other minds were attempting to outline the future course of the world monetary order. Two

principal plans emerged in the early 1940s: one British, one American.[13] Authored by John Maynard Keynes, the British plan envisaged something on the order of a world central bank to stand behind national central banks. World liquidity would be influenced by the bancor—a new international currency by which other national currencies would be valued. The Keynes plan also expected that exchange adjustments would be made by both deficit and surplus countries—not by the deficit country alone. The American plan, principally authored by Harry Dexter White of the U.S. Treasury, tied world liquidity to national currencies linked to gold and limited the central banker role of the proposed organization.* In addition, the White plan seemed to envisage relatively few exchange rate changes and then only for circumstances in which there was a "fundamental disequilibrium."[14]

By the time of the Bretton Woods conference of July 1944, a basically Anglo-American plan that had already been widely circulated was formally presented to the conference. Reflecting the military, industrial, and financial strength of the United States, the eventual agreement establishing the International Monetary Fund was basically drawn to American specifications.[15] Although the articles of agreement of the IMF envisioned ample world liquidity, stable exchange rates, and the removal of all current account restrictions, the postwar world created quite different demands. In all three of these areas the United States came to play a key role.

The IMF articles did not contemplate the creation of a new international currency but sought to assure world liquidity through a centrally held pool of funds made up of gold and certain key currencies. At the end of World War II, the United States held the bulk of the world's gold reserves. These reserves and a strong industrial economy undamaged by the war made the dollar the world's most sought-after currency. In fact, what emerged from the Bretton Woods system was a dollar/gold standard. Under this sytem world liquidity was crucially tied to increases in the gold supply and the existence of deficits in the U.S. balance of payments. Because of the liquidity-increasing nature of a U.S. balance of payments deficit, such deficits were tolerated and even welcomed throughout the 1950s and early 1960s. However, as modest deficits became large ones and as the U.S. gold stock was gradually reduced, dollar scarcity began to turn into a dollar glut.

---

*Keynes's concept of an interest-bearing, international currency, the bancor, to some extent anticipated the current form of the IMF's Special Drawing Rights. White's early plans did contain an international unit of account, the unitas, that was dropped from later versions of his proposal.

Lack of postwar liquidity was far from the only barrier to trade flows. The Great Depression and World War II had spawned a host of exchange rate controls that both protected domestic industry and worked to bring some stability into national balance of payments accounts. In part, the authors of the Bretton Woods agreement hoped to bring about the eventual demise of this panoply of controls. In particular, the United States sought to include provisions for the expansion of multilateral trade in the Articles of Agreement of the IMF.[16] Fund members are pledged to seek the removal of existing current account restrictions and further agree (Article VIII, sec. 2) not to impose additional restrictions without the permission of the IMF. Members were allowed to retain existing restrictions (Article XIV). If such restrictions were to be retained beyond 1952, however, the member was obligated to consult with the IMF.[17] Elimination of exchange restrictions between the industrialized countries proved to be a lengthy process. With heavy U.S. backing, the British attempted to move to full convertibility in 1947. The attempt, however, proved to be a failure and was abandoned in August of that year.[18] Although the members of the European Payments Unions allowed nonresidents of member countries to convert national currencies into dollars or gold, full convertibility for the major European industrial powers (France, Italy, the United Kingdom, and West Germany) did not come until February 1961.[19] Japan did not abandon the protections of Article XIV until 1964.[20]

No doubt the reasons for the slow move to convertibility are manifold. Some responsibility must surely lie with the IMF itself. No mechanism within the IMF was developed to facilitate a reciprocal removal of restrictions. Furthermore, the "division of labor which exists between the Fund and GATT has meant that it has been difficult to negotiate concessions in the field of payments in return for concessions in restrictions in trade."[21] Whatever the causes, the maintenance of exchange restrictions tended to discourage U.S. exports and encourage direct investments by U.S. multinationals to leapfrog any restrictions. Both these tendencies played their part in the determination of labor to seek a Burke–Hartke kind of solution to growing trade pressures.

The Bretton Woods preference for fixed exchange rates found expression in Article IV of the IMF agreement. Member currencies were defined in terms of gold. In spot transactions, the value of members' currencies was allowed to vary only within very tight limits.[22] Changes in exchange rates were to take place only in the case of a "fundamental disequilibrium."[23]

The original fund parities were set in an atmosphere of considerable uncertainty. It is not surprising that a number of currency valuation changes took place. France went so far as to establish a

free market for sterling and dollars in January 1948.[24] By allowing
the dollar to float upward relative to the pound, "exports to Britain
were curbed and those to the United States were encouraged."[25]
The British devalued the pound by 30.5 percent in 1949 and touched
off a series of other devaluations. A second British devaluation of
14.3 percent in 1967 again encouraged devaluations in several other
countries. Throughout the entire Bretton Woods period—1945 to
1971—there were only three revaluations. In 1961 the German mark
and Dutch guilder were both increased by 5 percent. In 1969 the
German mark was again increased, this time by 9.3 percent.[26]

By and large the IMF was not well suited to provide for adjustments in the value of national currencies. "Fixing the rate ensured
that no automatic corrective mechanism would be at work to prevent
deficits or surpluses from accumulating until they reached crisis
level."[27] And pressure for adjustment was generally placed overwhelmingly on the deficit country regardless of the political and
economic implications. By creating a system of relatively fixed
rates tied to a key currency, the Bretton Woods agreements made
the system more inflexible. It was difficult under this system to
deal with a fundamental disequilibrium—it was virtually impossible
where such a disequilibrium involved the key currency. No doubt
this was yet another factor that contributed to labor's break with the
free trade coalition.

INDUSTRIAL RECOVERY AND THE EMERGENCE
OF NEW TRADING POWERS

The U.S. assumption of international economic leadership at
Bretton Woods to a great extent determined the nature of both IMF
and GATT. In each case key economic concessions were made by
the United States so as to foster recovery in the industrial economies
ravaged by the war. The ability of parties to GATT to retain restrictions against new members, the predilection for fixed exchange rates,
and the role of the dollar as a key currency all contributed to the
eventual demise of the Bretton Woods system and the advent of protectionist forces in the United States.

However, the formal structure of the international economy
was not the only source of pressure on the U.S. balance of payments
and trade accounts. The industrial recovery of Western Europe and
Japan and the creation of regional trading blocs both played a part
in altering the international economic fortunes of the United States.
European cooperation began shortly after the end of World War II
and was carefully encouraged and nurtured by U.S. foreign policy.
The Organization for European Economic Cooperation (OEEC) was

created in 1948. The North Atlantic Treaty Organization came into being one year later. Six European countries (the Benelux nations, France, Germany, and Italy) established the European Coal and Steel Community in 1951. The same six later established the European Economic Community or Common Market in 1957. Failure of OEEC-sponsored negotiations to widen the EEC eventually led to the creation of the European Free Trade Association (EFTA) in 1960.[28]

From its inception, the EEC proved more dynamic and more successful than its rival, the EFTA. By extending trade preferences to many former French colonies in Africa and establishing special trade ties with various Mediterranean countries, the EEC greatly increased the scope of its trade. In January 1973 the United Kingdom, the leading industrial power of EFTA, along with Denmark and Ireland, became a member of the EEC. In a plebiscite the British electorate confirmed the United Kingdom's membership in the EEC. The EEC had taken a major step forward in both size and future importance; and there may be more steps to come. Several other European nations—Portugal, Spain, Greece, and Turkey—are candidates for EEC membership in the not-too-distant future.

And there is no question that the members of the EEC have registered impressive gains in terms of GNP. In 1955, two years before the formation of the EEC, the combined GNPs of current EEC members were slightly less than half that of the United States. By the early 1970s the combined GNPs had risen to roughly two-thirds of the U.S. total.[29]

Japan has shown an even more impressive rate of growth. GNP per capita in Japan increased from $270 in 1955 to $3,160 in 1972.[30] Between 1960 and 1972 the Japanese real GNP grew at an annual average rate of 10.1 percent.[31] By 1972 only the United States and the Soviet Union had larger GNPs.

Both Japan and the EEC countries have also achieved marked gains in world trade. The result was a clear erosion of U.S. dominance. For instance, between 1955 and 1972 the total U.S. share of world exports dropped from 16.7 percent to just over 11.9 percent.[32] During the same time period the share of EEC exports (including those of Great Britain) increased from 30.2 to 37.1 percent of the world total.[33] The increase in Japanese exports was even more striking. Growing at an average annual rate of 19.1 percent between 1960 and 1972,[34] Japanese exports increased their share of the world total from 2.1 percent in 1955 to 6.8 percent in 1972.[35]

The story was somewhat different with regard to imports. Between 1955 and 1972 the U.S. share of world imports increased slightly from 12.7 percent in 1955 to 13.6 percent in 1972. During the same period the EEC share actually dropped from 36.6 percent to 35.8 percent. Reflecting its rapid rate of growth, Japan increased its share of world imports from 2.5 percent in 1955 to over 5.4 percent in 1972.[36] Between 1960 and 1972, however, the rate of growth of Japanese imports trailed the rate of growth of exports by more than five full percentage points.[37]

This is not to say that the United States was no longer a world trade power. In 1972 it still had the largest dollar volume of exports of any country, but the gap had been dramatically narrowed. In 1955 U.S. exports of $15.6 billion were almost twice as large as the second-place $8.1 billion of the United Kingdom. By 1972, however, the $49.8 billion of the United States exceeded West Germany's $46.7 billion of exports by only $3.1 billion—a mere 6.6 percent.[38] In theory the economic impact of the EEC and EFTA on U.S. trade is indeterminate. A common external tariff may either increase or decrease imports from a particular area, depending on the existing pattern of trade and the level of the external tariff. In addition, the increased income that can be expected from a customs union may offset any adverse impact such a union may have on the exports of a particular country. In practice, it appears that the EEC's external industrial tariffs and common agricultural policy have combined to reduce U.S. imports below what they would have been without the emergence of the EEC. Although part of the increase in income attributable to the EEC union has gone to purchase American goods, this has generally not been enough to offset the impact of the common external tariff.[39]

Despite its growing importance, the United States was able to maintain a substantial level of exports to the EEC. The United States recorded a bilateral trade surplus with the EEC throughout the 1960s (see Table 11) and continues to experience a relative trade balance.

The most startling change, however, took place in the trade between the United States and Japan. After a series of bilateral trade deficits in the late 1950s and early 1960s, Japan began to register a large trade surplus with the United States. By 1971, the year in which President Nixon brought the Bretton Woods system to a close, Japan's exports to the United States exceeded imports by some $3.2 billion (see Table 12). By 1972 it may have been the single largest trade imbalance between two countries in the history of international trade.[40] The gap has continued to widen and reached $11.6 billion in 1978.

THE GROWTH OF THE U.S.-BASED MULTINATIONAL

The multinational firm itself is hardly a novel phenomenon, even in American garb. In modern times the multinational firm certainly dates back to the halcyon days of the East India Company

TABLE 11

U.S. Bilateral Trade with the EEC, 1958-74
(billions of dollars)

Year	Exports*	Imports*	Balance
1958	3.9	2.6	1.3
1959	4.1	3.7	.5
1960	5.7	3.4	2.3
1961	5.6	3.3	2.3
1962	5.9	3.6	2.3
1963	6.4	3.8	2.6
1964	7.2	4.1	3.0
1965	7.2	4.9	2.2
1966	7.6	6.2	1.4
1967	8.0	6.5	1.5
1968	8.7	8.3	.4
1969	9.7	8.3	1.4
1970	11.3	9.2	2.1
1971	11.1	10.4	.7
1972	11.9	12.5	-.6
1973	16.7	15.6	1.1
1974	22.1	19.2	2.9

*Exports are f.a.s. and imports are Customs values, generally
the market value in the foreign country.
   Source: Council on International Economic Policy, Annual
Report, 1975 (Washington, D.C.: U.S. Government Printing Office,
1975), Table 29, p. 134.

and possibly beyond. Nor are U.S. corporations particularly new
on the world scene. What is new is the extent and magnitude of their
foreign commitments. In 1950 the total book value of U.S. direct
foreign investments stood at $11.8 billion. By 1960 the total had
roughly trebled to slightly more than $32 billion. By 1971, the year
Burke-Hartke finally took legislative form, the total stood at more
than $86 billion.[41]

The growth of U.S. foreign direct investment was accompanied by changes in both the geographic distribution and the nature of the investment. New funds increasingly flowed to the developed European market rather than to Latin America. There was a parallel shift in emphasis from extractive to manufacturing investments. In Table 13 the marked tilt toward Europe is clearly shown.

But the geographical distribution of U.S. foreign direct investment was not the principal concern of the groups that supported Burke-

TABLE 12

U.S. Bilateral Trade With Japan, 1958-74
(billions of dollars)

Year	Exports*	Imports*	Balance
1958	1.0	0.7	0.3
1959	1.1	1.0	.1
1960	1.5	1.1	.3
1961	1.8	1.1	.8
1962	1.6	1.4	.2
1963	1.8	1.5	.3
1964	2.0	1.8	.2
1965	2.1	2.4	-.3
1966	2.4	3.0	-.6
1967	2.7	3.0	-.3
1968	3.0	4.1	-1.1
1969	3.5	4.9	-1.4
1970	4.7	5.9	-1.2
1971	4.1	7.3	-3.2
1972	5.0	9.1	-4.1
1973	8.3	9.7	-1.4
1974	10.7	12.5	-1.8

*Exports are f.a.s. and imports are Customs values, generally the market value in the foreign country.
Source: Council on International Economic Policy, Annual Report, 1975 (Washington, D.C.: U.S. Government Printing Office, 1975), Table 30, p. 135.

TABLE 13

Major World Area Shares of U.S. Foreign Direct
Investment, 1950, 1960, 1971
(percent of total book value at year end)

Area	1950	1960	1971
Canada	30.4	34.2	28.0
Latin American republics	37.7	24.5	
Other Western Hemisphere	1.1	2.7	
European Economic Community (6)	5.4	8.1	15.8
United Kingdom and other Western Europe	9.3	12.2	16.4
Africa			
Asia		omitted	
Oceania			
International shipping			

Sources: For 1950 and 1960, Vladimir N. Pregelj, Multinational Firm and Its Implications for the United States Foreign
Trade Policy (Washington, D.C.: Congressional Research Service,
1971), p. 10. For 1971, "The International Investment Position of
the United States: Developments in 1973," Survey of Current Business, August 1974, p. 16.

Hartke. Nor was there an anticipation of the energy-crisis-induced
concern with overseas investments in petroleum and other raw
materials. Rather, the focus was on the steady increase in the
amount of foreign direct investment in manufacturing plants abroad.
The trend to manufacturing investment was not new, but its cumulative effect had begun to concern much of the U.S. labor movement.
In 1950 somewhat more than 32 percent of U.S. foreign direct investment was in manufacturing facilities. In the next ten years the share
in manufacturing fluctuated slightly with a small increase to just
over 34 percent in 1960. But by 1971 there had been a noticeable
jump to 41 percent.[42] In simple terms, an increasing share of the
rapidly growing U.S. foreign direct investment was devoted to manufacturing abroad.

The impact of U.S. manufacturing investment abroad is clearly
reflected in the volume of sales by majority-owned foreign affiliates

(MOFAs) of U.S. firms. Between 1966 and 1972, sales of manufactures grew from $47 billion to more than $110 billion, an increase of well over 100 percent. The details of yearly sales by major industry are spelled out in Table 14. Exports of MOFAs to the United States over the same period showed an even more marked increase. From a level of 2.7 billion in 1966 they grew to 7.7 billion in 1972. The almost threefold increase in MOFA exports to the United States was cause of some concern to labor groups. Despite the rapid rate of growth of MOFA exports to the United States, they never constituted a large percentage of total MOFA manufactured sales. The story appears more vividly in Tables 15 and 16.

In response to labor claims about the growth of foreign sourcing from controlled affiliates, the multinationals contended that a large percentage of the MOFA exports were from Canada. The figures in Table 17 do go some way to substantiating the multinationals position. The heavy concentration of Canadian exports in the transportation equipment category reflects the impact of the Canadian Automobile Agreement. Designed to allow the duty-free exchange of automobiles and auto parts, the first five years of the pact effectively eliminated the trade surplus in transportation equipment that the United States had run with Canada. When exports from Canadian MOFAs are eliminated from total MOFA exports to the United States, the MOFA exports for most industries and for most years are around 2 percent (see Tables 18 and 19) of total MOFA sales of manufactured goods.

There is little question that the rapid growth of U.S. foreign direct investment has made many large U.S. firms increasingly dependent on their foreign operations. A 1970 profile of 50 large U.S. firms highlights the degree of dependence in terms of both sales and income (see Table 20).

Economic forces played an important role in the spread of the U.S. multinational, but government policy was also involved. In light of U.S. preeminence at the end of World War II, it was an obvious candidate to become a major capital exporter. To some extent existing tax policy was already structured to accommodate direct foreign investment by American firms. The practice of allowing foreign taxes to be credited against U.S. taxes and of deferring liability on foreign-source profits until they were actually repatriated eliminated potential domestic barriers to U.S. investments abroad.

Regardless of party, the U.S. government has sought to reduce international barriers to capital investment. For instance, both the Johnson and Nixon administrations brought steady pressure to bear on the Japanese to allow foreign direct investment in the technologically dynamic sectors of Japanese industry, particularly the computer field.

TABLE 14

Total Sales by Majority-Owned Foreign Manufacturing Affiliates by Industry, 1966–72 (millions of dollars)

Industry	Total Sales						
	1966	1967	1968	1969	1970	1971	1972
Manufacturing, total	47,374	52,372	59,583	67,739	77,000	92,604	110,404
Food products	5,644	6,172	6,286	6,907	7,624	9,850	11,238
Chemicals and allied products	7,421	8,635	10,006	11,039	12,615	15,130	18,516
Primary and fabricated metals	3,904	4,473	4,907	5,763	7,221	7,818	8,697
Machinery	10,902	12,145	13,519	16,183	19,244	22,995	27,319
Transportation equipment	11,156	11,551	13,804	16,135	16,708	20,203	24,118
Other	8,348	9,396	11,061	11,712	13,588	16,607	20,516

Source: "Aspects of International Investment," Survey of Current Business 54, no. 8, Part II (August 1974).

TABLE 15

Exports to the United States by Majority-Owned Foreign Manufacturing Affiliates by Industry, 1966–72 (millions of dollars)

Industry	Exports to the United States						
	1966	1967	1968	1969	1970	1971	1972
Manufacturing, total	2,679	3,318	4,098	5,346	5,514	6,383	7,694
Food products	188	197	181	197	261	235	240
Chemicals and allied products	171	138	165	169	162	205	211
Primary and fabricated metals	47	421	293	549	335	396	431
Machinery	444	313	435	578	864	680	1,177
Transportation equipment	D*	1,637	2,357	3,138	3,225	4,097	4,778
Other	D	612	667	715	667	770	858

*D = Suppressed to avoid disclosure of data of individual reporters.

Source: "Aspects of International Investment," Survey of Current Business 54, no. 8, Part II (August 1974).

TABLE 16

Export Sales by Majority-Owned Foreign Manufacturing Affiliates of U.S. Companies
as a Percent of Total Sales by Industry, 1966-72

Industry	1966	1967	1968	1969	1970	1971	1972
Total export sales	5.7	6.3	6.9	7.9	7.2	6.9	7.0
Food products	3.3	3.2	2.9	2.9	3.6	2.4	2.1
Chemicals and allied products	2.3	1.6	1.6	1.5	1.3	1.6	1.1
Primary and fabricated metals	1.2	9.4	6.0	9.5	4.6	5.1	5.0
Machinery	4.1	2.6	3.2	3.6	4.5	3.0	4.3
Transportation equipment		14.2	17.1	19.4	19.3	20.3	19.8
Other		6.5	7.1	8.5	4.9	4.6	4.2

Source: Calculated from figures contained in "Aspects of International Investment," Survey of Current
Business 54, no. 8, Part II (August 1974).

TABLE 17

Exports to the United States by Majority-Owned Foreign Manufacturing Plants in Canada by Industry, 1966-72

Industry	1966	1967	1968	1969	1970	1971	1972
Manufacturing, total	1,961	2,327	3,046	3,964	3,912	4,754	5,670
Food products	46	D*	36	68	76	73	86
Chemicals and allied products	118	86	91	98	75	121	121
Primary and fabricated metals	27	62	D	128	82	115	119
Machinery	186	D	D	239	337	225	513
Transportation equipment	948	1,480	2,116	2,856	2,821	3,608	4,186
Other	686	520	557	575	521	612	646

*D = Suppressed to avoid disclosure of data of individual reporters.

Source: "Aspects of International Investment," Survey of Current Business 54, no. 8, Part II (August 1974).

TABLE 18

Exports to the United States by Majority-Owned Foreign Manufacturing Affiliates Outside Canada by Industry, 1966–72

Industry	1966	1967	1968	1969	1970	1971	1972
Total export sales	718	991	1,052	1,382	1,602	1,629	2,024
Food products	142	D*	145	129	185	162	154
Chemicals and allied products	53	52	74	71	87	34	90
Primary and fabricated metals	20	359	D	421	253	281	312
Machinery	258	D	D	339	527	455	664
Transportation equipment	D	157	241	282	404	489	592
Other	D	92	110	140	146	158	212

*D = Suppressed to avoid disclosure of data of individual reporters.

Source: Calculated from figures contained in "Aspects of International Investment," Survey of Current Business 54, no. 8, Part II (August 1974).

TABLE 19

Export Sales by Majority-Owned Foreign Manufacturing Affiliates Outside Canada as a Percent of Total Sales by Industry, 1966–72

Industry	1966	1967	1968	1969	1970	1971	1972
Total export sales	1.5	1.9	1.8	2.0	2.1	1.8	1.8
Food products	2.5	n.a.	2.3	1.9	2.4	1.7	1.4
Chemicals and allied products	.7	.6	.7	.6	.7	.2	.5
Primary and fabricated metals	.5	8.0	n.a.	7.3	3.5	3.6	3.6
Machinery	2.4	n.a.	n.a.	2.1	2.7	2.0	2.4
Transportation equipment	n.a.	1.4	1.7	1.7	2.4	2.4	2.4
Other	n.a.	1.0	1.0	1.2	1.1	1.0	1.0

Source: Calculated from figures contained in "Aspects of International Investment," Survey of Current Business 54, no. 8, Part II (August 1974).

TABLE 20

Multinational Profits, 1970

Company	Net Sales (millions)	Estimated Foreign Sales (millions)	Percent Total	Net Income (millions)	Percent Foreign	Where the Profits Come From
Standard Oil (New Jersey)	$16,554	$8,277	50	$1,310	52	Worldwide
Ford Motor	14,980	3,900[a]	26	516	24[a]	Germany, Britain, Australia
General Motors	18,752	3,563[a]	19	609	19[a]	Worldwide
Mobil Oil	7,261	3,267	45	483	51	Canada, Middle East
International Business Machines	7,504	2,933	39	1,018	50	Worldwide
International Telephone & Telegraph	6,365	2,673[a]	42	353	35[a]	Canada, Europe, Latin America
Texaco	6,350	2,540	40	822	b	Worldwide
Gulf Oil	5,396	2,428	45	550	21[c]	Middle East, South America, Canada
Standard Oil of California	4,188	1,885	45	455	46[c]	Middle East, Indonesia, South America
Chrysler	7,000	1,700[a]	24	7.6[d]	b	Worldwide

Company					
General Electric	8,727	1,393	16	329	20	South America, Canada, Italy
Caterpillar Tractor	2,128	1,118	53	144	b	Export sales, Worldwide
Occidental Petroleum	2,402	1,105[a]	46	175	b	Middle East, South America, Africa
F. W. Woolworth	2,528	1,001[e]	35	77	61	Canada, Germany, Britain
Eastman Kodak	2,785	874	31	404	19	Worldwide
Union Carbide	3,026	870	29	157	b	Worldwide
Procter & Gamble	3,178	795	25	238	25	Britain, Europe, Latin America
Singer	2,125	775	37	75	b	Europe, Latin America
Dow Chemical	1,911	771	40	103	45[f]	Worldwide
CPC International	1,376	692	50	61	51	Worldwide
International Harvester	2,712	680	25	52	b	Canada, Europe, Africa
Firestone Tire & Rubber	2,335	677	29	93	39	Worldwide
Colgate–Palmolive	1,210	670	55	40	b	Worldwide
Honeywell	1,921	622	35	58	b	Europe, British Commonwealth
National Cash Register	1,421	643	45	30	51[f]	Worldwide
E. I. duPont	3,618	634	18	329	b	Export sales, Europe
W. R. Grace	1,938	633	33	30	39[a,f]	Latin America
Minnesota Mining & Manufacturing	1,687	605	36	188	b	Europe, Canada, Australia
First National City Corp.	1,704	600	35	139	40	Worldwide

(continued)

Table 20 (continued)

Company	Net Sales (millions)	Estimated Foreign Sales (millions)	Percent Total	Net Income (millions)	Percent Foreign	Where the Profits Come From
Englehard Minerals & Chemical	1,474	589	40	36	b	Britain, Europe, Japan
Sperry Rand	1,739	589	34	72	b	Europe, Japan
Xerox	1,719	518	30	188	38	Britain, Canada, Latin America
American Standard	1,418	511	36	13	33	Europe
Coca-Cola	1,606	498	31	147	b	Worldwide
Swift	3,076	492	16	29	b	Canada, Britain, Germany
General Foods	2,282	479	21	119	b	Canada
American Smelting & Refining	718	467	65	89	55g	Australia, Peru, Mexico
Monsanto	1,972	467	24	67	31	Canada, Latin America, Europe
Warner-Lambert	1,257	453	36	98	b	Worldwide
General Telephone & Electronics	3,439	441	13	236	7	Canada, Europe, Latin America
H. J. Heinz	990	433	44	38	44	Worldwide
Uniroyal	1,556	420	27	24	75	Canada, Mexico
Pfizer	870	412	47	81	55	Britain, Europe, Latin America

106

Litton Industries	2,404	409	17	69	b	Europe, Latin America
Schlumberger	579	341	59	49	b	France, Canada
Otis Elevator	601c	301	50	24	35	Worldwide
Gillete	673	289	43	66	50	Worldwide
USM	440	203	46	10	98	British Commonwealth, Europe, Latin America
Chesebrough-Pond's	261	111	43	21	40	Europe, Canada, Latin America
Black & Decker	255	107	42	20	50	Export sales

aExcludes Canada.
bNot available.
cContracts completed.
dDeficit.
ePercent based on consolidated sales and equity in unconsolidated subsidiary.
fPercent based on operating income.
gPercent based on earnings before taxes and extraordinary items.
Note: All oil company figures exclude excise taxes.

Source: The Multinational Corporation and The World Economy, Committee on Finance, U.S. Senate, 93d Cong., 1st sess. (Washington, D.C.: U.S. Government Printing Office, 1973), pp. 14-15. Reprinted from Forbes, November 15, 1971, p. 77.

Foreign direct investment by U.S. firms has also played an important role in the formulation of U.S. development policy. Investment guarantees originally devised to aid in the economic reconstruction of Europe were broadened to include developing countries in 1953. Until 1976 special rules governed the taxation of foreign-source income earned in developing countries. And both bilateral and multilateral assistance tended to emphasize the major infrastructure projects that make direct foreign investment in manufacturing both useful and profitable.

For some time discussion of U.S. foreign direct investment was centered on its impact on the host or recipient nation. Was foreign direct investment a natural and effective partner in the reconstruction of Western Europe or had it come to present an almost insurmountable challenge to European industry? Did the Alliance for Progress properly rely on the proven know-how of the U.S. corporations or were the U.S. corporations guilty of foisting inappropriate products and production techniques on an already beleaguered Third World?

In many ways Burke-Hartke marked a shift in the debate on the impact of foreign direct investment. Instead of concentrating on its role abroad, Burke-Hartke advocates questioned its impact on the domestic economy. What were the short-run implications for jobs, the balance of trade, and the overall balance of payments? Admitting the rather sizable dollar return on foreign direct investments (see Table 21), Burke-Hartke partisans nonetheless argued that foreign direct investment was made at the expense of domestic investment.

Although it was not central to either their concern or their case, the proponents of Burke-Hartke also began to question the popular concept of the service society. They suggested that if there is an eventual concentration of manufacturing in lower-wage, developing countries, the technological services that are currently provided by the developed world would soon follow the industrial base.

In seeking to control the multinational corporation and the flow of capital abroad, the drafters of Burke-Hartke may have reacted to a series of U.S. failures in the capital control area. Brought on by the balance of payments deficits of the 1960s, these policies ranged from the interest equalization tax on foreign securities to the Federal Reserve Board's voluntary program for U.S. banks. Rather than relying exclusively on direct capital controls, Burke-Hartke opted to change the rules for taxation of foreign-source income.

Burke-Hartke then was not a will of the wisp of organized labor nor the product of an aging but still cranky George Meany. A product of many forces, it nonetheless was a definite response to the then current rules of international commerce, a changing world economic

TABLE 21

U.S. Direct Investments Abroad, Direct Investment Interest, Dividends and Branch Earnings, and Direct Investment Royalties and Fees, 1960-71 (millions of dollars)

Year	A Direct Investment Outflows	B Direct Investment Interest Dividends and Branch Earnings	C Direct Investment Royalties and Fees	D B + C	E Net Balance of Payments Effect
1960	1,674	2,335	590	2,925	1,251
1961	1,598	2,768	662	3,430	1,832
1962	1,654	3,044	800	3,844	2,190
1963	1,976	3,129	890	4,019	2,043
1964	2,328	3,674	1,013	4,687	2,359
1965	3,468	3,963	1,199	5,162	1,694
1966	3,661	4,045	1,329	5,374	1,713
1967	3,137	4,518	1,438	5,956	2,819
1968	3,209	4,973	1,546	6,519	3,310
1969	3,254	5,658	1,682	7,340	4,086
1970	4,445	6,026	1,880	7,906	3,461
1971	4,943	6,385	2,161	8,546	3,603

Source: Survey of Current Business, June 1971, p. 32, and Survey of Current Business, June 1974, p. 34.

109

order, and the steady growth of the U.S.-based multinational firm. And it was very definitely the AFL–CIO's challenge to established foreign economic policy.

NOTES

1. See, for instance, U.S. Congress, House, Committee on Ways and Means, Foreign Trade and Tariff Proposals, Hearings, Part 3, June 11, 12, and 13, 1968 (Washington, D.C.: U.S. Government Printing Office, 1968), p. 925.

2. In 1953 the Economic and Social Council of the United Nations adopted the c.i.f. basis as the standard way of recording the transactions value of an import. See United Nations, Yearbook of International Trade Statistics, 1972–1973 (New York: United Nations, 1974), p. 4.

3. See U.S. Bureau of the Census, Title U.S. General Imports, (FT/135), January 1974 (Washington, D.C.: U.S. Government Printing Office, 1974), p. XI.

4. M. A. G. van Meerhaeghe, International Economic Institutions (New York: St. Martins Press, 1971), p. 90 et seq.

5. Ibid., p. 91.

6. Kenneth W. Dam, The GATT: Law and International Economic Organization (Chicago: University of Chicago Press, 1970), p. 11.

7. For a discussion of the GATT treatment of internal taxes, see ibid., Chapter 7.

8. See "Tax Adjustments in International Trade: GATT Provisions and EEC Practices," Executive Branch GATT Studies, Committee on Finance, U.S. Senate, 93d Cong., 2d sess., March 1974, p. 2.

9. For a brief discussion of the traditional view, see Richard Goode, The Corporation Income Tax (New York: John Wiley, 1951), pp. 46 et seq.

10. Harberger spells out the conditions under which labor would bear a portion of the corporate income tax. See A. Harberger, "The Incidence of the Corporation Income Tax," Journal of Political Economy, June 1962. For a general treatment of the question, see Richard A. Musgrave and Peggy B. Musgrave, Public Finance in Theory and Practice (New York: McGraw-Hill, 1973), Chapter 17. There is also a brief discussion of the issue in Dam, op. cit., p. 214 et seq.

11. See, for instance, Foreign Trade and Tariff Proposals, Hearings before the Committee on Ways and Means, 90th Cong., 2d sess., Part 1, p. 51 et seq.

12. Dam, op. cit., p. 348.

13. There are many summary discussions of these plans. See, for instance, Wilbur F. Monroe, International Monetary Reconstruction: Problems and Issues (Lexington, Mass.: D. C. Heath, 1974), pp. 20-23.

14. Monroe, op. cit., p. 22.

15. For a brief overview of the IMF, see van Meerhaeghe, op. cit., Chapter 1, pp. 21-55.

16. Ibid., p. 37.

17. See, for instance, Hans Aufricht, The International Monetary Fund, Legal Bases, Structure, Functions (New York: Frederick A. Praeger, 1964), pp. 23-24.

18. Van Meerhaeghe, op. cit., p. 38.

19. Ibid., p. 39.

20. Ibid.

21. W. M. Scammell, International Monetary Policy: Bretton Woods and After (New York: John Wiley, 1975), p. 138.

22. Originally, a 1-percent limit was established for the variance between maximum and minimum in spot transactions. This limit was changed to 2.5 percent in the Smithsonian Agreement of 1971. Ibid., p. 109.

23. Article 4, 5a and f as cited in Van Meerhaeghe, op. cit., p. 34.

24. Ibid., p. 36. As a result France was denied access to IMF resources until October 1954.

25. Ibid., p. 35.

26. Ibid., p. 36.

27. Scammell, op. cit., p. 110.

28. For a brief descriptive summary of these and other events, see The European Free Trade Association and the Crisis of European Integration, by A Study Group, Graduate Institute of International Studies, Geneva (New York: Humanities Press, 1968), pp. 308 to 319.

29. Council on International Economic Policy, Annual Report 1975 (Washington, D.C.: U.S. Government Printing Office, 1975), p. 122.

30. Ibid., Table 3, p. 122.

31. Ibid., Table 4, p. 123.

32. Figures are calculated from ibid., Table 17, p. 131.

33. Figures are calculated from ibid.

34. Ibid., Table 16, p. 130.

35. Figures calculated from ibid., Table 17, p. 130.

36. Figures calculated from ibid., Table 17, p. 131.

37. Figures calculated from ibid., Table 16, p. 130.

38. Figures calculated from ibid., Table 17, p. 131.

39. See, for instance, Lawrence Krause, <u>European Economic Integration and the United States</u> (Washington, D.C.: Brookings Institution, 1968), Chapter 2.

40. Or so opines Martin Bronfenbrenner in his "Japanese-American Economic War? Some Further Reflections," <u>Quarterly Review of Economics and Business</u> 13 (Autumn 1973):36.

41. Figures for 1950 and 1960 are from U.S. Office of Business Economics, <u>U.S. Business Investments in Foreign Countries</u> (Washington, D.C.: U.S. Government Printing Office, 1960) and the <u>Survey of Current Business</u> for 1962, as cited in Vladimir N. Pregelj, <u>Multinational Firm and Its Implications for the United States Foreign Trade Policy</u> (Washington, D.C.: Congressional Research Service, 1971), p. 8. The figure for 1971 is from "The International Investment Position of the United States: Developments in 1973," <u>Survey of Current Business</u>, August 1974, p. 16.

42. See Pregelj, op. cit., p. 11 for 1950 and 1960. For 1971 see J. N. Friedlin and L. A. Lupo, "U.S. Direct Investment Abroad in 1973," <u>Survey of Current Business</u> 54, no. 8, Part II (August 1974), Table 9, p. 17.

CHAPTER 5

EVOLUTION OF THE LABOR CASE

In discussing labor's break with the free trade coalition, considerable emphasis has been put on the impact of economic events. Fearful of rising imports and apprehensive about the multinational firm, the AFL-CIO altered both its position and its thinking on trade and investment. This chapter focuses on the changed economic reasoning that provided much of the rationale for the labor case.

In basic terms the labor argument was seemingly straightforward. Imports were growing more rapidly than exports, more and more of these imports competed with potential U.S. production, and imports thus were taking away more and more jobs from American workers. Although there were many causes for the persistent increase in imports, a principal cause was the phenomenal growth of the U.S.-based multinational corporation. The increased mobility of capital precipitated plant closings, retarded economic growth in the United States, and facilitated the rapid spread of U.S. technology.

So much for the basic outline of labor's position. How has it gone about proving its case? How did labor attempt to persuade the Congress and the country that U.S. foreign economic policy was in need of a sharp reversal? As mentioned in Chapter 1, this study does not focus principally on the back-door exercise of political or financial influence. There is no attempt here to make this an updated Washington Payoff in academic garb. Rather the emphasis is on the role of persuasion. Did labor rely on current economic theory or did it challenge an accepted orthodoxy? Were tightly reasoned studies the order of the day or did labor rely mainly on a series of working hypotheses, an aggregate of assertions? Did labor successfully adduce the necessary facts to make its case? This is not to say that the power and the politics of the entire arrangement were not crucially important, for they were. Once again, the emphasis is on how Congress assesses the problem while making up its own mind.

113

Once set, labor has presented its case before congressional hearings, in press conferences, in speeches in the labor press, in letters to congressmen, and in many personal contacts on Capitol Hill. The clearest, most comprehensive single expression of the labor case, however, can be found in a study commissioned by the AFL-CIO by Stanley H. Ruttenberg and Associates.[1] The Ruttenberg study is not designed for an audience of professional economists, but it does contain almost all the economic arguments made by the AFL-CIO in support of the Burke-Hartke Bill. Because it is so all-encompassing, the Ruttenberg volume provides an ideal point of departure for an analysis of the labor case. Throughout this chapter, Ruttenberg will be referred to not for his own views but rather as a spokesman for the AFL-CIO.

The Ruttenberg study is divided into four very different parts. First, there is an analysis of what Ruttenberg terms the "changing patterns of U.S. trade and investments." Second, there is an exposition of the forces behind this change—the labor theory behind Burke-Hartke. Third, there is a catchall section designed to rebut anticipated arguments or patch over possible weaknesses in the argument. And finally, there is the prescription for change—Burke-Hartke without the legislative language.

Unfortunately, Ruttenberg does not focus on economic theory. Even in his section presenting the labor view of the international economy, the labor position is neither integrated with nor contrasted with current economic thought. To put the Ruttenberg (and hence the labor) view in some sort of economic perspective involves a certain amount of academic reconstruction and more than a little intellectual interpolation. But the effort is well worth while. In making his case, Ruttenberg is relying on a variety of economic arguments and on more than one point he specifically attacks an only partially presented orthodoxy. In addition, Ruttenberg was widely judged on economic grounds by the Washington-based policy economists.

INCREASED MOBILITY OF CAPITAL, MANAGEMENT, AND TECHNOLOGY

To Ruttenberg and the AFL-CIO, the most important change in the world economy was associated with the increased mobility of most resources. Capital, management, technology, and technical know-how—but not labor—had become increasingly capable of traversing national boundaries. It was, of course, the "but not labor" that was of so much concern to the AFL-CIO.

An earlier chapter discussed a number of precedents in the academic literature for labor's apprehension about the possible costs of foreign direct investment. Labor did not, however, focus on either the potential for a diminished rate of return on existing foreign investments or for a worsened terms of trade. Rather, the concern of labor was with the implications of foreign direct investment for the level of manufactured imports, the future rate of domestic economic growth, and above all else for the level of domestic employment.

In the labor view, every dollar invested abroad was a dollar lost to capital investment in the United States. In rough terms the labor position corresponds to the "classical view" of foreign investment. A detailed discussion of classical substitution assumptions in a preceding chapter suggested that they had rather definite and adverse implications for labor's share in national income, the future rate of domestic growth in the donor country, and the level of employment.

The loss of domestic capital should reduce labor productivity and the real wage labor. On the other hand, capital owners should earn both a higher return domestically and participate fully in the return on the direct foreign investment. Unless the additional foreign direct investment reduces the return on existing foreign investments or the investment induces a demand for labor-intensive exports from the donor nation, labor's share in national income is sure to suffer.[2]

To the extent that capital investment is a prerequisite for future economic growth, the classical view suggests that future growth will be slowed by foreign direct investments. Although both capital owners and labor will suffer from slower domestic growth, capital owners will share in the rewards of faster economic growth abroad. The slower rate of growth could also reduce the future supply of jobs in the capital-dependent, manufacturing (and highly unionized) sector. It is possible, of course, that the higher domestic price for capital might bias technological change in a labor-using direction.[3]

Classical substitution assumptions also have possible implications for stabilization policy. If the direct foreign investment creates an equal demand for U.S. exports of capital equipment, no stabilization policy would be necessary. On the other hand, if the direct foreign investment is not fully transferred, there could be a multiple reduction of U.S. production and employment. Depending on whether the current administration was willing to pursue a full-employment policy, labor might suffer immediate losses in both jobs and job opportunities. The antiinflationary policies of the first Nixon administration may thus have had more than a little to do with labor's changed view toward both foreign direct investment and foreign trade. Nor can one ignore the effect of various stabilizing policies on labor. Musgrave notes that if taxes on capital are reduced to encourage more investment, stabilization policy will result in a further "internal distribution toward capital owners."[4]

The use of classical substitution assumptions does not describe the full range of the labor case. Ruttenberg and labor were at pains to stress the impact that reduced investment could have on both the use and generation of new technology. In part, labor could be viewed as stressing an embodied view of technological change and accepting the importance of innovation for economic growth.[5] In addition, technology appeared to be an important determinant of the U.S. export performance.

Ruttenberg and labor also feared that foreign direct investment would reduce U.S. exports not only to the host country but to third countries as well. In many cases labor feared that foreign countries would serve merely as "export platforms" directed toward the large U.S. market. The labor view with regard to export displacement is quite consistent with its adoption of essentially classical substitution assumptions. The displacement of U.S. exports abroad could have long-run implications for the balance of trade and might demand further stabilizing activity on the part of the government.

Ruttenberg spends as much time discussing the causes of foreign direct investment as he does on its possible effects. Although admitting that any particular investment decision may be motivated by a number of concerns, Ruttenberg focuses on low wages abroad and the U.S. taxation of foreign-source income. In a view that seems to roughly parallel Vernon's theory of the product cycle, Ruttenberg expresses the traditional labor concern with low foreign wage rates. To Ruttenberg it is "a general rule in industry [that] as a product becomes standardized, labor costs become more important than the technical skills which were critical in the early development. At this point, as the multinationals have discovered, the process of production is ready for export to a country where labor costs are lower."[6]

Although there is considerable controversy over the role taxes play in influencing capital flows,[7] Ruttenberg and labor both argue that the U.S. tax treatment of foreign-source income was "certainly a principal reason" for the increase in U.S. direct foreign investment.[8] Labor also contended that both the deferral privilege and the foreign tax credit constituted a considerable drain on the U.S. Treasury.* Musgrave has estimated the combined 1972 loss to the

---

*From the national point of view, one could argue that the return on direct foreign investment net of foreign taxes had to exceed

Treasury as in excess of $3 billion.[9] Ruttenberg also singles out for special mention the "preferential treatment that the U.S. tariff laws provide for products only partially fabricated outside U.S. borders."[10]

QUESTIONING COMPARATIVE ADVANTAGE

In the Ruttenberg study, labor also sought to raise some difficult questions about the utility of current economic theory for analyzing current trade and investment problems. Labor argued that the emergence of the multinational firm and an increasingly government-managed international economy had simply changed the nature of the U.S. comparative advantage. In fact, labor frequently spoke of the "repeal" of the law of comparative advantage. To labor the law of comparative advantage was neither descriptive of the present-day international economy nor any guide for government policy.

Perhaps because labor put so much emphasis on comprehensive import quotas, the labor questioning of the doctrine of comparative advantage was largely ignored. In part it also probably reflected the need for some further intellectual reconstruction. It is not completely clear what Ruttenberg means by comparative advantage. Although he mentions Ricardo, his argumentation is directed neither at the general formulation of Ricardo nor the more frequently used Heckscher-Ohlin model. In place of these two he appears to have tied the Vernon product cycle theory to an unexplored assumption concerning the continual creation of new technology.[11]

Ruttenberg specifically attacks what he labels the "two basic assumptions [of] the theory of comparative advantage . . . that the factors of production remain fixed and that there will be complete freedom of trade."[12] Instead, he stresses the extreme mobility of capital and the plethora of trade barriers that continue to clutter trade channels.

If Ruttenberg is attacking the descriptive powers of the HO model, he has made some proper criticisms. In a standard formulation,[13] the HO model does assume that while there is complete mobility of factors within a nation state (or trading unit), there is absolutely no international mobility of factors.[14] The HO formulation of comparative advantage generally makes assumptions about economies of scale, entry, and the initial number of firms so that competi-

---

the return on domestic investment gross of taxes. Under existing tax laws, the Treasury might seek to have taxable remissions equal the return on domestic investment gross of federal income taxes.

tive markets exist. Ruttenberg has thus raised reasonable questions about the validity of both assumptions.

Technology raises a more complicated point. An HO model generally assumes that the same technology is available to all trading partners. Labor has taken a quite different view. It contends that the United States had a large technological lead at the end of World War II that had been steadily eroded through the licensing and investment practices of the U.S.-based multinational firm. Labor also expressed concern about the future ability of the United States to generate technological change, a matter that does not readily fall within the ambit of the HO approach.

Labor has come to stress the dynamic aspects of an economy that are not easily contained within the confines of traditional trade theory. Although labor admitted the likelihood of continued technological innovation, it contended that mobile capital can so rapidly spread a new technology that "the time lag between shifts to new industries grows ever shorter; and consequent disruptions to our economy more severe."[15] Gilpin takes a similar position in a publication for the Joint Economic Committee.[16]

With so much international trade taking place within multinational firms rather than between competitive firms, Ruttenberg argues that the old rules of international trade no longer apply. It is certainly possible that private company calculations with regard to foreign tax rates or existing company assets may distort the pattern of trade from what it might have been. Although no settled view has emerged on this issue, both Corden[17] and Kreinen[18] have recently attempted to assess the implications of the multinational firm for trade theory.[19]

Ruttenberg does not, however, limit his questioning of the HO model to the growth of the multinational firm or general factor mobility. He also pointed to the emergence of preferential trading blocs and the widespread use of nontariff barriers. Considerable stress is placed on government intervention in the allegedly free channels of international trade. For instance, Ruttenberg contends that a partial explanation for America's worsening merchandise trade balance can be found in the success of other countries in isolating their export prices from the impact of a generalized inflation. Using IMF data for both export and domestic consumer prices, Ruttenberg noted that export prices in Japan, Italy, the United Kingdom, and France did not keep pace with the rise in domestic consumer prices. According to the labor view, these countries "were able (by government action) to suppress export prices."[20]

FOREIGN INVESTMENT, TRADE, AND
DOMESTIC EMPLOYMENT

The foregoing suggests that a strong, certainly an intelligent,
case could be built for labor's position on foreign trade and investment. In terms of the impact of direct foreign investment on jobs,
income, or growth, however, Ruttenberg was not particularly forceful in either presenting or proving the labor case. He does cite the
growing size of total U.S. direct foreign investment and the growth
in plant and equipment outlays of foreign subsidiaries controlled by
U.S. firms.[21] In an attempt to tie the U.S. multinational to specific
job losses, Ruttenberg cites 1970 congressional testimony of Paul
Jennings, president of the International Union of Electrical Radio
and Machine Workers.[22] The Jennings testimony contained several
instances of plants being transferred abroad by Zenith, Admiral,
Ford-Philco, and RCA.
    To make the link between foreign trade and a loss of domestic
employment, Ruttenberg relies principally on a Bureau of Labor
Statistics study of foreign-trade-related employment in 1966 and
1969.[23] That study attempted to compare export-related (both direct
and indirect employment) to the employment (both direct and indirect)
needed to produce the imports that competed with U.S. production.
According to the figures generated by this study, between 1966 and
1969 the number of jobs needed to produce competitive imports increased by 700,000. During the same period the number of export-
related jobs increased by 200,000. The net loss figure of 500,000
was a key figure in the Ruttenberg analysis and the rallying cry of
the AFL-CIO's jobs-lost-to-foreign-trade cause.* Any other figures
used by labor—at one time a 1-million-job figure was used—are extrap-
olations from the same basic BLS study.

---

*In a similar but more recent study, the Department of Labor
has calculated the number of jobs related to imports and exports
through 1975. According to this study, between 1965 and 1975 jobs
related to exports grew by 1,977,000 while jobs related to imports
grew by 1,688,000. The apparent net gain of 289,000 jobs would not
buttress the labor position. However, 1975 was a year of severe
recession. Imports had fallen sharply and the United States had a
$9 billion trade surplus. If one looks at 1973, the last preoil-shock
trade year, employment related to imports and exports looks quite
different. Between 1965 and 1973, jobs related to imports grew so
much faster than those related to exports that the figures show a new
loss of job opportunities of 812,000. In making these calculations,

In describing the employment situation, Ruttenberg argued
that "between 1966 and 1969 U.S. foreign trade produced the equivalent of a net loss of half a million American jobs" (emphasis added). [25]
The term equivalent actually begs a multitude of issues. Aside from
the complexities of the BLS estimates, they said little or nothing
about the employment level in the U.S. economy. They indicate
neither that jobs were lost nor that jobs were unavailable. In fact,
the years during which these apparent losses took place were years
of exceptionally low rates of overall unemployment.

Going beyond the overall employment figures of the BLS study
period, Ruttenberg attempts to tie apparent losses to real losses in
specific industries. Consumer electronics was one industry that
clearly followed the general outlines of the Ruttenberg case. Another
BLS study covering the period 1960-65 was cited to buttress the connection between the degree of import penetration and the rate of
increase of unemployment.

In the first two parts of his study, Ruttenberg concentrated on
spelling out the changes in the U.S. merchandise trade account and
attempting to tie those changes to the growth of the U.S.-based multinational corporation. Except for some of the material on comparative
advantage, most of the "reconstruction" of the labor position was
drawn from these two parts.

In the concluding two parts of his study, Ruttenberg presents
the Burke-Hartke proposal and attempts to meet some anticipated
arguments against it. In addition to criticizing the doctrine of comparative advantage, Ruttenberg seeks to dispose of the idea of a
service economy, the question of retaliation by our trading partners,
the possible role of trade adjustment assistance, the impact of international trade in raising wage standards around the world, and,
somewhat surprisingly, the importance of wages in determining
patterns of international trade. This section of the Ruttenberg study
does not attempt to tie all these different positions together in a
rigorous alternative to existing trade theory, although the general
theme of the erosion of technological dominance through the spread
of the multinational firm does appear throughout.

Trade adjustment assistance is dismissed as almost the classical example of a snare and a delusion. Reflecting the failure of labor
to secure an adjustment assistance ruling prior to 1969, Ruttenberg
argues that adjustment assistance is more fantasy than fact. The

---

the Labor Department looked at all manufactured imports rather
than only those that competed with U.S. production, a practice followed in the earlier study. [24]

Ruttenberg view finds a garden with too many thorns and not enough roses—even the levels of assistance were set unrealistically low. Beyond that, Ruttenberg suggests that adjustment assistance diverted the nation's view from the really vital issues in foreign trade. It should be noted here that although Burke-Hartke did seek to improve the administration and the terms of adjustment assistance, it was still widely referred to in the labor movement as "burial assistance."

In an equally sweeping manner, Ruttenberg seeks to dispose of other possible arguments against the Burke-Hartke position. The fear of foreign retaliation against the import quotas of Title III is rather emphatically dismissed. Ruttenberg argues that others already discriminate against us and are so dependent on foreign trade that they "dare not take lightly efforts by the United States to restore equity in the international trade picture."[26]

Ruttenberg is also at pains to reject the notion that free trade, however constituted, will lead to the long-time labor goal of international wage equalization. It is not exactly clear what Ruttenberg has in mind at this juncture, but it certainly is not the concept of factor price equalization. Equalization in these terms seems to imply a mix of catching up to current real levels in the United States and/or worldwide legislation mandating current real levels of the U.S. minimum wage. Lack of labor mobility is singled out as one cause and the plethora of unemployed in the developing world is identified as another. There is little or no discussion of the trade-development issue or an assessment of foreign direct investment on foreign wage structures. In conclusion, Ruttenberg identifies production in foreign (non-U.S. minimum wage) plants for the U.S. market as a method of circumventing current U.S. minimum wage legislation.

While suggesting the importance of low foreign wages in attracting foreign direct investment and increasing exports to the United States, Ruttenberg does not want to build a case for lower wage levels in the United States. This particular peregrination is accomplished by focusing on the large productivity differentials between U.S. and foreign labor. To maintain existing wage levels the United States must "maintain a sufficient lead in technology and productivity."[27] And by implication this line of reasoning flows quite naturally back into one of Ruttenberg's main themes: the growth of the multinational and the spread of U.S. technology.

Ruttenberg continues with a vision of the future that as much as anything may have accounted for labor's new approach to foreign trade and investment policy. Citing Labor Department projections of future employment opportunities, Ruttenberg foresees the laborer in the manufacturing plant caught between jobs that "either require considerably more education than most workers have, or less skill (and less pay) than the jobs they are losing." And so the labor view of the service economy.

But the Ruttenberg analysis foresees a danger far beyond losses to be suffered by those currently employed in industry. In his view the service economy suggests a stagnation or decline in the U.S. standard of living. The future occupational structure—divided between highly trained and paid professionals and low-skilled clerical or service types—will "destroy the great strength of the middle class on which democracy rests."[28]

Ruttenberg's presentation has been subjected to such close scrutiny here because it remains the most comprehensive statement of the labor view of proper foreign trade and investment policy. The positions sketched and the arguments expressed by Ruttenberg continue to appear in labor testimony before the Congress. Despite a close and rather exhaustive assessment, the Ruttenberg labor is such a mix of things that it defies easy evaluation. It ranges from a straightforward recitation of facts to some extremely speculative hypotheses. In between, it raises some very tough questions about the role of factor mobility and technology in foreign trade. But it also leans heavily on assertions and rather lightly on facts, often leaving the reader with a sense of intellectual vagueness.

Nor is the tying of the multinational corporation to the loss of jobs or job opportunities in the U.S. economy an entirely convincing performance. There is the casual and persistent confusion between foreign direct investment and actual plant closing in the United States. There is the failure to distinguish between long-term capital flows and the book value at year end of U.S. foreign direct investments. As Eurodollar borrowings grew in the 1960s, one could have expected a continuing divergence between the flow of direct foreign investment of capital out of the United States and the actual size of a particular foreign direct investment. Nor was there any attempt to contrast the capital flow for direct foreign investment to present or future current account flows reflecting the return on that investment. Following labor's classical substitution assumptions, a strong case could have been made that current capital flows could in no way be judged by current remissions on past capital flows. By ignoring the whole question, labor left itself open to business appeals for just such a comparison. A quick look back at Table 7 in Chapter 4 would then suggest that the impact on domestic investment may have been quite small.

A similar impreciseness permeates the discussion of actual job losses. Little attempt is made to distinguish between people actually put out of work due to an increase in imports or an actual plant transfer and an apparent loss of job opportunities in industries that make items directly competitive with increasing imports.

The Ruttenberg/labor case, however, cannot be examined solely on academic grounds. It was never designed to "sparkle with least squares" or flex its arguments with mathematical rigor. Rather, it was designed to persuade and disarm a very special readership: the limited fraternity that would be involved in the congressional debate on foreign trade policy. From this perspective the Ruttenberg treatment of comparative advantage takes on a quite different coloration. Faced with an audience that may know little more about trade theory other than the phrase "comparative advantage," Ruttenberg is at pains to raise legitimate doubts about the application of the theory. Much of the Ruttenberg argumentation can be viewed in a similar light.

A somewhat more informed reader might also be puzzled about one of the policies that Ruttenberg does not advocate. Ruttenberg presents an economy caught between rising export prices and a fixed exchange rate. The conditions that Ruttenberg describes—a declining merchandise trade account and a shift of labor-intensive production abroad—follow naturally from the inability to adjust exchange rates. Why then does Ruttenberg virtually ignore the possibility of devaluation? To some extent, the labor movement was probably caught by surprise. The key position of the dollar in the Bretton Woods system made devaluation seem virtually unthinkable. And the Burke-Hartke position had taken time to formulate and time to establish within the labor movement itself. As it turned out, the Nixon break with Bretton Woods (August 1971) came just a month before the introduction of Burke-Hartke (September 1971) and just two months before publication of the Ruttenberg study (October 1971).

Ruttenberg does acknowledge the possible benefits to be gained from the import surcharge and the devaluation of the dollar, but he suggests that neither represents a long-run solution to the foreign trade and investment problems of the United States. The import surcharge is dismissed as being "not only temporary" but "also quite limited in application."[29] After recounting the way in which devaluation can make U.S. goods "a better buy in foreign countries," Ruttenberg challenges devaluation's overall importance. In Ruttenberg's view,

> a more rational system to cope with the problem of
> exchange rates . . . will not solve the threats to this
> nation's jobs, or to its living standards, that are posed
> by (1) the unfair competition from imports produced
> under substandard conditions and (2) the export of job
> opportunities via the export of American capital, or
> American technology to low-wage countries. The
> longer-run multi-faceted solution recommended in this
> study is more and not less essential as a result of the
> August 15, 1971 actions of the Administration.[30]

And that remained the Ruttenberg/labor view throughout the foreign trade policy debate engendered by the Burke-Hartke Bill. Having committed itself to a particular course of action, the AFL-CIO probably found a change of direction quite difficult. Some years had been invested in evolving the Burke-Hartke position, selling it to the leadership of the constituent unions and the membership at large. No doubt the abstractions of international monetary reform were less appealing to the general AFL-CIO membership than statutory protection against imports.

Of equal importance, in the author's view, was the desire of the AFL-CIO to bring some sort of stability and job security to the industrial economy. The long-standing fears about automation and job displacement were easily transferred to the foreign trade arena. Unlike the general question of technological displacement, foreign trade was an area that was quite properly subject to federal control and congressional action. Although not a position stressed in the early 1970s, the AFL-CIO remains wary of a trade stability through an exchange policy approach. After all, neither devaluation or even a system of freely fluctuating exchange rates promised the kind of permanent market share stability envisioned by Title III of Burke-Hartke. In retrospect, what is surprising is how little attention was paid to the thinking behind the labor view of the international economy.

Much of the actual labor position could be reconstructed in terms of current foreign trade and investment theory. The various implications of the HO model did provide some broad description of labor action. A more detailed understanding of the labor position, however, demanded the relaxation of a number of assumptions usually made in the HO approach. In particular, the limitations on the mobility of labor and international mobility of capital played an important part in bringing labor to the position it advocated in Burke-Hartke.

An explicit recognition of the multinational corporation and the existence of international oligopoly added considerably to understanding the economic world that labor faced. The mobility of capital and the austere stabilization policies adopted in the early Nixon years also played a role.

The use of theory to predict organizational behavior is often fraught with difficulties. Economic theory may have been used to formulate a position or it may have been used to rationalize policies adopted for quite different means. It remains possible that, under considerable pressure from its members, the AFL-CIO found remedies first and reasons later.

The theoretical explanations also leave considerable territory either unexplained or unexplored. Organized labor's relations with large international oligopolies remains unclear. To some extent organized labor has shared in the fruits of oligopolistic structures, yet opposes their international operations even where they improve domestic profitability. Nor do the intricacies of labor's political maneuvering always fit neatly into a theoretical framework. The general success in maintaining a unified position, though constituent unions might have quite varied economic interests in the outcome of a foreign trade and investment debate, is not readily explained.[31] Nor does the opposition of the United Auto Workers to import restrictions on automobiles (see Chapter 8) follow unambiguously from existing trade theory.

Despite the preceding qualifications, economic theory does provide considerable insight into the labor position and suggests a framework in which further analysis can take place.

NOTES

1. Stanley H. Ruttenberg and Associates, Needed: A Constructive Foreign Trade Policy, Industrial Union Department, AFL-CIO (Washington, D.C.:1971).

2. This section closely follows Musgrave's approach in Peggy Musgrave, United States Taxation of Foreign Investment Income: Issues and Arguments (Cambridge, Mass.: The Law School of Harvard University, 1969), p. 23.

3. It is far from clear what the impact of relative factor prices is on the rate and direction of technical change. Habakkuk puts considerable stress on factor prices in explaining nineteenth-century technological development in the United States. H. J. Habakkuk, American and British Technology in the Nineteenth Century: The Search for Labor-Saving Inventions (Cambridge: Cambridge University Press, 1962), see especially Chapter IV on "Labor Supplies and Technology in the U.S.A.," pp. 91-131. Other commentators have remained more agnostic on the issue. In a series of factory interviews in Brazil, the author found only one instance of a machine actually redesigned to meet Brazil's conditions of smaller markets, cheaper labor, and higher prices in capital. See Kent Hughes, "Factor Prices, Capital Intensity, and Technological Adaptation in Brazil," in Contemporary Brazil: Issues in Economic and Political Development, ed. H. Jon Rosenbaum and William Tyler (New York: Praeger Publishers, 1972).

4. Musgrave, op. cit., p. 23.

5. Denison gives weight to this view in E. Denison, The Sources of Economic Growth in the United States and Alternatives Before Us (New York: Committee for Economic Development, 1962).

6. Ibid., p. 79.

7. Musgrave, op. cit., pp. 76-96, summarizes some evidence and suggests a possible role for taxes.

8. Ruttenberg, op. cit., p. 56.

9. See Musgrave, "Tax Preferences to Foreign Investment," in The Economics of Federal Subsidy Programs, Part 2, Joint Economic Committee, 92d Cong., 2d sess. (Washington, D.C.: U.S. Government Printing Office, 1972), p. 177.

10. Ruttenberg, op. cit., p. 56.

11. For a somewhat more elegant presentation, see Caves and Jones's discussion of the technological gap in Richard E. Caves and Ronald W. Jones, World Trade and Payments: An Introduction (Boston: Little, Brown, 1973), pp. 217-19.

12. Ruttenberg, op. cit., p. 102.

13. A recent exposition can be found in Caves and Jones, op. cit., pp. 162-81.

14. Kemp does relax some of the standard assumptions in what he terms a neo-Heckscher-Ohlin approach. See Murray C. Kemp, "The Gain from International Trade and Investment: A Neo-Heckscher-Ohlin Approach," American Economic Review 6, no. 4, Part 1 (September 1966):788-809. Kemp intends to show the interdependence of trade and investment and with that insight to "derive expressions for the optimal tariff and optimal tax," p. 789. He presents his analysis within the usual two-country, two-commodities, two-factors assumption but does allow technology to vary between countries.

15. Ruttenberg, op. cit., p. 104.

16. See Robert Gilpin, Technology, Economic Growth and International Competitiveness, Subcommittee on Economic Growth of the Joint Economic Committee (Washington, D.C.: U.S. Government Printing Office, 1975). See also Jack Baranson, "Technology Transfer Effects on U.S. Competitiveness and Employment," in U.S. Department of Labor, The Impact of International Trade and Investment on Employment (Washington, D.C.: U.S. Government Printing Office, 1978), pp. 201-02, and Robert Gilpin, U.S. Power and the Multinational Corporation (New York: Basic Books, 1975).

17. W. M. Corden, Trade Policy and Economic Welfare (Oxford: Clarendon Press, 1974), pp. 355-64.

18. Mordechai E. Kreinin, International Economics: A Policy Approach, 2d ed. (New York: Harcourt Brace Jovanovich, 1975), pp. 403-06.

19. Kreinin suggests that within a limited sphere, existing trade theory might still be useful in describing introcorporate trade flows. Ibid., pp. 405-06.

20. Ruttenberg, op. cit., p. 96.

21. Ibid., pp. 52-54.

EVOLUTION OF THE LABOR CASE / 127

22. Ibid., p. 81.
23. A discussion of the BLS study was appended to then
Secretary of Labor George P. Shultz's testimony before the House
Ways and Means Committee. See <u>Tariff and Trade Proposals</u>,
Hearings before the Committee on Ways and Means, U.S. House of
Representatives, Part 2, pp. 608-12. Possible implications of the
BLS study for the Leontief paradox were discussed in Chapter 1.
24. See Office of Foreign Economic Research, Bureau of
International Labor Affairs, U.S. Department of Labor, "The Impact
of Changes in Manufacturing Trade on Sectoral Employment Patterns,
Progress Report" (Washington, D.C.: U.S. Department of Labor,
November 15, 1978), pp. 10 and 24-27.
25. Ruttenberg, op. cit., p. 62.
26. Ibid., p. 109.
27. Ibid., p. 121.
28. Ibid., p. 105.
29. Ibid., p. 10.
30. Ibid., p. 11.
31. See, for instance, Philip Shabecoff, "Unions also are
Split into Rich and Poor," New York <u>Times</u>, December 31, 1978.

CHAPTER 6

THE BUSINESS RESPONSE

Although long lines of special business interests populated the Smoot-Hawley hearings in 1930, it has been largely since the passage of the Trade Expansion Act of 1962 that business has become increasingly aware of the importance of foreign economic policy to its own well-being.[1] In part, this reflected the tremendous growth in the amount of foreign direct investment by U.S. firms. It was also partly in response to the growing economic power of Europe and Japan. Foreign multinationals were an increasingly large fact of competitive life for many U.S. firms.

The government has also become more active in the setting of foreign economic policy. In addition to the establishment of quotas for domestic oil producers and for a number of agricultural interests, the government had begun to intervene in the workings of the multinational corporation. Faced with persistent balance of payments deficits, the U.S. government had instituted a number of policies to restrict the flow of capital abroad. Ranging from an interest equalization tax to direct controls, the U.S. program did not appear to have had much of an impact on the expansion of U.S. firms abroad. But it did put the regulatory foot in the multinational's door.

In addition, the long-time free trade coalition appeared to be in real danger. From 1968 onward, big labor appeared increasingly restive with the results of the Trade Expansion Act of 1962. Their catalog of complaints—the failure of trade adjustment assistance, the surge in imports, the growing tendency to manufacture here but assemble abroad—became longer and longer. Gradually, labor seemed to shift its focus from isolated trade issues to the broader spectrum of foreign economic policy. There was still talk about low-wage foreign labor, but the multinational corporation became more and more of a preoccupation.

In this atmosphere big business began to respond to the potentially volatile nature of foreign economic policy. New organizations were formed and established organizations became more active in the area of the multinational corporation. The Emergency Committee for American Trade (ECAT) was one of the first of the business organizations to focus on the multinational corporation. Founded in 1967, the 55 ECAT members were drawn from the ranks of the largest of the U.S.-based multinational firms.[2] Headed by Donald Kendall, board chairman of the Pepsi Cola Company, ECAT became one of the leading lobbyists in the Burke-Hartke debate.

The traditional business groups—the National Association of Manufacturers and the Chamber of Commerce—also became strong advocates of the multinational corporation. In 1970 the Chamber of Commerce established a Task Force on Multinational Enterprise; Lee Morgan, an executive vice-president of Caterpillar Tractor Company, was made chairman of the group.[3] A year later the National Association of Manufacturers established an Ad Hoc Committee on International Trade with a Multinational Corporation Task Force. The Task Force was chaired by J. Standford Smith, group vice-president of the General Electric Company.[4]

A REACTION TO QUOTAS

The introduction of the Burke-Hartke Bill in September 1971 brought big labor's view of foreign economic policy into sharp perspective. In terms of traditional free trade concerns, the bill was a radical departure. In place of a free trade policy qualified with a few exceptions, Burke-Hartke proposed across-the-board market shares for all goods that competed with American products.

That demand alone might have been enough to stimulate action on the part of the multinationals. Some firms did ship a substantial portion of their production back to the United States and would be hurt by the quota and rollback provisions of the bill. Others with substantial investments around the world may have feared retaliation from governments stung by the economic consequences of the rollback implicit in the 1965-69 base on which market shares would be calculated. Retaliation could take so many forms. Aside from the imposition of further trade barriers, the U.S.-based multinational firms might have been faced with a growing web of restrictions on their foreign activities. The possibility of European Community strictures on multinationals, Canada's foreign investment review board, and the Andean code on direct foreign investment were the type of impediments that might have proliferated in response to a partial closing of the American market.

Yet it is doubtful that the quota provisions themselves would have been of overriding concern to the bulk of multinationals. First of all, relatively little of the foreign production of U.S.-based multinationals was actually shipped back to the U.S. market. Exclusive of exports from Canada that were heavily influenced by the Canadian Automobile Pact, exports from the foreign affiliates of U.S.-based multinationals to the United States amounted to about 2 percent of total foreign affiliate sales. Second, it is unlikely that business ever thought that the rollback features of Burke-Hartke had much chance of enactment. As important as they may have been in constructing internal AFL-CIO support for Burke-Hartke, the base period (1965-69) proved to be a point of negotiation.* Third, most multinational businesses operate throughout a world dotted with trade barriers. In fact, trade barriers can be an incentive to direct foreign investment. It is doubtful that a U.S.-market-shares approach to imports would have proved an insurmountable obstacle to U.S.-based multinationals.

Nor was business always unanimous in its evaluation of import quotas. The oil industry and certain segments of agriculture had long benefited from import protection. The cotton textile industry had received special consideration in the Long Term Textile Agreement and was continuing to seek quota protection from competitive man-made fibers as well. Shoes, steel, and electronics have long sought and continue to seek congressional action against imports at one time or another. Like textiles, steel had garnered some relief with a voluntary agreement.

Even individual firms could be badly split on the import quota issue. Particularly in the large diversified companies that were often among the first to go international, the division could be present. The General Electric Company is an interesting example of just this phenomenon. "As a diversified company, made up of many smaller companies, some of which tend to be protectionist, GE must be careful to maintain company harmony."[5]

The same type of balancing appeared in several other companies. For instance, a number of Connecticut ball-bearing firms supported a bill introduced by Congresswoman (now Governor) Ella Grasso of Connecticut, which would have limited ball-bearing imports to "the same share of the domestic market they had during the period 1961-1966 or 6.3 percent, a percentage considerably less than" the 9.6

---

*Eventually, Congressman James Burke (D-Mass.), coauthor of the Burke-Hartke Bill and a member of the House Ways and Means Committee, offered in committee to drop the rollback provision altogether.

percent share imports captured in 1972.[6] Interestingly, the four companies in Grasso's district included divisions of Textron, Ingersoll Rand, TRW, and General Motors—large multinational companies that were generally opposed to import quotas.

Multinational companies have continued to pursue a multiplicity of divisional interests. In October 1977 testimony at a congressional hearing conducted in Corning, New York, Thomas A. MacAvoy, president of Corning Glass, raised some questions about the benefits of unrestricted free trade. Although Corning Glass earns almost one-third of its total income from exports or overseas operations, its production of glass for TV picture tubes had already been severely affected by import competition. MacAvoy went so far as to point out that the United States seemed "to have no philosophical reservations in regulating our so-called free enterprise system," and he wondered why we should have any reservations "in regulating our free trade system."[7]

Some of the national business organizations had internal splits over trade legislation as well. The National Association of Manufacturers (NAM) was firmly against Burke-Hartke but did not take a position on the foreign trade question. NAM argued that the major issue involved in Burke-Hartke was the "political control of direct foreign investment."[8] The Chamber of Commerce, also under some pressure from import-competing industry, was structured to avoid fights over individual quotas but could oppose them in general.[9] Only the Emergency Committee for Free Trade, with a small membership entirely composed of multinational firms, had no such difficulties.*

A FOCUS ON TAXES

It was Burke-Hartke's explicit attack on the multinationals themselves that so mobilized the business groups. The proposed restructuring of U.S. taxation of foreign-source income would have been an immediate blow to the current and future profitability of multinational firms. Under Burke-Hartke, the foreign subsidiaries of U.S.-based firms would have been forced to pay taxes on a current basis. Present law defers tax liability until the profits are actually repatriated. Burke-Hartke would have replaced the foreign tax credit with a deduction. In addition, Burke-Hartke would have forced all

---

*According to the trade specialist at ECAT, membership was open only to multinational firms that had demonstrated a commitment to the free flow of goods and capital in international commerce.

companies to figure their depreciation on a straight line rather than an accelerated basis.

A chorus of multinationals argued that the Burke-Hartke provisions would have proved to be devastating. According to a number of firms the loss of the foreign tax credit alone could boost the combined U.S.-foreign tax burden to 75 percent.* In addition, corporations argued that they would be unable to compete against the increasingly aggressive multinationals of European or Japanese origin.

Burke-Hartke also contained two proposals that could greatly expand government control over the multinationals. Under Burke-Hartke, both capital and technology flows would be subjected to government scrutiny. Where an individual export of either technology or capital would have an adverse effect on domestic employment, the president would be empowered to prevent the transaction. Proposals by the United Auto Workers went much further in their attempt to subject capital flows to some sort of federal control. Despite the long-run implications of such proposals, they did not play much of a role in the Burke-Hartke debate.

It was the tax provisions more than any other feature of the bill that concerned the multinationals. Costly, disruptive, possibly endangering their worldwide competitive position, the proposed tax changes of the Burke-Hartke Bill posed a significant threat to the companies. Labor was strongly convinced that current U.S. tax laws favored direct foreign investment at the expense of domestic investment. In addition, they contended that foreign and domestic subsidiaries of U.S.-based firms should be treated in an identical fashion. Labor wanted all income of U.S. firms to be taxed currently and would allow income taxes paid to a foreign government the same deduction allowed income taxes to a state government in the United States. The deferral privilege and foreign tax credit were to be eliminated. Frequently labor presented its case as a question of "simple equity." Senator Hartke was particularly fond of arguing

---

*The calculations were usually made on the assumption that foreign jurisdictions had a corporate income tax similar to that of the United States. In such a case, foreign-generated profits would be taxed by a foreign government at about 50 percent. In the case of $100 of foreign profit, the Burke-Hartke Bill would permit a deduction of $50 (.5 × 100). The remaining $50 ($100 - $50) would be subject to the American corporate tax—again at a level near 50 percent. The corporation would be left with $25 ($50 - .5 × $50). The combination of foreign and U.S. corporate taxes would thus amount to 75 percent.

that these changes would simply put foreign income on the same ground as domestic income.

In effect, labor was arguing for a mix of equity and domestic neutrality in determining the nature of U.S. tax laws. In theory, domestic neutrality requires that the burden of taxes on profits must be the same regardless of the location of the investment. There is little question that, standing by itself, the deferral of taxation on foreign-source income does violate the standard of domestic neutrality. But given the existence of other distortions and imperfections, the removal of the deferral might not actually lead in the direction of domestic neutrality. To be sure the tax burden is on the same level, one must see that taxable income and the tax rate are the same, the shifting of direct and indirect taxes is identical in all jurisdictions, and government tax receipts must benefit foreign and domestic firms in the same way. Leaving the complexities of foreign tax systems to one side, one can still identify a number of features of the U.S. tax code that favor domestic over foreign investment. For instance, no investment tax credit may be taken on the investment of a foreign subsidiary, and the rules for carrying losses either forward or back are more restrictive for a foreign investment. By either reducing or deferring taxes, the Domestic International Sales Corporation (adopted in 1971) and the Western Hemisphere Trade Corporation both favor domestic over direct foreign investment. One recent study of the deferral question suggested achieving domestic neutrality by repealing the deferral while at the same time extending the benefits of the investment tax credit and accelerated depreciation to direct foreign investments.[10] In any case, given the complexity of the U.S. code, the elimination of deferral may or may not bring one closer to domestic neutrality.

Although politically appealing, the equity argument was somewhat harder to maintain on the merits. The equity test simply demands that all firms or individuals that are similarly situated and located in the same tax jurisdiction must be subjected to the same tax burden. Even if foreign and domestic subsidiaries are, in fact, in the same tax jurisdiction, it is still not clear if they are more comparable to their foreign or domestic counterparts.

Aside from their financial implications, the multinationals generally felt that the tax provisions had a much greater chance of enactment than other major sections of the bill. Unlike the proposal for virtually universal import quotas, some of the proposed tax changes had fairly extensive academic backing.[11] The generally firm alliance between academics and the national press in support of free trade could not be counted on to stand as firmly against the change in tax treatment of the multinational firm.

The tax aspects of Burke-Hartke could be easily severed from the bill and acted on separately. They required no new Foreign Trade

and Investment Commission, invited no retaliation from foreign
countries, would have abrogated no international treaties. In fact,
the repeal of the deferral privilege did appear in various tax reform
measures introduced in the 92nd Congress.[12] Senator Hartke frequently introduced the tax provisions of Burke-Hartke in the form
of proposed amendments to a number of pieces of legislation.

In addition to the immediate threat of the proposed tax changes,
the multinationals were concerned about the wide number of economic
charges that labor had ranged against them. In a survey of multinational firms, the Government Research Corporation, a private,
Washington-based research firm, found that multinationals were
"just as troubled by the impact the [Burke-Hartke] controversy
might have on their image."[13] No doubt such fears were exacerbated
by the establishment in 1972 of a Subcommittee on Multinationals by
the Senate Foreign Relations Committee.[14] Although not explicitly
concerned with the impact of multinationals on the domestic economy,
the subcommittee proved a ready forum for a wide range of critics
of the multinational firms.

Faced with an immediate economic threat and the prospect of
growing public scrutiny, it is not surprising that big business took
an active role in the discussion of foreign trade and investment policy.
In an attempt to counteract the initial impetus of the Burke-Hartke
Bill, business relied on a whole gamut of activities. Industry groups
and individual firms have made studies to show the favorable impact
of their international activities on the domestic economy. The studies,
speeches by leading business spokesmen, and special press conferences were all used to try the business case in the national press.
National industry groups and individual firms embarked on grass
roots campaigns to mobilize support against the Burke-Hartke Bill.
Direct efforts on Capital Hill ranged from presidential letters to
various congressmen to personal visits. Certain individual firms
and business groups proved to be active and consistent witnesses
before congressional committees.

An interesting aspect of the corporate campaign was that it
was essentially defensive. They were clearly in the position of
arguing for the status quo in the face of a number of labor claims
about their economic activities. Their essentially negative status
was not altered until President Nixon introduced the Trade Reform
Act in January 1973, which was aimed at trade liberalization.

After passage of the Trade Act of 1974, multinational business
has had to return to a largely defensive posture, in the sense that it
still must react to continuing attempts to circumscribe its activities.
In recent years most of the pressure has been on the tax side. Congressional tax reformers have succeeded in reducing tax breaks for
income from direct foreign investments in developing countries,

eliminating the use of the per-country method of calculating the foreign tax credit, restricting the use of DISCs, and making major changes in the rules for the taxation of foreign-earned income.[15]

Two factors may put multinational business back on a more aggressive footing. First, President Carter has notified the Congress of his intention to enter into a multilateral trade agreement.[16] If for no other reason than to keep international economic peace, multinational business has a major stake in the successful passage of the trade agreements. Second, the partially successful attacks on DISC and on the taxation of income earned by Americans working overseas have affected large multinational businesses. The president's effort to restore some favorable treatment to foreign-earned income and his announcement of a new export policy have presented the multinationals with concrete legislative goals.[17]

In their early response to labor's tax arguments, business essentially argued for foreign as opposed to domestic neutrality. Foreign neutrality suggests that foreign subsidiaries of U.S. firms should be subjected to the same tax burden as their competitors in a foreign jurisdiction. Foreign neutrality, however, proves to be a difficult guide for domestic tax policy. For instance, if the foreign subsidiary of a U.S. firm in Germany is to meet the competition of a local German firm, the U.S. tax system would have to become essentially similar to the German code. Not only does this have the foreign tail wagging the domestic dog, but it may confound any easy choice as domestic policy would have to adapt to the varying codes of different foreign countries. In practice, the multinationals sought equal treatment with foreign-based multinational firms. Regardless of French treatment of French domestic firms, the U.S.-based multinational wanted to compete in Germany on an equal footing with the French multinational. In most cases this boiled down to an argument for the status quo, which in turn depended on the benefits or costs of direct foreign investment to the home country.

THE CAUSES OF DIRECT FOREIGN INVESTMENT

With regard to investment, business made quite different assumptions from those that stood behind labor's analysis. On the one hand, they described most direct foreign investments as defensive in nature.[18] If a U.S.-based multinational had not made the investment, foreign local interests or non-U.S.-based multinationals would have filled the gap. On the other hand, most U.S.-based multinationals contended that their foreign investments did not reduce their level of domestic investment. In Hufbauer and Adler's terminology, most business groups and individual businesses adopted "reverse classical" investment substitution assumptions.[19]

The implications of reverse classical assumptions are quite different from those of the classical assumptions made by labor. Since the level of domestic investment is unaffected, there will be no direct impact on the future rate of domestic growth nor on the domestic generation of new technology. Nor would there be any additional need for stabilization policy. The investment would leave things much as they were.

The ability to invest abroad without reducing domestic investment, however, does suggest one of three things. The domestic economy is running at less than full employment, which has left individual firms with idle cash balances; the domestic firm is able to borrow abroad the full extent of the direct foreign investment, or so little of the investment is actually transferred in terms of resources that stabilization policy can restore the preinvestment level of domestic economic activity. Business never clearly addressed any of these three alternatives. Despite some evidence that relatively few national resources actually were transferred to complete foreign investments of British origin,[20] business chose to emphasize exports actually generated by the investment. The probable need for some further stabilization effort was studiously ignored.[21]

By adopting essentially reverse classical assumptions, business was able to minimize the export displacement effect of U.S. direct foreign investment. Since the foreign investment would have been made by somebody, export losses were inevitable. Business also placed considerable stress on the flow of returns on direct foreign investment. They noted that the flow of dividends, interest, royalties, and management fees was a major contributor to the U.S. Current Account. In fact, business frequently pointed out that the flow of returns actually exceeded the outflow of direct foreign investment, although under most assumptions,[22] the reflow and the outflow were quite different matters.

In responding to labor's views on foreign trade, business groups and individual multinational firms virtually ignored the question of comparative advantage. Market imperfections such as the growth of common markets and free trade zones were generally used to justify the need to leap tariff and other trade barriers by means of direct foreign investment. Instead, business concentrated on rebutting labor's charges that the U.S.-based multinationals had reduced U.S. exports, increased U.S. imports, and decreased the level of U.S. employment.

BUSINESS STUDIES OF TRADE AND INVESTMENT

Much of the early business response was based on a series of economic studies conducted by the principal industry groups. The

Emergency Committee on American Trade[23] and the U.S. Chamber of Commerce[24] both conducted survey studies of American-based multinational companies. Not surprisingly, their studies found that the multinational companies have increased their domestic employment and exports at a more rapid rate than has U.S. industry as a whole.

The survey study has a number of inherent weaknesses. The responses may be skewed rather than random and the information itself may be questionable or selective. Firm names are kept secret, so independent verification is impossible. In addition, neither the ECAT nor the Chamber studies attempted to correct for acquisitions. Although the 1960s was a major era of merger and conglomerate growth, these two studies completely ignore the possibility that the figures for growth in exports or domestic employment might have been caused through merger.

Business International, an independent consulting group based in New York and headed by ex-Secretary of Agriculture Orville Freeman, has also done a survey study.[25] Alone among those done and published by private groups, the Business International survey did attempt to correct their figures for growth in domestic employment for the effect of mergers. They did not, however, extend that attempted correction to the alleged growth in exports.

Despite the many limitations of these particular studies, they received wide and generally uncritical coverage in the national press. Although Senator Hartke noted the failure to correct for mergers in an open letter to the U.S. Chamber of Commerce, it received no mention in the press.[26] Similar criticisms of the survey were contained in subsequent labor testimony before congressional committees but likewise got no coverage.

Other industry groups also made studies in response to Burke-Hartke. Generally relying on published sources, the NAM came up with conclusions quite similar to those of the survey studies.[27] The American Importers Association (AIA) has also published a study designed to appeal to consumer interests. Authored by C. Fred Bergsten, then of the Brookings Institution, the AIA study attempts to assess the extra costs to the consumer of the Burke-Hartke Bill.[28]

In a somewhat more scholarly tone, the International Economic Policy Association (IEPA) launched a series of studies on the multinational firm. Acting through its Center for Multinational Studies (established in 1971), IEPA contracted with the New York University Graduate School of Business for the bulk of the research work on the multinationals.[29]

Somewhat surprisingly, the Committee for a National Trade Policy (CNTP) was not a leader in the research effort against the Burke-Hartke Bill. In fact, its principal publication was a brief

pamphlet entitled "Hartke-Burke in a Nutshell."* A leading business
group in previous foreign trade debates, CNTP continued to play an
active but somewhat less public role.[30] They were, however, regularly called to present testimony at the important congressional
hearings on Burke-Hartke. David Steinberg, the former president
of CNTP, continues to support unfettered world trade and to appear
before congressional committees in his new role as president of the
U.S. Council for an Open World Economy.[31]

Individual firms have also been active in opposing the labor
drive to control imports and limit capital flows. A number of firms
have made studies to assess the particular impact of their international
activities on the domestic economy. In some cases, for instance the
Caterpillar[32] and Union Carbide[33] studies, the firms garnered considerable favorable publicity.

Although the individual company studies may have been accurate
enough, few implications should have been properly drawn from them.
Who, after all, would release a study unless it was beneficial to their
own position? The possible impact of the Burke-Hartke Bill had been
well known since late 1971—any company with resources to make such
a study and the overseas investments to make it interesting would
surely release only a "white-hat" result.

In many ways, business behavior is very much in line with the
implications developed in Chapter 2. Assuming that the United States
is indeed capital intensive, business was quite consistent in seeking
to pursue further trade liberalization and in opposing attempts to
impose comprehensive import quotas. The product cycle theory and
Caves's work on oligopoly and foreign direct investment were largely
consistent with business behavior during and after the Burke-Hartke
debate. Both theories had in fact been developed from rather close
attention to the present workings of the international economy.

The almost complete unity of business on the question of both
trade and foreign direct investment is rather surprising. After all,
capital is not perfectly mobile domestically. Plant and equipment

---

*The Foreign Trade and Investment Act of 1972 (later 1973)
was referred to both as Burke-Hartke (generally used in this study)
and Hartke-Burke. Some argue that the constitutional precedence
granted the House Ways and Means Committee in tax (and hence tariff)
matters dictates giving the congressmen precedence. Following that
convention, the bill emerges as the Burke (for Congressman James
Burke) Hartke Bill. Others contend that the senior body should be
given precedence—hence Hartke (for Senator Vance Hartke) Burke.
Needless to say, the legislative staff of Senator Hartke inclined toward
the latter view.

designed for the production of labor-intensive goods might well find themselves joining labor's efforts in behalf of Burke-Hartke. And even in the early 1970s there were some signs of dissension within the business community. The refusal of the NAM to take a position on trade indicated some internal opposition. Ball-bearing manufacturers sought separate quota assistance. Specialty steel manufacturers expressed interest in the Burke-Hartke approach to trade. But only a shoe industry group actually went so far as to endorse Burke-Hartke. Other sectors that were particularly hard hit found an answer to their import problems through either foreign direct investment or ad hoc government action. In summary, electrical appliances and electronic goods went abroad while steel and textiles secured a variety of protective agreements.

Domestic industries pressured by import competition have continued to press for some sort of protection. Textile and apparel firms sought stricter limits in a renewed international trade pact governing natural and man-made fibers (the Multifiber Arrangement) and exemption from tariff cuts at the current round of multilateral trade negotiations.[34] Steel firms, footwear manufacturers, makers of color television receivers, and producers of specialty steel items have all sought temporary surcease from import competition under the Trade Act. In many cases industry pressure has brought labor and management into closer harmony on trade questions. As yet, however, there is no indication that major trade associations have adopted import restriction as a formal trade policy.

The continuing key to business unity seems to lie in the emphasis business has put on the foreign direct investment issue. There was never any ideological opposition to taking care of any particular industry. The import-affected industries in turn were not threatened by investment flows.

Business behavior in the ongoing congressional debate over foreign trade and investment policy appears to be consistent with the predictions of economic theory. The economic interest of business lay in the further liberalization of trade and capital flows, not in their restriction. But Burke-Hartke and subsequent tax reform proposals also threatened an immediate tax loss to a large number of multinational companies and the possibility of curtailed foreign operations. The multinationals may have been reacting as much to the prospect of short-term injury as to a perception of long-run economic self-interest.

NOTES

1. For an interesting look at past business lobbying on trade matters, see Raymond A. Bauer, Ithiel de Sola Pool, and Lewis

Anthony Dexter, <u>American Business and Public Policy: The Politics of Foreign Trade</u> (Chicago: Aldine, Atherton, 1972, first published in 1963).

2. For a more detailed description of ECAT, see <u>The Politics of Foreign Trade, Tax and Investment Policy</u> (Washington, D.C.: Government Research Company, 1972), pp. 150-57.

3. For further information on the activities of the Chamber of Commerce, see ibid., pp. 140-45.

4. For more information on the NAM's campaign against the Burke-Hartke Bill, see ibid., pp. 177-85.

5. <u>The Politics of Foreign Trade</u>, p. 159.

6. Richard S. Frank, "Trade Report/Black Olives and Ball Bearings Lobby Groups Attempt to Restrict Competing Foreign Imports," <u>National Journal</u>, August 8, 1973, p. 1225.

7. Thomas C. MacAvoy, in "Implications of Our International Trade Policy for American Business and Consumers," Hearing before the Subcommittee on International Trade, Investment and Monetary Policy of the Committee on Banking, Finance, and Urban Affairs, U.S. House of Representatives, 95th Cong., 1st sess., October 8, 1977, Corning, N.Y. (Washington, D.C.: U.S. Government Printing Office, 1977), p. 19.

8. William R. Pollert, director of international economic affairs for the NAM, as quoted in Charles Culhane, "Economic Report/Labor and Industry Gear for Major Battle Over Bill to Curb Imports, Multinationals," <u>National Journal</u>, January 15, 1972, p. 115.

9. According to Article VIII of the Chamber's by-laws, the Chamber can act only upon proposals that are national in character. The board of directors of the Chamber has interpreted Article VIII to mean that the Chamber "should not take a position on . . . specific tariff rates, [or] quotas . . . applicable to any imported product or commodity." See Bylaws of the Chamber of Commerce of the United States, Washington, D.C., 1975, Article VIII, Section I (p. 15) and Board Rules and Administrative Policies, 1975, Scope of Chamber Action: Paragraph 3. According to a staff member of the Chamber's international division, the board's interpretation of Article VIII permitted the Chamber to take no position on the textile and shoe provisions contained in the Trade Act of 1970, while allowing the Chamber to oppose the more far-reaching Byrnes-basket approach.

10. C. Fred Bergsten, Thomas Horst, and Theodore H. Moran, <u>American Multinationals and American Interests</u> (Washington, D.C.: Brookings Institution, 1978), p. 466. The authors' discussion of deferral and domestic neutrality (capital export neutrality in their terminology) can be found at pp. 196-202.

11. See, for instance, Lawrence B. Krause and Kenneth W. Dam, <u>Federal Tax Treatment of Foreign Income</u> (Washington, D.C.:

Brookings Institution, 1964). Much of the discussion on tax equity and domestic and foreign neutrality follows the treatment in Krause and Dam. See also Peggy Musgrave, The Economics of Federal Subsidy Programs, A Compendium of Papers, Submitted to the Joint Economic Committee, Congress of the United States, Part 2, International Subsidies (Washington, D.C.: U.S. Government Printing Office, 1972).

12. See, for instance, S.3378, 92d Cong., 2d sess. (Senator Nelson) and H.R. 15230, 92d Cong., 2d sess. (Congressman Mills).

13. The Politics of Foreign Trade, op. cit., p. 50.

14. Current rules of the U.S. Senate require that "measures to foster commercial intercourse with foreign nations and to safeguard American business interests abroad" be submitted to the Committee on Foreign Relations. See Standing Rules of the United States Senate, Committee on Rules and Administration, U.S. Senate (Washington, D.C.: U.S. Government Printing Office, 1975). In practice the Subcommittee on Multinationals has focused on a range of topical interests: the operations of ITT in Chile, the international oil companies, and the question of destabilizing currency speculation by the multinationals. More recently, the committee has begun to direct some of its attention to the impact of the multinational corporation on the domestic economy. In June 1975 the committee published a study by Peggy Musgrave on effects of direct foreign investments on the U.S. economy. See Peggy Musgrave, Direct Investment Abroad and the Multinationals: Effects on the United States Economy, Subcommittee on Multinational Corporations, Committee on Foreign Relations, 94th Cong., 1st sess. (Washington, D.C.: U.S. Government Printing Office, 1975).

15. For a discussion of the specific tax changes involved, see Chapter 2.

16. A copy of the proposed agreement can be found in Federal Register 44, no. 5 (January 8, 1979):1933 et seq.

17. A copy of the president's statement outlining his new export policy can be found in U.S. Congress, Senate, Committee on Commerce, Science, and Transportation, National Export Program, Hearings, 95th Cong., 2d sess. (Washington, D.C.: U.S. Government Printing Office, 1978), pp. 73-76.

18. Hufbauer and Adler briefly review some studies that reached a "defensive" conclusion. See G. C. Hufbauer and F. M. Adler, Overseas Manufacturing Investment and the Balance of Payments, Tax Policy Research Study No. 1 (Washington, D.C.: U.S. Treasury Department, 1968), pp. 5, 90-92. Reddaway gives some support to this view by adopting what Hufbauer and Adler termed reverse classical substitution assumptions. See W. B. Reddaway et al., Effects of U.K. Direct Investments Overseas; An Interim Report (Cambridge: Cambridge University Press, 1967).

19. Ibid., p. 6. Recent business behavior suggests that the adoption of "reverse classical" assumptions may have been at least partially self-serving. Although direct foreign investment by U.S.-based multinationals has continued into the 1970s, the business community also sought tax relief on the basis that there is a growing shortage of domestic capital.

20. Reddaway et al., op. cit., pp. 89-95.

21. On the other hand, academic analysts are usually quite explicit about the need for stabilization policy. See, for instance, Peggy Musgrave, United States Taxation of Foreign Investment Income: Issues and Arguments (Cambridge, Mass.: The Law School of Harvard University, 1969), especially pp. 10-25.

22. Hufbauer and Adler refer to a mid 1960s study by the National Industrial Conference Board that adopted an "organic" view of direct foreign investments. In effect, the Conference Board argued that the annual increments of investment are necessary to insure the total sum of remissions. See Hufbauer and Adler, op. cit., p. 4.

23. Emergency Committee for American Trade, The Role of the Multinational Corporation (MNC) in the United States and World Economies (Washington, D.C.: Emergency Committee for American Trade, 1972). A copy of the ECAT study can be found in Multinational Corporations, A Compendium of Papers, Submitted to the Subcommittee on International Trade of the Committee on Finance of the United States Senate, 93d Cong., 1st sess. (Washington, D.C.: U.S. Government Printing Office, 1973), pp. 733-968.

24. Chamber of Commerce of the United States, United States Multinational Enterprise, Report on a Multinational Enterprise Survey (1960-1970) (Washington, D.C.: 1972). A copy of the Chamber study can be found in ibid., pp. 607-52.

25. Business International, The Effects of U.S. Corporate Foreign Investment 1960 to 1970 (New York: Business International Corporation, 1972).

26. A copy of Hartke's letter appears at page S2234 of the Congressional Record 118, no. 24 (February 22, 1972).

27. National Association of Manufacturers, The U.S. Stake in World Trade and Investment: The Role of the Multinational Corporation (New York, 1971).

28. C. Fred Bergsten, "The Cost of Import Restrictions to the American Consumer (New York: American Importers Association, 1972).

29. The first of these studies appeared in February 1972. Robert G. Hawkins, "U.S. Multinational Investment in Manufacturing and Domestic Economic Performance" (New York: IEPA, 1972). The impact of foreign direct investment on the home economy has begun to attract a good deal of academic attention. In a study con-

ducted for the Department of Labor, Robert Frank and Richard Freeman found, among other things, that foreign direct investment lowered the real wage, labor's share of national income, and national income itself. See their "The Distributional Consequences of Direct Foreign Investment," in The Impact of International Trade and Investment on Employment, U.S. Department of Labor (Washington, D.C.: U.S. Government Printing Office, 1978). In the same volume, Thomas Horst was much more agnostic in not finding "any consistently strong statistical relationship between U.S. investments abroad and any any of [his] measures of trade performance." See Thomas Horst, "The Impact of American Investments Abroad on U.S. Exports, Imports, and Employment," ibid., pp. 139-51. A more extensive treatment of Horst's approach can be found in Bergsten, Horst, and Moran, op. cit., pp. 45-99.

30. For a discussion of past CNTP activities on behalf of free trade legislation, see Bauer, Pool, and Dexter, op. cit., pp. 375-87.

31. For instance, see his testimony before the Ways and Means Subcommittee on Trade in Exemption of Certain Products from Tariff Reductions Negotiated in the Multilateral Trade Negotiations (MTN), Hearing before the Subcommittee on Trade of the Committee on Ways and Means, House of Representatives, 95th Cong., 2d sess. (Washington, D.C.: U.S. Government Printing Office, 1978), pp. 302-11.

32. See The Politics of Foreign Trade, p. 140.

33. Union Carbide, Union Carbide's International Investment Benefits the U.S. Economy (New York, 1972). A copy of the Union Carbide study can be found in Multinational Corporations, A Compendium of Papers, op. cit., pp. 445-543.

34. See, for example, Exemption of Certain Products, op. cit.

CHAPTER 7

THE CONGRESSIONAL SETTING

Although the fights over trade policy are generally waged in a variety of forums, final action eventually devolves on the Congress. To understand the manner in which business and labor presented their respective cases, one must take at least a brief look at the structure of economic decision making in the Congress. The way in which Congress judged the economic issues raised by Burke-Hartke was also influenced by the nature of congressional structure, procedures, and personalities. Recent changes in congressional structure are likely to have a similar influence on trade decisions in the 96th Congress.

THE COMMITTEE SYSTEM AND INTERNATIONAL ECONOMIC POLICY

Congressional decisions emerge from a highly decentralized process in which there are many points at which various interests can plead their case or exercise their power. In many cases the nature of congressional decision making contrasts sharply with the approach taken by the Executive Branch. Fiscal policy is one particularly interesting example.*

---

*Congressional treatment of monetary policy may appear even more confused. Although Congress does retain legislative authority over the Federal Reserve System, they do not generally benefit from the informal, off-the-record, and presumably candid discussions between the administration and the chairman of the Board of Governors

The executive is subject to a host of competing departmental pressures but contains a clear mechanism for turning bureaucratic fantasies into workable priorities. Within the executive office of the president, a mix of economic and political advisors suggests appropriate fiscal aggregates. The Office of Management and Budget translates these aggregates into policy by reconciling the competing demands of individual executive departments.

Although legislation to extend the public debt and major tax bills often provided a forum for the congressional consideration of fiscal policy, until 1974 Congress had no mechanism for reconciling expenditures and revenues. There simply was no congressional fiscal policy. Following lengthy consideration in the 93rd Congress, however, the Congress finally adopted what may prove to be a revolution in the making of U.S. fiscal policy. The Congressional Budget and Impoundment Control Act of 1974 (P.L. 93-344) established the new process.

House and Senate Budget Committees are now charged with formulating an overall limitation on spending in light of projected revenues and needs. In addition, the two Budget Committees have some influence on setting budgetary priorities by proposing the allocation of national expenditures along functional (so much for national defense, so much for international affairs) lines. The activities of the two Budget Committees are backed by their own substantial staffs, a new Congressional Budget Office, and expanded staffs in the Congressional Research Service and the General Accounting Office.

Although the Budget Committees are a growing force in both houses of Congress, most individual spending and taxing decisions are still made much as they have been throughout the post-World War II era. The process remains tortuous, diffuse, and complex.

By virtue of the U.S. Constitution, tax bills must begin in the House of Representatives and by virtue of custom they begin in the House Ways and Means Committee. Tax legislation is ordinarily subjected first to public hearings and then to the actual writing or "marking up" of the bill by the committee. Before consideration by the full House, the Ways and Means Committee must obtain a rule from the House Rules Committee. The rule generally specifies how much debate will be permitted on a particular bill and to what extent amendments may be offered from the House floor.

Following passage in the House, the process of hearings and final committee changes in the bill must be repeated in the Senate.

---

of the Federal Reserve System. Despite recent attempts to exercise greater congressional control over the Federal Reserve System, it has succeeded in retaining its independent status.

Because of Senate rules on unlimited debate, rules for discussion of the bill in the Senate are generally established by unanimous consent or in extreme cases by cloture. A successful motion for cloture, however, must be supported by 60 Senate votes.

The outcomes are seldom the same, particularly because the Senate allows great discretion to individual members. Differing bills must be reconciled in a conference committee made up of senators and congressmen. If the conferees reach agreement, both houses of Congress are allowed to vote to either accept or reject the conference report. If the bill clears all these hurdles, it must be reconciled with the president's view of fiscal necessity. Although vetoes of major revenue bills are rare, they remain a potential source of fiscal instability.

The entire process is further complicated by the Budget Act. The Congress adopts an overall budget resolution that contains guidelines for total federal revenues. Although the decision on individual tax bills is left to the House Ways and Means and Senate Finance Committees, the revenue totals must be compatible with the congressional resolution.

The Budget Act has brought some overall order to the expenditure side of fiscal policy. At the time of the debate over Burke-Hartke and the proposed Trade Reform Act of 1973 (1971-74), decisions on aggregate spending were startlingly diffuse. House and Senate Appropriations Committees tended to consider proposals on a department-by-department basis, never as a whole. Major spending programs were and still are handled by other committees. The House Ways and Means and the Senate Finance Committees controlled expenditures from the social security trust fund. Revenue-sharing funds are now controlled by the House Government Operations Committee but were previously under the aegis of Ways and Means. The Finance Committee still retains jurisdiction over revenue sharing on the Senate side.

The congressional process for dealing with the international economy has been equally disjointed. Even the Executive Branch has not been particularly aggressive in this area. President Nixon did establish a Council on International Economic Policy that floundered, then languished, and was finally eliminated at the suggestion of President Carter.

Despite rather sweeping changes in the jurisdiction of a number of House committees, the structure for international economic decision making remains much as it was throughout the Burke-Hartke debate. A major effort to shift responsibility for trade legislation to the House Committee on Foreign Affairs proved unsuccessful.

The bulk of foreign trade and investment legislation passes through the House Ways and Means and the Senate Finance Committees.

Tariffs were at one time an important source of national revenue and were only incidentally used as a means of regulating foreign commerce. Because of the historic tie between tariffs and taxes, the tax-writing committees have retained jurisdiction over foreign trade legislation, though tariffs are now only one of many devices used to regulate foreign trade. The taxation of foreign-source income also lies within the purview of the tax-writing committees, but tax treaties are submitted to the Senate Foreign Relations Committee.

Although the control of imports is handled by one set of committees, the responsibility for export promotion is divided among a number. The House and Senate Commerce Committees consider a variety of programs to promote exports as well as measures that could lead to the establishment of international standards and the consequent lowering of major nontariff barriers. Tax incentives for exports remain with Ways and Means and Finance while the House and Senate Committees on Banking control policies that would lower the price of U.S. goods on the foreign market through changes in U.S. foreign exchange policy.

On August 15, 1971, President Nixon notified the world that the dollars in their hands were no longer redeemable in gold. At that time the question of dollar convertibility was one problem confronting the Congress. How to deal with it? Ways and Means could consider tighter investment controls or restrictive trade policies that would have an impact on our balance of payments. With or without the formal acquiescence of the banking committees, the falling value of the dollar will encourage exports, converting foreign-held dollars into U.S. goods. But the banking committees also control legislation dealing with export controls, a policy pushed by the Nixon administration and approved by the Congress to fight domestic inflation. The potential for hodge-podge decision making is obvious.

More scholarly work on legislative problems often emerges from the Joint Economic Committee (JEC). Although the committee did not focus directly on the foreign-trade aspects of Burke-Hartke, a JEC-sponsored study of federal subsidies in the international sphere included a rather extensive treatment of the taxation of foreign-source income.[1] Written by Peggy Musgrave of Northeastern University, the study did receive some notice on Capitol Hill and at least brief mention in the national press. A key limitation of the JEC, however, is that it writes no legislation. Its influence comes through capturing congressional attention, by way of the national press or even by helping to build the case for a member who sits on both the JEC and a legislative committee.

As is mentioned in Chapter 8, the Senate Labor and Public Welfare Committee also contracted for a study on the multinational firm. Although interesting and suggestive, the study came too late

to be of much importance in the struggle over Burke-Hartke.[2] In
the case of the Burke-Hartke Bill, it fell quite unambiguously within
the purview of the House Ways and Means and the Senate Finance
Committees. Its two principal provisions dealt with trade and the
taxation of foreign-source income, both prime responsibilities of
Ways and Means and Finance. Any ancillary features of the bill that
might have fallen within the jurisdiction of another committee could
be handled by the tax committees on the basis of something analogous
to federal "pendant" jurisdiction.*

In the context of a generally diffuse congressional process,
the formal structure, membership, and chairman of an individual
committee can often play a crucial role in the way a particular piece
of legislation is actually decided. Both the Ways and Means and
Finance Committees are interesting cases in point. Under the chairmanship of Congressman Wilbur Mills, the House Ways and Means
Committee exercised almost unparalleled congressional power. In
no small measure a reflection of Mills political sagacity and substantive expertise, tax and trade bills from the Ways and Means Committee regularly received a closed rule (precluding amendments
from the floor) from the House Rules Committee.

Generally conservative in makeup, the House Ways and Means
Committee exerted unique authority over its own membership. During
the Mills tutelage of the committee, its members acted as the "committee on committees" for the Democratic majority. In other words,
Ways and Means Committee members decided which Democrats were
to be elevated to which committees, including much-coveted positions
on the tax-writing committee. The committee itself was structured
so as to enhance Mills's individual control over various bills. House
and Senate committees generally operate with an extensive subcommittee structure. In most instances these subcommittees can hold
hearings, consider actual legislation, and have considerable influence
in molding a bill before action by the full committee.

In the early 1970s, however, Ways and Means was a very different story. Despite a very heavy load of legislative responsibility—
health care legislation, unemployment compensation, revenue sharing,
taxation, foreign trade—Ways and Means operated without a subcommittee structure. All hearings and legislative drafting took place in
the full committee. Committee staff was responsible to Chairman
Mills rather than to a host of subcommittee chairmen.

---

*Under pendant jurisdiction, federal courts are allowed to
treat state questions that arise in a case that principally involves
federal questions.

By tradition, by rule, and by practice, the U.S. Senate is a far more open body than the House. The closed rule so often used to limit amendments in the House is virtually unknown in the Senate. The terms under which a bill is to be considered are generally determined by the Democratic leadership with the unanimous consent of the Senate. Nothing analogous to the House Rules Committee even exists in the Senate.

Despite this tradition of openness, the Senate Finance Committee has developed a relatively closed structure. Major pieces of Senate Finance Committee legislation are frequently reported out at the very close of a congressional session. The Trade Act of 1970 and the State and Local Fiscal Assistance (Revenue Sharing) Act of 1972 are two of many examples. In effect, the Senate Finance Committee appears to have adjusted its legislative calendar to the lack of a closed rule in the Senate.

With responsibilities roughly comparable to the House Ways and Means Committee, the Finance Committee began to move to a subcommittee system only in 1971. At first the subcommittees were investigative rather than legislative; that is, they could hold hearings but the full committee made all decisions on actual legislative proposals. Throughout the Burke-Hartke period, the Finance Committee operated with a bipartisan staff. In theory, the staff was available to serve any senator on the committee. In practice, the staff was appointed by and responsive to the chairman.

Both the Ways and Means and Finance Committees also relied on the very strong staff of the Joint Committee for Internal Revenue Taxation. The Joint Tax Committee was made up of senior members of the two tax-writing committees with a chairmanship that alternated between the chairmen of the House Ways and Means and Senate Finance Committees. Ostensibly designed to serve all the tax-writing members of Congress, in fact the staff of the Joint Tax Committee dealt largely with the chairman of each committee.

PROCEDURAL REFORM IN THE HOUSE AND SENATE

Since consideration of the Burke-Hartke Bill and eventual passage of the Trade Act of 1974, the Congress and particularly the House have undergone rather startling changes. In the House the Ways and Means Committee has experienced a considerable erosion of its powers. Although successful in fending off an attempt to strip it of trade-making authority, Ways and Means lost its committee on committees role to the Democratic Steering and Policy Committee and to the Democratic Caucus.

Under considerable personal duress, the longtime chairman of the House Ways and Means Committee, Wilbur Mills, resigned his chairmanship toward the end of the 93rd Congress. The absence of Mills, the large reform-minded class of Democratic freshman in the 94th Congress, and a series of previous changes in House Rules led to further alterations in the Ways and Means structure. In fact, tight central control of the committee was shattered. In its place a host of specialized legislative subcommittees sprang up. Particularly in the House, procedural reform has had the effect of increasing the power of the Speaker and of the subcommittee chairman. As a result, the control of the committee chairman over the pace and content of legislation has been considerably diluted. For instance, under the new regime the Speaker could send a bill to more than one committee, could split up a bill, or could send portions of it to different committees.[3]

Would the fate of Burke-Hartke or the Trade Act of 1974 have been different under these changed circumstances? As always it is hard to say, but the thought of Congressman James Burke as chairman of an active subcommittee suggests that the considerations of trade questions in the early 1970s might well have been different. Perhaps a strong pro-Burke-Hartke stance in the subcommittee coupled with an open rule in the House might have led to a flood of protectionist amendments.

At any rate, it is enough to point out that the previous congressional structure did have some influence on the way in which Burke-Hartke was considered and its eventual legislative fate. What will the new openness mean for trade and investment issues in the 1970s? The multilateral trade agreements themselves will not be the best test case. As long as the president stays within the authority delegated by the Trade Act of 1974, tariff agreements under the Multilateral Trade Negotiations enter into force automatically. Congressional approval, however, is required for the nontariff barrier aspects of any MTN agreement.

The MTN agreement, however, will not be considered like any other bill. The Trade Act of 1974 set out a number of special provisions—prohibiting amendments to the implementing legislation, provision for discharge from committee, limitation on floor debate, and a 60-day time limit on the final vote—for consideration of the agreement.[4] It is other trade and investment bills, whether stimulated by the debate over the MTN or introduced in response to individual trade problems, that will provide the better measure of how new procedures will influence policy.

NOTES

1. Peggy Musgrave, "Tax Preferences to Foreign Investment," in The Economics of Federal Subsidy Programs, Part 2, International Subsidies (Washington, D.C.: U.S. Government Printing Office, 1972).

2. Robert Gilpin, The Multinational Corporation and the National Interest, Prepared for the Committee on Labor and Public Welfare, U.S. Senate (Washington, D.C.: U.S. Government Printing Office, 1973).

3. For a discussion of House procedural reform in the 1970s, see Lawrence C. Dodd and Bruce I. Oppenheimer, "The House in Transition," in Congress Reconsidered, ed. Lawrence C. Dodd and Bruce I. Oppenheimer (New York: Praeger Publishers, 1977), pp. 21-32.

4. Trade Act of 1974, P.L. 93-618, Sec. 151.

CHAPTER 8

BUSINESS AND LABOR
BEFORE THE CONGRESS

Congressional assessment of the labor-business debate over trade and investment policy takes place in a variety of ways. Private meetings with business and labor leaders play a part. Alternative legislative proposals often act as trial balloons designed to test the political forces at work. But the heart of the congressional process remains the committee hearing. The hearings offer an unparalleled opportunity to see both the interest group arguments at their fullest and to observe the public deliberations of the Congress.

This chapter focuses on the business and labor presentations to the House Ways and Means and the Senate Finance Committees from 1970 to the close of the 95th Congress in 1978. Historical material is added to help frame the individual hearings to suggest the various economic pressures that influenced business and labor.

LABOR AT THE WITNESS TABLE

The Ruttenberg study analyzed in Chapter 5 was the single most comprehensive presentation of the labor position on foreign trade and investment. It was not, however, the principal vehicle through which the labor case reached the Congress. Private correspondence and personal visits were vitally important to the political maneuvering that accompanied Burke-Hartke and other labor proposals but did little to amplify the economic justification for their approach. In terms of formal argumentation, labor relied principally on direct testimony before a number of congressional committees and to some extent on the national press.

The labor position can be found in a series of congressional hearings conducted on foreign trade policy and foreign economic policy during the 1970s. In most cases the testimony either anticipated the rough lines of the Ruttenberg analysis or followed the more explicit contours of the published Ruttenberg study. Even after passage of the Trade Act of 1974, the basics of the labor case remained the same.

Generally the testimony of the AFL-CIO and constituent unions follows a similar pattern. The statement of George Meany or a high-ranking official will set the AFL-CIO position fairly early in the hearings. Big labor is almost always one of the first of the non-governmental witnesses called before a tax or trade committee. Somewhat later in the set of hearings a spokesman for the Industrial Union Department (IUD) will appear; until his retirement, I. W. Abel as the IUD's president was its most frequent representative. Many of the constituent unions will also testify in person, although they tend to add little to the generally voluminous testimony of the AFL-CIO. During the period leading up to passage of TA-74, only the testimony of two groups of constituent unions was singled out for special attention. First, there was the testimony of Paul Jennings, president of the International Union of Electrical, Radio and Machine Workers, AFL-CIO, and his chief assistant, George Collins. Second, there was the testimony of Howard Chester, executive secretary of the Stone, Glass and Clay Coordinating Committee. The Coordinating Committee represented six individual AFL-CIO unions. Jennings, Collins, and Chester all played active parts in the Burke-Hartke controversy. Chester eventually was named to head a special Burke-Hartke task force created by the AFL-CIO.

Concern with jobs and stability in the economy was hardly new to the U.S. labor movement. The shift on the trade issue became most evident in the 1970 House Ways and Means Committee hearings on the proposed Trade Act of 1970. Speaking on behalf of George Meany, Andrew Biemiller, legislative director of the AFL-CIO, basically anticipated the Ruttenberg line of attack.[1] His opening remarks stressed the "major changes in the world economic relationships in the past 25 years. . . ."[2]

Biemiller identified what he felt to be a major change in the composition of U.S. foreign trade and stressed the labor-intensive nature of imports that led to "significant losses of job opportunities, particularly for semiskilled and unskilled production workers. . . ."[3] Biemiller found a quite different shift in the make-up of U.S. exports. According to Biemiller, "during the 1960s, the expansion of manufactured exports was strongest in products which are based on advanced technology such as computers, jet aircraft, control instruments, and some organic chemicals. Such industries are generally capital intensive, with relatively few production and maintenance workers for each dollar of production"[4] (emphasis added). Interestingly enough, no one queried Biemiller on his apparently special definition of the labor component or on his general thesis. To buttress his case, Biemiller (speaking for Meany throughout) relied on the BLS study on the impact of foreign trade on job opportunities in the 1966-69 period and one or two newspaper accounts. That was all.

Throughout the presentation, much of the focus remained on the multinational corporation. At this point restrictions on imports were still advocated primarily as a stop-gap measure. In the labor view, the multinational firm was simply a new and more threatening version of the runaway plant. Biemiller stressed the potential impact of a deteriorating foreign trade position on the "collective bargaining strength of unions" as well as on jobs and wages.[5]

What also emerges from the Biemiller testimony is apprehension, not so much with foreign trade per se, but rather about jobs and economic stability. As far as Biemiller was concerned, "production and maintenance workers—usually the unskilled, semiskilled and the most vulnerable—are being forced to bear most of the burden of the deterioration of the U.S. position in foreign trade."[6] But trade was not the only disruptive factor on the economic scene. Continuing, Biemiller contended that "this is the same group of non-supervisory workers . . . that bear most of the heavy burden of the administration policy of severe economic restraint, as well as the impact of radical and rapid technological change."[7] In sum, Meany, through Biemiller, was mixing the black adage with some comments on structural change: first fired, no place to be rehired.

Biemiller ended his testimony with a series of recommendations. AFL-CIO backing was given to Congressman Burke's Orderly Marketing Bill (H.R. 9912), to efforts to tighten the escape clause, and to Congressman (and then still Ways and Means Committee chairman) Wilbur Mills's bill to repeal the tariff on value-added-only, contained in Item 807 of the Tariff Schedule of the United States (H.R. 14188).

A few days later the Meany presentation was followed by the testimony of Jacob Clayman, administrative director of the IUD speaking for I. W. Abel. Most of the testimony paralleled that of the Meany statement: the litany of changes in the world economy backed up by the BLS study and a series of assertions.

The Clayman testimony did attempt to anticipate one of the major arguments of the opponents of orderly marketing agreements: the alleged pressure that foreign trade put on the price of domestic goods. Implicitly, Abel argues that the multinational corporations so control the market that their shifting of plants abroad merely results in a cutting of costs and not prices. But again the argument is stated in crude, almost petulant terms. Clayman, speaking for Abel, contends that "to expect these firms to cut their consumers in on what they feel is a good deal, is about as naive as Chase Manhattan

hiring 'Bonnie and Clyde' as bank guards."[8] This particular point
is further weakened by the not-infrequent focus on electronic items—
either wholly made abroad or partially made here and assembled
abroad. But the experience of almost every consumer had been one
of steadily declining prices for TV sets, radios, and stereo equipment
in apparent contradiction of the Clayman argument. There may be
a variety of causes for this phenomenon—scale economies, technological breakthroughs, market economies, and so forth—but they
must be explored. After all, congressmen are consumers too. In
addition to the expected call for controlling the multinationals and
establishing orderly marketing agreements, Clayman adds an appeal
for clearly labeling imports, for public ownership of patents developed
with public funds, and for a cabinet-level department of foreign trade.

The congressional questioning was interesting but not generally
very pointed. Congressman Ullman (chairman of the House Ways and
Means Committee in 1975) focused on the deficiencies of GATT. He
wondered out loud about a possible return to bilateral negotiations.
Congressman Burke, the future coauthor of the Burke-Hartke Bill,
emphasized the relationship between domestic minimum wage legislation and imports produced by low-wage foreign labor. And how might
the United States facilitate the growth of international wage standards?
Clayman agrees that the level of U.S. tariffs would be one way,
treaties another, and the exercise of U.S. influence a third. Whether
it was the switch in labor's position, the administration efforts to aid
the Southern textile mills, or changes in the world economy, the Ways
and Means Committee did report a bill that took two definite steps to
establishing quotas on industrial products—one step for textiles and
the other for shoes.

In Senate Finance Committee hearings on the trade bill, the
labor testimony followed the general outline already etched by the
Meany/Abel statements. Continuing the practice of one labor leader
reading another's statement, Nathaniel Goldfinger, then director,
Department of Research, AFL-CIO, spoke on behalf of the absent
Andrew Biemiller.[9] Although endorsing portions of the Ways and
Means bill, Goldfinger notes that the bill fails to deal with the tariff
on the value-added-only feature contained in Item 807, the tax treatment of foreign-source income, the question of capital controls, or
the issue of international fair labor standards. Goldfinger was particularly critical of a new tax feature contained in the House bill: the
Domestic International Sales Corporation. In general terms the
DISC proposal offered an indefinite deferral on half the export earnings of a U.S. firm as an incentive to boost exports.

The congressional questioning was generally wide ranging rather
than focused. At times it bordered on the irrelevant. Senator Ful-
bright, who was well known for his lack of interest in Finance Com-

mittee matters, seized the opportunity to inveigh against government guarantees to encourage foreign direct investment and to criticize U.S. spending in Southeast Asia. At two points it appeared that Goldfinger was not as well briefed as he might have been. After excoriating the DISC proposal, Goldfinger was forced to admit that he had not done a study of DISC's costs and benefits. A little later, during a discussion of agricultural exports, Goldfinger noted that only agriculture currently received quota protection. When pressed for specifics, he was able to mention only sugar.

The Senate Finance Committee adopted most of the Ways and Means Committee's bill, deleted the provisions repealing the American Selling Price system, and attached the trade measures to a number of social security amendments. The entire package died on the floor of the Senate at the end of the 91st Congress. Following the defeat of the Ways and Means-Finance approach to foreign trade, labor broadened and hardened its position. In September 1970 Goldfinger prepared a "Labor View of Foreign Investment and Trade Issues," a paper that showed considerable evolution in the thinking of the AFL-CIO.

In the foreign economic policy field, 1971 was to be a year of intensive labor activity. In May 1971 at a meeting in Atlanta, the 35-member executive council of the AFL-CIO adopted a "detailed statement urging new trade and investment legislation."[10] The Atlanta resolution contained Burke-Hartke in all but legislative form. Before the year was out, the AFL-CIO had launched a full trade and investment campaign. In July the AFL-CIO sponsored a national conference on jobs that brought some 600 labor delegates to Washington.[11] The Burke-Hartke Bill was introduced at the very end of September. The Industrial Union Department of the AFL-CIO held a one-day rally for Burke-Hartke just prior to their biennial convention in Washington. IUD director Jacob Clayman estimated that they attracted about "4,000 delegates from all over the country."[12] In the afternoon chartered buses carried the labor delegates to Capitol Hill. Some 15 to 20 Washington lobbyists for international unions accompanied them.[13]

The AFL-CIO had made arrangements for the largest delegations to meet with their congressmen in the Capitol. In some cases the meetings bore almost immediate fruit. For instance, on October 18, 1971, Congressman Thomas E. Morgan (D-Pa.), chairman of the House Committee on Foreign Affairs (now International Relations) wrote to President Nixon urging a vigorous reassessment of our foreign-trade policies. Letters advocating early hearings on the Burke-Hartke Bill were sent to Senator Long (D-La.) and Congressman Mills. There was to be little actual consideration of trade or investment legislation in 1971, but hearings conducted by the Subcommittee on International Trade of the Senate Finance Committee did offer the AFL-CIO a convenient congressional forum.

Presidential authority for trade negotiations had expired in 1967. Despite attempts by both Presidents Johnson and Nixon, no legislation had passed the Congress to create new authority. However, the administration was expected to make a second attempt at trade legislation, possibly a more ambitious approach than that taken in Nixon's proposed Trade Act of 1969.

With this prospect of trade legislation in mind, the Subcommittee on International Trade scheduled five days of hearings. In some ways it was unusual for the Senate Finance Committee to hold hearings in absence of any specific legislation and before the House Ways and Means Committee had taken some trade-related action. However, at that time the Subcommittee on International Trade was purely investigative in nature and had not been delegated any legislative authority by the full committee. In other words, no legislation would ever be formally considered or altered by the International Trade Subcommittee.

George Meany, president of the AFL-CIO, personally presented the labor case before the subcommittee during its May 1971 hearings.[14] In his opening statement, Meany reiterated the familiar testimony about the multiple changes in the world economy with the usual emphasis on the growth of the multinational firm and the spread of U.S. technology. Meany also took up the theme of labor immobility:

> Workers have great stakes in their jobs and their communities. They have skills that are related to the job or industry. They have seniority and seniority-based benefits such as pensions, vacations, and supplemental employment benefits. Workers have investments in their homes, a stake in the neighborhood schools and churches.[15]

Admitting the lack of concrete data on the impact of foreign trade on domestic employment, Meany blamed the "indifference . . . and lack of interest by foreign trade experts in Government and business."[16] In sum, there was little change in the labor thesis, facts to support that thesis, or in specific policy recommendations. Burke-Hartke was still to come.

The congressional questioning of Meany was neither pointed nor particularly insightful. Some of the senators appeared to use the hearings more as a platform for set positions rather than an opportunity to explore the labor position. In most cases congressional questioners reflected little knowledge of or concern with what economics had to say about foreign trade and investment issues. One interchange between Senator Long, chairman of the Senate Finance Committee, and George Meany is particularly instructive in this regard. Long asks if Meany was aware "that the purist, in terms of free trade, thinks in terms of a free flow of capital to go wherever it can produce goods more cheaply?"[17]

Although not using the term, Meany replies by relying on an externalities argument in criticizing the "pure theory." He paints a hypothetical picture of a middle-aged worker in the one-factory town. In Meany's presentation, labor immobility brings lost jobs, costly moves, sacrificed skills, and lost pension rights. In responding, Long expresses basic agreement with the Meany point of view. To Senator Long the pure theory "is sort of like saying that . . . in the long run everything is going to be all right." In a paraphrase of Keynes, Long goes on to note that "in the long run we are all going to be dead in our graves." He ends with praise for Meany having taken "a practical, commonsense point of view"[18] (emphasis added).

Senator Talmadge (D-Ga.), ranking Democrat on the Finance Committee, focused most of his questioning on the impact of foreign trade on the domestic textile industry. Much of his questioning reads like an excerpt from the Congressional Record prepared for home consumption. He did lead Meany into a discussion of the various labor intensities involved in foreign trade. Although Meany remained critical of the DISC program, labor had still not done a study of its costs or benefits. In response to questioning by Senator Bennett (R-Utah), labor made such a study and submitted it for the record. Senator Hansen (R-Wyoming) quoted from a recent statement by Henry Ford II, president of the Ford Motor Company, to the effect that every percentage point of penetration of the U.S. market by foreign automobiles cost the United States 20,000 jobs. Based on a penetration figure of 20 percent, Hansen calculates the job loss at something near 400,000 in autos alone. Why then, asks Senator Hansen, had the United Auto Workers (UAW) resisted a move to the type of orderly marketing sought by the AFL-CIO? Meany had no real answer.

Before following the AFL-CIO testimony to its final conclusion, it is important to take a quick look at the UAW. As much as any major American union, the UAW has been exposed to the problems of foreign trade and the questions raised by the multinational corporation. The auto industry was among the first U.S. industries to go international. The response of the UAW has been to seek broad ties with unions in other countries. Through the International Metalworkers Federation in Geneva, the UAW has "forged international links with more than 11 million metal workers in more than 50 countries. . . ."[19] Included in those totals are some 3 million auto workers in more than 20 countries. The UAW has sought to share information on existing contract provisions on a worldwide basis. The UAW position on trade is also something of an anomaly. Despite heavy penetration of the U.S. automobile industry by foreign manufacturers, for the most part the UAW remained a staunch advocate of freer trade. Only at the height of the energy crisis in 1973 did the UAW issue a call for temporary quotas on automobile imports.

The history of foreign auto penetration of the U.S. market is well known to almost any American consumer. Although the Volkswagen success was temporarily stalled by the American compacts, the compacts quickly grew in both size and price. Imports resumed their growth, this time under both German and Japanese labels. The American response to the rapid upsurge of the foreign-made subcompacts raised interesting questions about the viability of using foreign trade to make domestic industry more competitive. In place of domestic production, the multinational auto makers at first attempted to respond to Japanese and German competition with in-house imports. General Motors touted the Opel, Ford brought in a limited number of Anglias and other English Fords, and Chrysler made some attempts to introduce Simca, made by their French subsidiary.

As the German penetration continued and the Japanese presence proved to be more successful and persistent, there was finally an attempt at a totally domestic response. General Motors, in what must have appeared as the classic American strategy, adopted highly capital-intensive techniques in producing the Vega. Ford followed a middle path by combining considerable U.S. production with foreign parts (engine and transmission) and some Canadian assembly in the Pinto. Chrysler alone followed the older strategy. Following a sizable investment in Mitsubishi the Japanese agreed to import a number of Chrysler-produced cars (from Chrysler of Australia) and Chrysler in turn agreed to market the Japanese Colt as its own product. Chrysler also pushed the English Cricket but did not attempt to compete with the subcompacts through domestic production.

In late 1973 the United States was hit by the twin problems of rising petroleum prices and an oil embargo imposed by a number of Arab oil producers. One of the many results of the embargo-price rise was massive layoffs in the automobile industry. Pressed by their membership and fearful that domestic demand for automobiles would move to energy-efficient foreign models, the UAW leadership called for temporary import quotas. The quotas were justified on the grounds that U.S. industry needed time to shift to the production of more energy-efficient models.

Even with such provocation the move to quotas was a reluctant one. The UAW never sought permanent market shares but rather temporary quotas. And the leadership began to move away from the quotas as early as March 1974. Final repudiation of the quota approach came in June at the UAW's 24th constitutional convention.[20] Instead of quotas or increased tariffs, the basic UAW position was a two-pronged approach designed to reduce the impact of foreign trade on the individual worker. On the one hand, the UAW has advocated much more extensive provisions for trade adjustment assistance, especially for displaced workers. Under the UAW scheme, workers put out of work because of imports would be "granted 100 percent adjustment assistance; . . . be compensated for loss of seniority rights; [be] retrained for other jobs, [and be] paid for any relocation costs which they incur."[21] On the other hand, the UAW favors capital controls. At one point the UAW spoke in favor of requiring firms to specifically request permission to close a plant with a proviso that if such a closing was not economically necessary (as opposed to desirable), the firm would have to pay a portion of the adjustment costs incurred by the workers. The UAW also is willing to consider "the use of a temporary, phased-down tariff" where there is sudden market disruption.[22] They cited the ball-bearing industry as a case in point.

The UAW position on quota legislation seems to have reflected three very different forces. First, there was the long tradition of internationalism that had been started by Walter Reuther. In a number of interviews conducted in July 1976, international specialists from labor, business, the administration, and Capitol Hill all stressed the Reuther tradition. Leonard Woodcock, then president of the UAW, was very much brought up in the Reuther mold.

Second, the UAW had a substantial Canadian membership. With an economy that was overwhelmingly dependent on industrial exports to the United States, the Canadian members were understandably apprehensive. The Canadian automotive workers were provided some protection by the Canadian Automobile Agreement, which governed trade with the United States in automobiles and auto parts. Burke-Hartke did exempt existing trade treaties from the ambit of the mandatory quota provisions. But the tenor of Burke-Hartke suggested that revisions in the automobile pact inimical to Canada would be a real possibility.

Finally, the UAW also represents a large number of workers in the aircraft industry, which is heavily export oriented. In addition, the UAW includes a substantial number of workers in the farm implement industry, which is export oriented in its own right and heavily dependent on American agriculture, which is also a major exporter. A number of individuals in the international trade field indicated that the multinational firms had been successful in persuading their employees of the link between direct foreign investment and export sales and export sales and their particular jobs.

It is interesting to compare the position of the UAW with that of the International Association of Machinists (IAM), a member of the AFL-CIO. Except for automobile workers, the IAM has a similar membership to that of UAW with extensive representation in the aircraft and farm implement industries. The IAM also has a substantial (around 6 percent) Canadian membership. Although the IAM endorsed Burke-Hartke, it was not actively involved in the formulation of the quota provisions. From the start the IAM urged that import quotas not be applied to Canada. According to an IAM staff member, Burke-Hartke was opposed by some members in export-oriented industries.[23] Subjected to similar pressures but with a markedly different tradition and different institutional loyalties, the IAM was able to support Burke-Hartke with some reservations and a solid emphasis on the investment rather than the trade aspects of the bill.

Despite evident import pressures and its own highly restrictive proposals for controlling foreign direct investment, the UAW kept to the sidelines in the foreign trade and investment debate. The AFL-CIO would have to go it alone with Burke-Hartke. Despite the failure of the UAW to fully support the Burke-Hartke approach, the AFL-CIO managed to set the terms of the foreign trade and investment debate throughout 1972. The multinational firms saw Burke-Hartke as a direct attack on their worldwide operations. A number of individual companies and industry groups published studies that sought to demonstrate that direct foreign investment increased both exports and domestic employment.

The initial debate over the AFL-CIO proposals took place in a year that saw both general economic improvement and a growing trade imbalance. During 1972 the economy showed definite signs of recovery from the preceding two years of slow growth. The overall unemployment rate for all civilian workers edged down from 6.0 percent in 1971 to 5.6 percent in 1972. The changes for manufacturing employment were much more marked. For instance, in durable manufacturing the rate of unemployment dropped from 7.0 percent in 1971 to 5.4 percent in 1972, a fall of 1.6 percentage points.

Trade figures, however, painted a different picture. In 1971 the U.S. suffered its first trade deficit since figures had been recorded, a deficit of some $2.7 billion. At close to $7 billion, the 1972 deficit was almost three times as large. Import penetration continued to put pressure on a number of industries. The U.S. trade deficit widened in motor vehicles, textiles and footwear, steel, and consumer electronics. There was even considerable deterioration (although still a sizable surplus) in the trade balance of the aircraft industry.

For most of 1972 the administration had resisted any efforts to present a new trade bill to the Congress. There was considerable

internal debate over when the administration should advance trade
legislation and indeed even some speculation that none would be forth-
coming at all. Toward the end of the year, however, there were
indications of movement on the trade issue. In a GATT speech
delivered in November 1972, Ambassador Eberle, the U.S. Special
Representative for Trade Negotiations, broached the possibility of
the long-run elimination of tariffs on industrial goods.[24] In December George Shultz was made chairman of the new cabinet-level Council
on Economic Policy. Early in the new year Shultz was pushing the
administration to prepare trade legislation.[25]

The administration moved with particular force in February
1973. Faced with renewed speculative pressures on the value of the
dollar, the U.S. announced a further 10 percent devaluation, released
plans to end controls on U.S. investments abroad, and indicated the
intention to seek new trade-negotiating authority. Trade legislation
was finally presented to the Congress in April.

Following the introduction of President Nixon's Trade Reform
Act of 1973, the House Ways and Means Committee initiated hearings
on the measure. For the most part the AFL-CIO testimony remained
the same. Amendments were made to deal with other aspects of the
president's program[26]—pension reform or the proposed change in
unemployment compensation. There was also an attempt to respond
to a number of studies made by groups representing the multinational
corporation that purported to show the multinationals had not "exported
jobs" or otherwise injured the American working man.

I. W. Abel, in his role as chairman of the AFL-CIO Economic
Policy Committee, presented the heart of the labor case. After
repeating the general warnings about the changed world economy,
the growth of the multinational firm, and the spread of U.S. technology, Abel moved on to specific criticisms. As could be expected,
the special feature applying the tariff to value-added-only was roundly
excoriated. To buttress the case about U.S. technology, Abel referred to a recent AFL-CIO disclosure "that the ThorDelta launch
rocket and its entire missile launch system . . ." was in the process
"of being sold to the Japanese by McDonnell-Douglas Corporation,
[a] multinational corporation."[27]

Labor also was at some pains to rebut a series of studies done
by a number of business groups. The studies were roughly similar,
involving surveys of the membership with regard to their employment
and export performance over the past several years. Abel's criticism of these studies was twofold. First, he noted that most of the
survey studies did not correct for acquisitions or mergers. Second,
he argued that because the multinational firms were the leading
sectors of the economy, their employment was largely determined
by what happened "in the American economy . . . not what [happened]

as a result of their foreign operations."[28] Following his oral testimony, Abel added a number of appendixes.[29] One of these was specifically directed at the multinational studies and the contention that the operations abroad actually spurred job growth in the United States. In part, the appendix relies upon a lengthy Tariff Commission study that reached widely different conclusions depending upon which assumptions were adopted. Abel's criticism was directed at the multinationals' use of the Tariff Commission findings only under the most favorable assumptions. The study of the Emergency Committee for American Trade was singled out for special attention. Abel noted that when ECAT figures are corrected for mergers, they reveal a rate of job growth lower than that experienced by the overall economy.[30] In the appendix Abel also cited Labor Department statistics to show "substantial job losses between 1966 and 1972 in major industries at home in which direct foreign investment by multinationals expanded rapidly."[31] All in all it was not an overwhelming performance.

Ways and Means Committee members reflected a wide range of interests in their subsequent questioning of Abel. Ullman (D-Ore.) expressed interest in the question of industrial versus service employment. Conable (R-N.Y.) pressed Abel on why the AFL-CIO is not more of an international labor movement. It is hard to determine exactly what prompted Conable's question: whether pointing out the difference between the AFL-CIO and the UAW or focusing on the contrast of helping the American worker at the expense of his foreign counterpart. No one suggested that Conable was advocating yet another "international." The increasingly maligned academic theorists were in for more trouble. Waggoner (D-La.) expressed his "total disagreement . . . with some college professors who in my opinion are theorists who take the position that we in this country should not do anything. . . ."[32]

In response to questions from Chairman Mills, Goldfinger made the first public break with the language of the Burke-Hartke Bill. He indicated that the base period for the quota, in Title III, was very definitely negotiable.[33] In the final markup sessions, Congressman Burke was to move to eliminate any rollback at all, but this major concession came far too late. Goldfinger also attempted to shore up Burke-Hartke against the impact of cutting the dollar free from gold. Naming devaluation as the "free traders'" alternative to Burke-Hartke, Goldfinger argued that devaluation was too inflationary.[34]

Subsequent labor testimony added little to the Abel presentation. George Collins, assistant to the international president, International Union of Electric, Radio and Machine Workers, appearing with several other labor witnesses, did add something of interest.[35] In the course

of applying the spread of technology argument to the electronics
industry, Collins cited unattributed figures to the effect that during
the period 1960–70 the government provided 57.5 percent of all
research funds.[36] He also specified actual job losses in the electronics industry rather than relying on the loss of job opportunities.
After appending a series of specific plant closings by multinational
firms, he concluded with strong support of the Burke-Hartke Bill.

In the questioning period, labor again was forced to deal with
the impact of devaluation in stemming the flow of imports. Schneebeli
(R-Pa.) reported on a recent tour of an electronics plant in his district. Schneebeli noted that the manager of the plant said that the
first devaluation did not have "too much of an impact as far as imports
from the Far East were concerned. But he felt sure that the second
devaluation would have a very positive effect on imports"[37] (emphasis
added). Schneebeli went on to say that the manager expected that
much of the company's Singapore operation would be transferred
back to the United States. In his prepared statement, Collins had
argued that the devaluation coupled with yen revaluation had merely
shifted the source of imports from Japan to Taiwan and Mexico.[38]

Collins's testimony did break once with established Burke-
Hartke policy. He suggested that Burke-Hartke be amended to provide
for negotiation of a compact with Canada "aimed at preventing the
international trade abuses that have damaged both nations."[39] Burke
complimented Collins for comments on Canada. This particular trial
balloon may well have reflected the reported restlessness of Canadian
affiliates of AFL-CIO internationals.[40] The Ways and Means Committee concluded its hearings in June 1973. In early July the committee decided to drop consideration of the administration proposal
to preclude the deferral of tax liability of certain limited types of
foreign-source income. Although labor considered the administration's tax plan totally inadequate, they had hoped to have tax and trade
issues linked in one piece of legislation as they were in the Burke-
Hartke Bill.

At a July 12th strategy session, Congressman Joseph E. Karth
(D-Minn.) and four or five other Ways and Means Committee "members considered sympathetic to labor met for breakfast with AFL-
CIO legislative director Andrew J. Biemiller and assistant, Ray
Dennison, head of a special task-force on the trade bill."[41] Every-
one agreed that Burke-Hartke was not going to pass. Karth and other
committee members offered to "take a look" at any labor amendments
to the administration trade bill. If the amendments met with their
general approval, they expressed a willingness to propose the amendments "during the course of the committee meeting."[42] Karth indicated that he never heard from labor.

A well-placed House staffer felt that labor amendments could have had a considerable impact, particularly in the safeguards and injury-from-imports area. Labor, however, was convinced that no amendments of any substance would have been accepted by the committee. Dennison was quoted as saying that to have offered amendments to the bill would have put "labor in the position of asking for 'yes' votes on the amendments and 'no' votes on the bill itself."[43]

In the face of negative prospects for Burke-Hartke, the AFL-CIO did make one serious attempt at compromise. In mid July 1973, Burke (of Burke-Hartke) made two separate motions in the Ways and Means Committee. "First, he proposed to set automatic quotas on imports when they capture 15 percent of the domestic market. Then he moved to limit imports to the 1973 levels. . . . The committee voted more than two to one to defeat Burke's . . . proposals."[44]

Changing economic conditions almost surely had some influence on the deliberations of the Ways and Means Committee. When the administration bill was introduced in April, the United States was "already more than $800 million in deficit for the first three months of the year."[45] While the committee was actually considering the bill, the trade figures began to improve with surpluses recorded in April, July, and August. The employment situation also continued to improve. With an unemployment rate of around 5 percent when the Trade Reform Act of 1973 was introduced, the rate fell to 4.5 percent just "as the committee concluded its deliberations."[46]

Although Ways and Means had definitely turned away from the Burke-Hartke approach, the president did not get all that he hoped for either. Presidential control was carefully circumscribed, the removal of a nontariff barrier was subject to veto by either House of Congress, and adjustment assistance was to be both retained and amplified. The committee left the Burke-Hartke tax proposals for another day and ignored the plea for comprehensive import quotas entirely. Where the committee came closest to Burke-Hartke was in the provisions for speeding up the procedures for unfair import competition (countervailing duties and antidumping hearings) and easing the standards for relief from general import penetration (escape clause action and trade adjustment assistance).

Even before final House action on the trade bill in December of 1973, the terms of the foreign trade debate had changed. From 1970 through the early part of 1973, the focus of the trade debate had been on the multinational firm, the importance of foreign direct investment, and the impact of imports on the future of the U.S. industrial economy. But in 1973 the debate on the trade bill began to focus on the issue of extending most-favored-nation status to the Soviet Union. Almost all political and economic debate also began to reflect the growing influence of the Watergate scandal.

Labor's testimony before the Senate Finance Committee did adjust to these changes. But the basics of the labor case remain the same. In March 1974 testimony before the Senate Finance Committee, Meany made another attempt to deal with the question of devaluation.[47] He noted that "in spite of the dollar devaluations, there was no surplus of <u>manufacturing exports over imports</u>"[48] (emphasis added).

Questioning by the committee elicited little of merit. Much of the questioning was done with the home folks in mind or to buttress an existing senatorial position. In response to a question from Senator Byrd (Ind-Va.), Meany backed away from the specifics of the Burke-Hartke solution. Stressing that the world had changed since Burke-Hartke was introduced, Meany appealed to Congress to write a law that would keep trade from being a one-way street.

After an exchange with Senator Packwood (R-Ore.) about the national loyalties of a multinational firm, the discussion turned to the question of repealing the foreign tax credit. Meany made no bones about repealing the foreign tax credit as a punitive measure designed to keep American capital at home.[49] In somewhat later testimony, Abel, this time speaking as president of the United Steelworkers of America, reiterated the standard labor case.[50] Noting that the Industrial Union Department's "first concern is to advance the interests of working men and women—and particularly to advance the interests of working men and women in the United States," Abel emphasized his concern with the "erosion of the U.S. industrial base. . . ."[51]

Continuing his testimony, Abel took a rare but quite explicit swipe at the old nemesis, comparative advantage. In Abel's view, "we still cling to the myth that the free market principle of comparative advantage will work. The fact is that the development of managed economies and of monopolistic industries, such as the oil industry, have long since relegated such theories to the scrap heap."[52] Senator Ribicoff quickly joined in to agree that "the theory of comparative advantage certainly goes out the window."[53]

In attempting to deal with the 1973 trade surplus, Abel zeroed in on the manufactured items. He found virtually no change in the trade balance of classified manufactured goods (such as steel) and an increase in the deficit of miscellaneous manufactured goods (such as scientific goods).

Abel continued Meany's step toward compromise on Burke-Hartke—in fact the phrase "Burke-Hartke" does not appear in Abel's testimony. In place of Burke-Hartke's rigid 1965-69 base period for regulating competitive imports, Abel advocated a "flexible system" with some type of a "triggering arrangement."[54] Subsequent labor testimony followed the outlines laid out by Meany and Abel.[55]

Congressional questioning of these witnesses bordered on the per-functory.

There has not been a great deal of trade and investment activity in either the 94th or 95th Congress. First recession and then infla-tion were the major economic preoccupations of the country. With a Democrat in the White House for the first time in eight years, the AFL-CIO concentrated its limited lobbying resources on matters of immediate labor concern (such as labor law reform) or broad social policy (such as the Humphrey-Hawkins Bill).

Despite the fact that there were few specific legislative targets, labor continued to press its case before the Congress. The funda-mental position of labor has not changed much. The unions continue to stress the economic impact of the multinational corporation on the flow of goods, capital, and technology. In addition, there are one or two slight shifts of emphasis. If anything, they have put greater weight on the asymmetry between the relatively open trading practices of the United States and the relatively closed policies of the rest of the world. One can also detect a growing apprehension about the economic potential of the developing world.[56]

Although hearings serve many purposes—building a record, offering interested parties a public day in court, insuring the appear-ance of objectivity, providing the congressmen an opportunity for either local or national coverage—they are also a genuine source of information and ideas on matters of public debate. But they are certainly not the sole means nor always the principal means by which congressmen garner information. In addition, there are old friends from the district, the college roommate, a favorite academic, trusted lobbyists, the congressmen's personal or committee staff, and general newspaper articles.

None of the many sides in a policy dispute can influence a con-gressman's choice of college roommate or old, valued friends. Briefings for the staff and the congressmen are quite another matter. And labor was efficient in getting its letters to the right people, gain-ing entry to various offices, and counting congressional noses. But they were not very successful in reaching either the congressmen or their staffs by indirect means: labor failed to successfully make its case both in the universities and in the national press.

Certainly one would be hard pressed to find much sympathy for the Burke-Hartke Bill in university circles or in academic publica-tions. To some extent the distance between labor and the academic community has been narrowed. During a recent (June and July 1976) attempt to repeal the deferral provisions, the AFL-CIO received considerable academic support. In a press bulletin released in early June, the AFL-CIO included a statement by many of America's best known economists endorsing the elimination of "inefficient tax expendi-tures like . . . tax deferral, for multinational corporations."[57]

The multinational corporation also came under more careful
scrutiny. Not all the findings, of course, were supportive of the
labor position. But there were scholarly papers contending that the
multinational corporation had reduced labor's share of national income, had accelerated the change in the U.S. comparative advantage,
and was in general inimical to U.S. national interest.

But at the time of Burke-Hartke, the AFL-CIO felt that the
academic community was indifferent to its interests and unresponsive
to the labor view of the changing world economy. It is hard to calculate the cost incurred by simply writing off the academic community.
But labor certainly made no attempt to cloak its arguments in language
that would appeal to either theoretical or practical economists. Even
labor's congressional allies were unable to bridge that particular
gap. Eventually the Senate Labor and Public Welfare Committee,
generally composed of senators friendly to labor, published The
Multinational Corporation and the National Interest.[58] Prepared
by Robert Gilpin of Princeton University, this study remained relatively agnostic about many of the issues raised by the AFL-CIO.
After opening with quotes from Keynes expressing some reservations
about the wisdom of direct foreign investment, Gilpin proceeded to
find merit in both sides of most of the controversies.

Gilpin did come down solidly on the side of eliminating the tax
deferral provision, but he found the heart of the matter to depend
upon an imperfect corporate structure. In Gilpin's view, "the high
rate of foreign investment by American corporations is largely the
consequence of an imperfect capital market abetted by present tax
laws."[59] Faced with a choice between expansion of existing product
lines and the development of new lines of business, the large U.S.
corporation will generally choose the former strategy. Foreign
investment—coupled with tax deferral and trade barriers—both
facilitates expansion and limits future competition.

But Gilpin provided little support for the controversial quota
provisions (Title III) of the Burke-Hartke Bill or the attempts to
apply direct controls to capital and technology exports. And his
views came very late in the day: a good part of the Ways and Means
Committee die had already been cast. Nor did Gilpin's study receive
much play either on Capitol Hill or in the national press. The first
tentative bridge between the academics and the labor movement had
gone virtually unnoticed.

This was not an isolated instance of labor's failure with the
press. No doubt the AFL-CIO had a particularly rough row to hoe
with most national newspapers. Editorials were generally hostile
toward quotas[60] and articles frequently showed a similar predilection
for free trade.[61] Mass-circulation publications were often just as
critical.[62] The bill itself was greeted with general hostility on the
principal editorial pages.[63]

The liberal press was also inimical to the AFL-CIO posture on trade questions. For instance, the New Republic treated the quota sections of Burke-Hartke with a mix of apprehension and disdain. In a December 4, 1971, column, the New Republic commented on a proposal to permit the president permanent authority to impose a 15 percent surcharge on imports in the case of a balance of payments emergency.[64] The New Republic quoted Senator Javits to the effect that the proposal would be the "economic counterpart of the Gulf of Tonkin Resolution."[65] The tendency to raise trade barriers was viewed in the light of the "notorious Smoot-Hawley Act of 1930."[66] In a subsequent (1973) column, the New Republic noted that there were no disinterested studies available on the economic impact of the multinational companies. The column went on to attack the protectionist spirit in Congress and the potential cost to consumers of the quota sections of the "now-celebrated Burke-Hartke bill."[67]

Aside from the generally hostile editorial coverage, the Burke-Hartke Bill received little serious treatment from either the economic reporters or the columnists. In the constant competition for congressional time and attention, the national economic reports and columnists have a large following both by congressional staffs and by the congressmen themselves. Although labor did get an occasional thoughtful column on its problem,[68] the proposed solutions were generally treated with derision.[69]

This is not to say the labor position received no dispassionate consideration in the press. There were articles that stressed the economic adjustments forced by imports[70] and the labor focus on jobs.[71] But for the most part labor failed with the national press as it had failed with the academics.

In sum, the labor approach has been weak on studies and strong on the political approach. In the legislative battle leading up to the Trade Act of 1974, they lost both the academics and the press. In no small measure they had failed to meet the burden of successfully challenging the status quo in terms of policies and analysis.

Hemmed in between limited resources for research and an always ambitious legislative program, labor was angered that the data-gathering agencies of the government had not been put to work answering some of the questions they raised. When seeking evidence of the impact of the multinationals on domestic employment from an AFL-CIO staffer, author Irwin Ross was met with: "Let the government get the data. Why is it up to us?"[72] Following the election of President Carter, the Department of Labor did begin to explore at least some of the issues posed by labor.

In the period following the passage of the Trade Act of 1974, labor has continued to build its case around a limited number of studies and a long list of individual examples: plants moving abroad, discriminatory practices against U.S. exports, the impact of imports

on employment, and unfair trade practices of foreign exporters.
But labor still has a tendency to show the flag rather than the figures,
to emphasize power over persuasion. This attitude was particularly
strong during the legislative battle over Burke-Hartke. In this context the author is reminded of an open briefing for congressmen and
their staffs at which an AFL-CIO representative made his case over
the opposition of administration spokesmen, including Paul Volcker,
then the undersecretary of the Treasury for monetary affairs. The
union man, who had been poorly briefed and led into considerable
embarrassment, stressed the importance of showing the administration
"where labor stood." This "where labor stands" rather than "why
labor stands" has too often characterized the AFL-CIO approach to
the problem. Beset with limited research money, a press that is
viewed as hopelessly hostile, and an economic theory that did not
seem to fit the working man's reality, labor relied heavily on the
game it played best: power politics.

BUSINESS TESTIFIES

Business has also sought to present its views in a variety of
ways. A few of the individual firms made films depicting the relationship between their overseas activities and increased domestic employment. The link between exports and home-plant employment was
given understandable emphasis. The films, however, were specifically designed to be shown to their own workers rather than for
general distribution to business groups.
    Letters from company presidents were sent to individual con-
gressmen and senators. In some cases the letters were followed
up by visits of a major corporate spokesman, in a few instances the
president himself. For the most part, however, the personal call
was left to the Washington representative of the company involved.
The companies were at some pains to plead their case in the national
press, with empirical studies, and in a series of personal contacts.
They were just as active in presenting their case to the more formal
congressional court: the committee hearings.
    Despite the growing change in big labor's attitude toward the
multinationals, the House Ways and Means trade hearings of 1970
gave little indication that the multinationals were about to come under
very severe attack. The testimony of business groups was generally
directed to opposing any gradual drift to import quotas, defending
the special tariff provision that taxed only the portion of an import
actually produced abroad (Items 807 and 806.30), and discussing
other features of the Nixon administration's proposed Trade Act of
1969.

In 1967 a group of concerned businessmen had formed the Emergency Committee for American Trade in response to a surge of protectionist legislation in the Congress. Although that particular "emergency" passed, ECAT remained on the scene as a specialized spokesman for the multinationals on a broad range of tax, trade, and investment issues. The 1970 ECAT testimony is particularly interesting for its avowedly pragmatic tone and its almost traditional concern with government regulation. In discussing the nature of the organization, ECAT president Donald Kendall stressed the fact that "ECAT members are practical, working businessmen."[73] Eschewing any ties to higher economics, Kendall went on to note that ECAT members are not "free trade theorists but, rather, have concentrated on specific issues and have supported the reciprocal trade program, because [they] know it has worked."[74]

ECAT opposed quotas for many of the expected reasons but also expressed some fear over the possibility of further governmental intrusion in the private sector. One of the ECAT spokesmen, Ellison L. Hazard, suggested that quotas would

> place in the hands of Government officials the power to favor one firm over another, one region over another, one set of labor practices over another, or what-have-you. No matter how skilled their administration, they are the hall mark of a "planned" as against a "market" economy.[75]

ECAT was not adamant against the use of import protection devices, however, as were some business groups. They specifically favored the administration proposal to break the link between tariff concession and injury in escape-clause actions. The U.S. Chamber of Commerce, for instance, took a directly opposed position.

In general the ECAT testimony portrays an "all is well with the multinationals" point of view. The attitude is particularly evident in its treatment of the debate over whether to expand the purview of Sec. 252 of the Trade Expansion Act of 1962. Sec. 252 specifically authorized U.S. retaliation against countries that discriminated against U.S. agricultural exports. Although unused throughout the TEA-62 era, a number of groups had suggested expanding the ambit of Sec. 252 to include industrial goods. ECAT wanted to take the process one step further. It advocated extending Sec. 252 to include discrimination against U.S. investments. In Kendall's words, ECAT had "worked for recognition of the important fact that when a country restricts our investment, it also damages our trade since investments almost always result in substantial exports of machinery, parts, and

the like."[76] That particular link was about to become the subject
of very heated discussion indeed.

The congressional questioning of the ECAT witnesses was not
particularly pointed, nor did it always grow out of the subject of the
testimony. Gibbons (D-Fla.) did attempt to follow up the ECAT discussion of Sec. 252 in the context of investment discrimination. He
also asked about the advent of the metric system. Vanik (D-Ohio)
renewed his quest for corporate information by asking for "a trade
balance sheet" for each of ECAT's members.[77]

The presentation of the U.S. Chamber of Commerce was equally
interesting. Speaking through Walter Sterling Surrey, a member of
the Chamber's International Committee, the Chamber expressed its
general support for the administration bill (H.R. 14870).[78] Surrey
went on to advocate a three-pronged approach based on the control
of domestic inflation, export financing, and tough negotiations to open
up foreign markets to U.S. exports.

Although de facto devaluation was little more than a year away,
most congressional witnesses did not treat it as much of a factor in
setting trade policy. The Chamber was certainly not unconcerned
about the impact of exchange rates on the pattern of trade. In discussing the changes in the world economy, Surrey noted that "since
the end of the Kennedy Round, a number of nations have made currency
adjustments, many of which had the effect of making their goods
cheaper here and our goods more expensive there—to the obvious
detriment of our trade balance."[79] But Surrey placed these devaluations in that generally uncomfortable category of necessary misde-
meanors. In Surrey's view, "such adjustments have been necessary,
in the absence of more automatic flexibility in exchange rates, to
restore imbalances which otherwise would threaten the climate for
our expanded trade"[80] (emphasis added).

In other words, changes to the detriment of our trade were
necessary for a climate that would expand it. Interestingly enough,
Surrey made no effort to apply the devaluation lesson to the U.S.
case. The "brooding omnipresence" of Bretton Woods may have
been too overpowering. At the end of his testimony, Surrey did
make an attempt to reply to some of the criticisms of multinational
corporations made by Andrew Biemiller (see discussion of labor
testimony above).

Congressional questioning of the Chamber witnesses was somewhat more extensive. Barber Conable (R-N.Y.) engaged one of the
Chamber witnesses, John E. Field, in an extensive discussion about
the Item 807 (tax on value-added-only) provision of the tariff code.
Field indicated that the 807 program had allowed the companies to
keep the "highly skilled capital-intensive" manufacturing operation
in the United States while performing the labor-intensive assembly

work abroad. By following the most efficient method of production, semiconductors dropped in price. The result has been a considerable expansion of semiconductor production and a consequent increase in U.S. employment. Then Conable asked if there would not have been "a substantial increase in the number of jobs under any circumstances" because of growth in the use of semiconductors in a wide variety of electronic equipment. Field responded in the negative and Conable went on to say: "In other words, you think there is a connection between the reductions in cost that could come from this and the increased demand quite apart from the soaring demand, itself?" Field agreed that substantial price reductions occurred because of the foreign assembly operations and that demand expanded markedly in response to lowered price.[81] Chairman Mills asked Surrey a series of tough questions on the status of U.S. trade policy. He also elicited a second defense by Surrey of the multinational firm.

If neither the Chamber nor ECAT displayed much anxiety about the position of either U.S. trade policy or the multinational firm, the Committee for a National Trade Policy was still strong on the trail to bar any retreat from existing free trade standards.[82] Not only did they oppose breaking the link between tariff concessions and injury in escape clause but they also suggested that "if [the president] decides to impose restrictions, he should report to the Congress on the cost of such restrictions to the national interest, and do so every year until the controls are removed."[83]

Taft and CNTP economist Steinberg placed great weight on the possibilities of far-ranging adjustment assistance and industrial adaptation. Taft endorsed an early warning system for industries that may suffer from import competition. In response to a congressional query, Steinberg seemed to go so far as to suggest differential taxes and depreciation rates for different industries.

Faced with such strong free traders, the congressional questioning zeroed in on what relief there would be for firms that do not meet the "tariff concessions test" of existing escape-clause procedures. Perhaps Congressman Burke (D-Mass.) best summed up the congressional concern for troubled economic times. "But what do you do," he asked, "when you represent a district that is losing thousands of jobs every year and there are no new jobs coming to replace them?"[84]

Even some industries that had suffered severe import competition remained divided with regard to the future of U.S. trade policy. For instance, the testimony of the Electronics Industries Association (EIA) contained no ringing call for import protection.[85] In fact, the main thrust of its testimony was to oppose the repeal of Item 807 of the tariff schedule. Relying on an analysis by Robert Stobaugh of Harvard Business School, they did attempt to describe their particular

industry in terms of the product cycle theory. Considerable stress
was laid on the mix of stable and dynamic technologies that could be
found in the electronics industry.

Despite the narrowed focus offered by a single industry, congressional questioning remained diffuse. Noting that Butler, the EIA
president, had limited his testimony to an endorsement of Item 807,
Conable asked if that meant that on other issues the industry will
"be all over the map."[86] Butler indicated that there would be agreement on some but not all issues.

Although the committee did not take up the opportunity to explore
the product cycle theory, Congressman Morton (R-Md.) did ask for
specific information on future trends in U.S. versus foreign costs
in the assembly of electronic items. Butler seemed unprepared for
the question, other than to say that Japanese costs were rising. In
terms of the future impact of Item 807, Morton's question was both
obvious and pertinent. Yet apparently neither the committee, the
committee staff, nor the interested witnesses were prepared to provide even an educated guess.

Industry divisions were even more apparent in the consumer
products division of the electronics industry.[87] Hoffman, chairman
of the consumer products division of EIA, acknowledged that

> a number of individuals and groups are urging the Con-
> gress to roll back present consumer product import
> levels and to provide that in the future such imports
> continue to be controlled in relation to domestic consump-
> tion of these products at lower levels than prevail today.[88]

Hoffman noted that similar proposals were made in 1968. Although
a majority still opposed the import quota approach, there was considerable feeling that the electronics industry was subject to unfair
competition from foreign firms. Hoffman urged the committee to
direct the Tariff Commission (now the International Trade Commission) to make such a study. Congressman Ullman saw the Hoffman
request as a Congress-like solution to a frequent congressional
dilemma. Ullman suggested that the "industry has one foot planted
firmly on each side" of the issue. "Up here on the Hill," continued
Ullman, "when that is the situation we call for a study, and that is
obviously the conclusion you arrived at also."[89]

Eventually the Trade Act of 1970 foundered in the Senate.
Itself the subject of much criticism, the bill was further weakened
by its association with controversial proposals for welfare reform
and national health insurance. Nor was formal Senate consideration
of the bill of much interest—two days of hearings called at a moment's
notice.[90] What they got was largely a rerun of earlier testimony
before the House.

Following the failure of the administration-proposed Trade Act of 1969, the Nixon administration was understandably reluctant to present new trade legislation to Congress. Certainly, if the relatively modest request for negotiating authority contained in the Trade Act of 1969 was suspect, a request for more general authority would almost surely be met with hostility.

The lack of legislation, however, did not prevent Congress from continuing to build a formal record on trade and investment issues. In a series of May hearings, the newly formed Subcommittee on International Trade of the Senate Finance Committee provided a new public forum for interested parties.

Despite the continuing problems with the U.S. balance of payments and the growing pressures for action on imports, the committee uncovered little change in the position of leading business organizations. Fred J. Borch, chairman of the board of the General Electric Company, did present a somewhat novel analysis of recent slippage in the U.S. merchandise trade account. Borch thoroughly discarded the frequently heard allegation that domestic inflation (and hence deficit spending) was the principal culprit. Although many of our principal trading partners had significantly higher rates of inflation than did the United States, Borch noted that they successfully contained their export prices. He concluded that the United States had simply been outmaneuvered on the international economic front. Borch went on to mention the "combination of export rebates, dual pricing, tilted tax structures, indirect export subsidies, import restrictions, nontariff barriers, restrictive procurement policies for national governments and the like, which [the United States faces] in international competition."[91]

Only a few months away from the first of the Nixon shocks, Borch did mention devaluation, but only in the context of the United States being the one country that could not devalue.[92] Borch anticipated policy to some extent. In place of devaluation he suggested an across-the-board import duty coupled with an export rebate. He noted the former policy was specifically permitted by GATT for balance of payments purposes. The Nixon import surcharge and the soon-to-be-passed DISC proposals came quite close to the Borch position.

Although somewhat constrained by his membership in the Williams Commission,[93] Borch showed little compunction in expressing sympathy for an occasional quota arrangement. Borch suggested that where U.S. "employment . . . is badly hurt like on steel, or on textiles, shoes, things" of that kind, one must move to an "arrangement which permits the foreigners to share in the growth of the market."[94]

Orville Freeman, president of Business International, displayed a growing concern about the criticisms of the multinational corpora-

tions. Freeman indicated that Business International was embarked
on a search for the facts about the multinational corporation. In
addition, he specifically endorsed negotiating an international code
of behavior for the multinationals.[95]

As the U.S. merchandise account slipped further into the red,
the Nixon administration bided its legislative time. Instead, labor
and business were allowed to plead their case before the public and
the Congress. There was to be no trade legislation proposed by the
Nixon administration during the 92nd Congress. Throughout this
period, however, the Subcommittee on International Trade remained
active in the foreign trade and investment debate. The Subcommittee
asked the Tariff Commission to evaluate the impact of the multinational corporation on the domestic economy.[96] In addition, the
subcommittee invited interested parties to submit papers on the
multinational.[97]

In early 1973 the subcommittee released both the Tariff Commission study and the compendium of submitted papers. Senator
Ribicoff announced several days of hearings to take place in late
February 1973.[98] With a tight time schedule, witnesses were limited
to the leading representatives of the administration, big labor, and
big multinational business. ECAT, General Motors, and IBM presented the business point of view. Business took the approach that
had already been established in its numerous studies and public
statements. As if one organization, business considered labor's
charges against the multinationals as a serious case of "mistaken
identity."[99]

Despite the clear focus of these hearings, they did not finally
dispose of any of the labor charges concerning the multinationals.
Although the theory behind Burke-Hartke had been battled to a stand-
still on an empirical level, it remained very much alive as a legislative force. But it has not again occupied center stage as it did
throughout late 1971 and 1972. In April the administration finally
came forward with its long-awaited trade proposal, the Trade Reform
Act of 1973. Other international issues crowded aside concern with
the multinationals: the question of detente with the Soviet Union, the
oil embargo, and the emigration of Soviet Jewry all clamored for
scarce congressional attention and concern.

The change shows up as early as the House Ways and Means
Committee Hearings on the Trade Reform Act of 1973.[100] Both
ECAT and NAM focused their testimony on support for the Trade
Reform Act of 1973. More attention was paid to the possibilities of
trade adjustment assistance and the implications of the administration's proposals for changes in the taxation of foreign-source income
than on defense of the multinationals. In fact, NAM's strong stand
against the administration's rather modest tax proposals suggests
that business felt the legislative tide had turned against Burke-Hartke.

This is not to say that the economic impact of the multinationals was not still of concern to either the committee or the witnesses. Business International's Freeman continued to cite the results of its survey study of U.S.-based multinationals. A thumbnail description of the results that Freeman had distributed to the committee proved to be the basis of lively and often intelligent questioning.[101]

Freeman came across as a well-informed witness with specific detail at his fingertips. Landrum (D-Ga.) asked if the Business International study uncovered any companies in which employment actually decreased in the United States. Freeman admitted that there were certain such companies but they were a distinct minority. Although there were certain companies that located abroad to ship back to the United States, the Business International study indicated that "the amount sent to the United States as a percentage of sales had increased from 0.6 percent to 0.8 percent or only two-tenths of 1 percent."[102]

In an apparent effort to establish the domestic investment records of the multinational companies, Conable asked if those that invested abroad also invested domestically. Freeman responded in the affirmative with some general assertions:

> I think very definitely that they invest more in the United
> States by virtue of having invested abroad because this
> has made it possible for them to diversify their base.
> It has provided an operation which can finance very
> expensive research and development. It has helped
> some companies, and this is a matter of public record,
> to make difficult transitions themselves into new tech-
> nology. In the cases of Burroughs and National Cash
> Register, for instance they have made it very clear
> that they could not have moved from mechanical
> machines to electronic computer machines if it had
> not been for substantial foreign operations which
> carried them through some critical years.[103]

The question of capital investment was not allowed to rest there, however. Vanik (D-Ohio) came closest to forcing Freeman into what might have been a very damaging admission. Vanik expressed some puzzlement over the Business International figures showing that the "larger the foreign investment, the faster the employment growth in the United States."[104] Freeman gave a "many factors" were involved response. Vanik continued to question: "Capital creates jobs wherever it is, but would you say that the foreign invested capital does a better job of creating jobs than domestically invested capital?"[105] In effect, Vanik was questioning the business position that "reverse classical" assumptions apply to the U.S. economy. In response, Freeman admitted, first, that the domestic investment would have a larger impact if the rates of return were the same, and, second, cited the previous examples of firms that were able to increase their domestic investments because of foreign earnings. And with a final admission that there are many "unknowns," Freeman moved on to other issues.

The business witnesses generally agreed that the devaluation of the dollar would act to correct the existing trade deficit. At least one business spokesman saw this as a permanent change in the rules of the trade game. Pointing to the growing use of Special Drawing Rights in the IMF, Lee L. Morgan, president of the Caterpillar Tractor Company, contended that the United States "will no longer be at the mercy of other countries in adjusting exchange rates."[106] The multinationals were back in business.

In the ensuing period (1975 through 1978), there has been no broadbased legislative attack on the multinationals. Rather, the last two Congresses have seen a series of skirmishes over particular trade and tax measures. In some cases the multinationals have suffered small but definite losses. The limitations on the calculation of the foreign tax credit, restrictions on the use of DISC, and other measures were victories for labor-backed tax reformers.

With the exception of further consideration of the tax on the foreign value-added-only feature of the tariff code (Item 806.30 and 807), the question of imports was basically an industry-by-industry or even sometimes a firm-by-firm affair.[107] Business testimony was limited to representatives of individual industries.

The basic posture of the multinational firms has remained unchanged. They continue to favor the free flow of capital goods and the preservation of existing laws on the taxation of foreign source income. In testimony over the extension of the Export-Import Bank, the AFL-CIO stressed the future impact on the economy of many capital goods exports, noting that casting capital goods upon the waters could bring back a much larger stream of manufactured goods.[108] At the same hearing, the National Association of Manufacturers emphasized the short-term contribution of capital goods exports to the U.S. balance of payments and domestic employment.[109]

Like labor, the multinationals have shifted their emphasis to match the changing economic times and have added new issues to their international economic list. Since large multinational firms are also, for the most part, major exporters, it is to be expected that they have lined up in support of the president's new export policy.[110] In a similar vein, they have not hesitated to point out the foreign practices that discriminate against U.S. exports.[111]

Throughout the 1970s the business response to labor's insistence on curbing trade and investment flows has proved to be diverse and largely effective. During the debate over Burke-Hartke and the Trade Reform Act of 1973, a number of the major business groups published studies on the impact of the multinational firm on the domestic economy. Not only did the studies garner generally favorable publicity in the national press but they also played an important role in blunting labor's challenge to the multinationals. By preempting the foreign trade field, labor had forced the multinationals into an essentially defensive posture. The business studies appear to have had the effect of "shifting the burden of going forward" back onto labor's shoulders.

Certainly, business benefitted from having a basically friendly administration in the White House. For the most part, business and the Nixon administration saw eye to eye on the broad questions of the role of the multinational corporation and the specific issue of the Burke-Hartke Bill. But the business effort itself was generally well coordinated and effective. Relative to past efforts, the business activities were impressive indeed.[112]

Business has continued to be successful in the years following the Trade Act of 1974. Although it did suffer some early defeats on the tax front, it has already begun to recoup lost ground. The 95th Congress restored much of what it had lost in the taxation of foreign earned income, and proposals to repeal deferral and DISC were both rejected.

Business no longer has a Republican friend in the White House, and it might well have been apprehensive about the victory of a Democratic president elected on a tax-reform platform with strong (and crucial) labor backing. But storm clouds of tax reform proved to have several silver linings for business, including a reduction in the capital gains tax. The multinationals remain a formidable and effective force on foreign trade and investment issues.

NOTES

1. Statement of Andrew J. Biemiller, Legislative Director, AFL-CIO, Tariff and Trade Proposals, Hearings, Committee on Ways and Means, U.S. House of Representatives, Part 4 (Washington, D.C.: U.S. Government Printing Office, 1970), p. 1001. The Biemiller testimony is also discussed in a previous chapter.
2. Ibid., p. 1001.
3. Ibid., p. 1003.
4. Ibid.
5. Ibid., p. 1008.
6. Ibid.
7. Ibid.
8. Statement of Jacob Clayman, Administrative Director, Industrial Union Department (AFL-CIO), Presenting Statement of

I. W. Abel, President, accompanied by Philip Daugherty, Legislative Representative, and George Collins, International Union of Radio and Machine Workers of America, Tariff and Trade Proposals, Hearings before the Committee on Ways and Means, U.S. House of Representatives, 91st Cong., 2d sess., Part 6 (May 22 and June 1, 1970) (Washington, D.C.: U.S. Government Printing Office, p. 1777).

9. Statement of Nathaniel Goldfinger, Director, Department of Research, AFL-CIO, accompanied by Ray Denison, Legislative Department, AFL-CIO, in Hearings and Informal Proceedings before the Committee on Finance, U.S. Senate, 91st Cong., 2d sess., on Amendments 925 and 1009 to H.R. 17550, Amendments to Incorporate the Text of The Trade Act of 1970, Part 1 (Washington, D.C.: U.S. Government Printing Office, 1970), p. 62.

10. Charles Culhane, "Economic Report/Labor and Industry Gear for Major Battle over Bill to Curb Imports, Multinationals," National Journal, January 15, 1972, p. 109.

11. Ibid., p. 111.

12. Ibid., p. 112.

13. Ibid.

14. Statement of George Meany, President, American Federation of Labor-Congress of Industrial Organizations, Hearings before the Subcommittee on International Trade of the Committee on Finance, 92d Cong., 1st sess., on World Trade and Investment Issues, Part 1 (Washington, D.C.: U.S. Government Printing Office, 1971), pp. 167-213.

15. Ibid., p. 171.

16. Ibid., p. 172.

17. Ibid., p. 187.

18. Ibid., p. 188.

19. Charles Culhane, "Washington Pressures/UAW Narrows Lobbying Focus, Stresses Issues Vital to Members," National Journal, July 3, 1971, p. 1412.

20. Much of the preceding material is based on a June 1976 interview conducted at the Washington Office of the UAW.

21. Remarks of Leonard Woodcock, President, UAW, before the National Foreign Trade Convention, November 14, 1972, New York. Also see Statement of Douglas A. Fraser, Vice President, UAW, in Hearings on Adjustment Assistance, Subcommittee on Foreign Economic Policy, House Foreign Affairs Committee, May 17, 1972 (Washington, D.C.: U.S. Government Printing Office, 1972), p. 315.

22. Woodcock, op. cit., p. 5. A number of UAW locals in the ball-bearing industry actually supported legislation that would have imposed quotas on ball-bearing imports. The legislation would have entailed a significant rollback on imports. See Richard S.

Frank, "Trade Report/Black Olives and Ball Bearings Lobby Groups Attempt to Restrict Competing Foreign Imports," National Journal, August 8, 1973, pp. 1224-25.

23. Interview conducted in July 1976.

24. Richard S. Frank, "Trade Report/Administration Torn Between Domestic, Overseas Interests in Drafting Trade Bill," National Journal, January 13, 1973, p. 46.

25. Ibid., p. 44.

26. Discussed in Chapter 8.

27. Statement of I. W. Abel, Chairman, Economic Policy Committee, American Federation of Labor-Congress of Industrial Organizations, accompanied by Nat Goldfinger, Director, Research Department, and Ray Denison, Legislative Department, in Hearings before the Committee on Ways and Means, House of Representatives, 93d Cong., 1st sess. on H.R. 6767, The Trade Reform Act of 1973, Part 4 (Washington, D.C.: U.S. Government Printing Office, 1973), p. 1209.

28. Ibid., p. 1214.

29. Ibid. Appendix 5, pp. 1239 et seq.

30. Ibid., p. 1240.

31. Ibid.

32. Ibid., p. 1276.

33. Ibid., p. 1280.

34. Ibid., p. 1281.

35. Panel consisting of George Collins, Assistant to International President, International Union of Electrical, Radio and Machine Workers; Anthony P. Bellissimo, Assistant to International President, International Brotherhood of Electrical Workers; and Gerard Borstel, Publicity and Publications Department, IUE, in Hearings before the Committee on Ways and Means, U.S. House of Representatives, 93d Cong., 1st sess. on H.R. 6767, The Trade Reform Act of 1973 (Washington, D.C.: U.S. Government Printing Office, 1973), p. 1239.

36. Ibid., pp. 1441-42.

37. Ibid., p. 1451.

38. Ibid.

39. Ibid., p. 1449.

40. See, for instance, Irwin Ross, "Labor's Big Push for Protectionism," Fortune, March 1973, pp. 93 et seq.

41. Richard S. Frank, "Trade Report/Administration's Reform Bill Threatened by Dispute Over Relations With Russia," National Journal, December 24, 1973, p. 1752.

42. Ibid.

43. Ibid.

44. Charles Culhane, "Trade Report/Labor Shifts Tactics on Administration Bill, Seeks Concessions on Imports, Multinationals," National Journal, August 28, 1973, p. 1095.

45. Frank, "Trade Report/Administration's Reform Bill," op. cit., p. 1742.

46. Ibid.

47. Statement of George Meany, President, AFL-CIO, accompanied by Andrew Biemiller, Director, Department of Legislation, and Nat Goldfinger, Director, Department of Research, in The Trade Reform Act of 1973, Hearings before the Committee on Finance, U.S. Senate, 93d Cong., 2d sess., March 27, 1974, pp. 1135-1238.

48. Ibid., p. 1137.

49. Ibid., p. 1155.

50. Statement of I. W. Abel, President, United Steelworkers of America, AFL-CIO, accompanied by Jacob Clayman, Secretary-Treasurer, Industrial Union Department, AFL-CIO, in Hearings before the Committee on Finance, U.S. Senate, 93d Cong., 2d sess., on H.R. 10710, Part 4 (Washington, D.C.: U.S. Government Printing Office, 1974), p. 1329.

51. Ibid., p. 1330.

52. Ibid., p. 1331.

53. Ibid.

54. Ibid., p. 1333.

55. See, for example, Trade Reform Act of 1973, Hearings, Senate Committee on Finance, Statement of George Collins, Assistant to the President, International Union of Electrical, Radio and Machine Workers, Part 4, p. 1686 et seq. In discussing the Mexican border program, Collins was virtually alone in admitting that foreign direct investment can aid the host country.

56. See, for instance, the testimony of Rudy Oswald, Director, Department of Research, AFL-CIO, before the House Ways and Means Trade Subcommittee in Causes and Consequences of the U.S. Trade Deficit and Developing Problems in U.S. Exports, Hearings before the Subcommittee on Trade of the Committee on Ways and Means, U.S. House of Representatives, 95th Cong., 1st sess., November 3 and 4, 1977 (Washington, D.C.: U.S. Government Printing Office, 1977), pp. 262-88.

57. In addition, Joseph A. Pechman and Stanley S. Surrey edited a "Compendium of Papers on Tax Reform," June 7, 1976, which were prepared by a number of tax economists. Included in the set of papers was one analyzing the implications of tax deferral and calling for its repeal.

58. Robert Gilpin, The Multinational Corporation and the National Interest (Washington, D.C.: U.S. Government Printing Office, 1973).

59. Ibid., p. 51.

60. See, for instance, "The Cost of the Textile Quotas,"
Washington Post, October 18, 1971, p. A22; and "The Folly of Protectionism," Wall Street Journal, March 10, 1970, p. 22.

61. See, for instance, "Hartke Bill's Tax Steps Scored,"
Journal of Commerce, June 28, 1972, p. 3; "'Hands Off' World Trade
Urged," Journal of Commerce, August 17, 1972, p. 9; and "Burke-
Hartke Bill Seen Striking Hard Blow to State," Journal of Commerce,
April 18, 1973, p. 11. Even balanced articles carried headlines that
cast Burke-Hartke in a negative light. For instance, "Protectionist
Action Unlikely in First Trade-Bill Skirmish," Christian Science
Monitor, January 27, 1972, p. 9.

62. See "No Winners in a Trade War—And One is Getting
Started," U.S. News and World Report, September 14, 1970, pp.
46-48; and "We Must Stop This Isolationist Trade Bill," Readers
Digest, August 1972, pp. 150-53. The U.S. News and World Report
article does give some points on both sides of the trade issue. The
Readers Digest piece, however, is unrelenting anti-Burke-Hartke.

63. See, for instance, "The Unions Against Their Members,"
Wall Street Journal, April 14, 1972, p. 14; "Memories of Smoot-
Hawley," Christian Science Monitor, March 15, 1972, p. 16; and
"Labor's Protectionist Swing," New York Times, March 4, 1973,
Section 3, p. 2. In a more general editorial, the Wall Street Journal
asked, "Did Protectionism Create Hitler?" October 26, 1971, p. 20.

64. The proposal was contained in the Senate-passed version
of the Revenue Act of 1971 (P.L. 92-178). The provision was dropped
in conference. Similar authority, however, was contained in Section
122 of the Trade Act of 1974 (P.L. 93-618).

65. "Economic Warfare," New Republic, December 4, 1971,
p. 7.

66. Ibid.

67. Robert W. Dietsch, "Maneuvering around Tariff Barriers,"
New Republic, April 21, 1973, p. 10.

68. See Edwin L. Dale, Jr., "'Situation Report' on an Import
Bill," New York Times, January 23, 1972, Section 3, p. 5; and
Edwin L. Dale, Jr., "Should We Forget About Trade," New York
Times, March 18, 1973, Section 4, p. 3.

69. Hobart Rowen of the Washington Post was particularly
single-minded in his opposition to the Burke-Hartke Bill. He gave
a high profile to the potential impact of Burke-Hartke quotas on the
consumer. See Hobart Rowen, "AFL-CIO Quota Drive Ignores Consumer," Washington Post, August 9, 1970, Section E, p. 1; "Proposals for Trade Quotas Could Harm All Consumers," Washington
Post, January 23, 1972, Section E, p. 1; "Burke-Hartke Bill: Higher
Prices, Fewer Jobs," Washington Post, March 5, 1972; and "Cost

of Tariff Barriers Put Over \$7.5 Million," Washington Post, March 5, 1973, D12. (The figure should have read 7.5 billion.) By way of contrast, Rowen was full of praise for the UAW's stress on adjustment assistance: see "UAW Points the Way, Washington Post, May 4, 1972, A27.

70. See, for instance, Ed Townsend, "Imports Nettle Labor," Christian Science Monitor, July 16, 1971, p. 7.

71. See, for instance, Richard Nenneman, "Jobs: Key Issue Behind Trade Talks," Christian Science Monitor, February 17, 1973, p. 4; and Albert R. Hunt, "Labor, Business Square Off in Trade Fight Even Though Key Bill Has No Chance in '72," Wall Street Journal, May 15, 1972, p. 34.

72. Ross, "Labor's Big Push for Protectionism," op. cit., p. 172.

73. Statement of Donald M. Kendall, Chairman, Robert L. McNeill, Executive Vice Chairman; Ellison L. Hazard; and Lynn Townsend, on behalf of the Emergency Committee for American Trade, Tariff and Trade Proposals, Hearings before the Committee on Ways and Means, House of Representatives, 91st Cong., 2d sess., Part 3 (Washington, D.C.: U.S. Government Printing Office, 1970), p. 739.

74. Ibid.

75. Ibid., p. 750.

76. Ibid., p. 747.

77. Ibid., p. 845.

78. Statement of Walter Sterling Surrey, Member, International Committee of the Chamber of Commerce of the United States; accompanied by Mrs. Kay Vest, Manager, International Group, John E. Field, and F. Taylor Ostrander, Jr., Tariff and Trade Proposals, Hearings before the Committee on Ways and Means, House of Representatives, 91st Cong., 2d sess., Part 4 (Washington, D.C.: U.S. Government Printing Office, 1970), p. 1039.

79. Ibid., p. 1043.

80. Ibid.

81. The entire interchange takes place in ibid., pp. 1048-49.

82. Statement of the Hon. Charles P. Taft, Chairman, Committee for a National Trade Policy; accompanied by John W. Hight, Executive Director and David J. Steinberg, Secretary and Chief Economist, Tariff and Trade Proposals, Hearings before the Committee on Ways and Means, House of Representatives, 91st Cong., 2d sess., Part 3 (Washington, D.C.: U.S. Government Printing Office, 1970), p. 852.

83. Ibid., p. 855.

84. Ibid., p. 871.

85. Statement of George D. Butler, President, Electronic
Industries Association; accompanied by Jay Price, Director of Public
Affairs, and Alfred R. McCauley, Special Counsel, Tariff and Trade
Proposals, Hearings before the Committee on Ways and Means,
House of Representatives, 91st Cong., 2d sess., Part 10 (Washington,
D.C.: U.S. Government Printing Office, 1970), p. 2827 et seq.
86. Ibid., p. 2863.
87. Statement of Charles N. Hoffman, Chairman, Consumer
Products Division, EIA; accompanied by Jack Wayman, Staff Vice-
President, and Alfred McCauley, Special Counsel, Tariff and Trade
Proposals, Hearings before the Committee on Ways and Means,
House of Representatives, 91st Cong., 2d sess. (Washington, D.C.:
U.S. Government Printing Office, 1970), p. 2870 et seq.
88. Ibid., p. 2871.
89. Ibid., p. 2874.
90. See Trade Act of 1970, Amendments 925 and 1009 to H.R.
17550, Social Security Amendments of 1970, Hearings and Informal
Proceedings before the Committee on Finance, U.S. Senate, 91st
Cong., 2d sess., Parts 1 and 2 (Washington, D.C.: U.S. Government
Printing Office, 1970). According to a number of witnesses, they
had only two days of notice before the Senate hearings.
91. Statement of Fred J. Borch, Chairman of the Board,
General Electric Company, in Foreign Trade, Hearings before the
Subcommittee on International Trade of the Committee on Finance,
U.S. Senate, 92d Cong., 1st sess., Part 1 (Washington, D.C.: U.S.
Government Printing Office, 1971), p. 509.
92. Ibid., p. 522.
93. The President's Commission on International Trade and
Investment Policy, Chaired by Albert L. Williams.
94. Ibid., p. 522.
95. Statement of Orville L. Freeman, President, Business
International Inc., in Foreign Trade, Hearings before the Subcommittee on International Trade of the Committee on Finance, U.S.
Senate, 92d Cong., 1st sess., Part 1 (Washington, D.C.: U.S.
Government Printing Office, 1971), p. 481.
96. United States Tariff Commission, Implications of Multinational Firms for World Trade and Investment and for U.S. Trade
and Labor, Report to the Committee on Finance of the U.S. Senate
and Its Subcommittee on International Trade, On Investigation No.
332-69, Under Section 332 of the Tariff Act of 1930 (Washington, D.C.:
U.S. Government Printing Office, 1973).
97. Multinational Corporations A Compendium of Papers,
Submitted to the Subcommittee on International Trade of the Committee
on Finance of the U.S. Senate (Washington, D.C.: U.S. Government
Printing Office, 1973).

98. Multinational Corporations, Hearings before the Subcommittee on International Trade of the Committee on Finance, U.S. Senate, 93d Cong., 1st sess. (Washington, D.C.: U.S. Government Printing Office, 1973).

99. The Politics of Foreign Trade, Tax and Investment Policy (Washington, D.C.: Government Research Company, 1972), p. 50.

100. Trade Reform, Hearings before the Committee on Ways and Means, House of Representatives, 93d Cong., 1st sess. on H.R. 6767, The Trade Reform Act of 1973, Parts 1 to 15 (Washington, D.C.: U.S. Government Printing Office, 1973).

101. "Statement of Hon. Orville I. Freeman, President, Business International, accompanied by Richard P. Conlon," in Trade Reform, Hearings before the Committee on Ways and Means, U.S. House of Representatives, 93d Cong., 1st sess. on H.R. 6767, The Trade Reform Act of 1973 (Washington, D.C.: U.S. Government Printing Office, 1973), pp. 607-58.

102. Ibid., p. 639.

103. Ibid., p. 640.

104. Ibid., p. 642.

105. Ibid., p. 643.

106. Statement of Lee L. Morgan, President, Caterpillar Tractor Company, in ibid., p. 988.

107. See, for instance, Special Duty Treatment of Repeal of Articles Assembled or Fabricated Abroad, Hearing before the Subcommittee on Trade of the Committee on Ways and Means, U.S. House of Representatives, 94th Cong., 2d sess., March 24, and 25, 1976 (Washington, D.C.: U.S. Government Printing Office, 1976).

108. See the testimony of Andrew J. Biemiller, Director, Department of Legislation, AFL-CIO, To Amend and Extend the Export-Import Bank Act of 1945, Hearings before the Subcommittee on International Trade, Investment and Monetary Policy of the Committee on Banking, Finance and Urban Affairs, 95th Cong., 2d sess., March 13, 15, 16, and 17, 1978 (Washington, D.C.: U.S. Government Printing Office, 1978), pp. 208-32.

109. See Testimony of Lawrence A. Fox, Vice-President for International Economic Affairs, National Association of Manufacturers, in ibid., pp. 267-68.

110. See testimony of William L. Wearly, Chairman and Chief Executive Office, Ingersoll-Rand Co. and Chairman, International Economic Affairs Committee, National Association of Manufacturers, in U.S. Congress, Senate Committee on Commerce, Science, and Transportation, National Export Program, Hearings, 95th Cong., 2d sess. (Washington, D.C.: U.S. Government Printing Office, 1978), pp. 43-71.

111. See, for instance, testimony of Raymond Garcia, Vice
President, Emergency Committee for American Trade, in U.S.
Congress, House Committee on Banking, Finance, and Urban Affairs,
Trade Policy and Protectionism, Hearings before the Subcommittee
on International Trade, Investment, and Monetary Policy of the
Committee on Banking, Finance, and Urban Affairs, 95th Cong., 2d
sess. (Washington, D.C.: U.S. Government Printing Office, 1978),
pp. 28-31.

112. Raymond A. Bauer, Ithiel de Sola Pool, and Lewis
Anthony Dexter, American Business and Public Policy: The Politics
of Foreign Trade (Chicago: Aldine Atherton, 1972), pp. 105-242
and 321-87.

CHAPTER 9

THE EXECUTIVE BRANCH: FROM THE FALL OF BRETTON WOODS TO THE STRAUSS WALTZ

For most of the post-World War II era, it has been the president and not the Congress who has been dominant in setting foreign economic policy. The president's constitutional prerogatives in foreign policy, the ability of presidents to make domestic concessions for foreign policy purposes, and the relative independence of the U.S. economy all enhance presidential authority in international economic affairs.

The Nixon presidency was as active as any in foreign economic policy since the end of World War II. In 1971 the Nixon administration refused to exchange U.S. gold holdings for dollars at the old price of $35 to the ounce. The Bretton Woods system that had ordered international monetary affairs in the postwar period was at an end. At the same time the administration imposed an across-the-board surcharge on U.S. imports. Then there was the quest for detente with the Soviet Union and the political opening to the People's Republic of China. Both initiatives had definite commercial overtones. The boldness of the Nixon administration's domestic economic policies also affected our international economic relations. In 1973 a temporary embargo was placed on soybean exports in an attempt to hold down domestic prices.[1] In the same year the president introduced his Trade Reform Act of 1973, the most far-reaching trade proposal to come from an administration since the Trade Expansion Act of 1962.

The Carter administration has had to face a growing range of international economic problems. Massive trade deficits in 1977 ($31 billion) and 1978 ($35 billion) contributed to a sharp drop in the international value of the dollar. President Carter sought to stabilize the dollar by attacking inflation, one of the underlying causes of dollar stability, but exchange markets did not react favorably to his antiinflationary program. As a result, on November 1, 1978, the administration and the Federal Reserve system adopted a major dollar support program.

The liberalized import relief sections of the Trade Act of 1974 have also forced the president to make a number of trade-related decisions. During the first two years of the Carter presidency, the International Trade Commission has recommended restraints on imports of such widely diverse products as sugar and color televisions. In some cases the president has modified the ITC recommendations and in others rejected them outright.

President Carter has also continued to press for a final agreement at the multilateral trade negotiations in Geneva. Some measure of the importance the president attaches to a successful completion of the current round of trade negotiations can be found in his decision to appoint Robert Strauss as his Special Trade Representative. Prior to President Carter's victory, Strauss had served as chairman of the Democratic party. Although no specialist in trade matters, Strauss was generally viewed as a consummate negotiator who could bring considerable skill to the bargaining table.

The president also ordered a review of current U.S. export policy, and in late September 1978 he announced the first phase of a new export policy to help bring new companies to world export markets. Export potential was also one of the many factors that led President Carter to normalize relations with the People's Republic of China. Since his announcement, a growing number of U.S. firms have announced their intention to pursue the China trade.

Trade matters are likely to weigh heavily in the president's relations with the 96th (1979-80) Congress. On January 4, 1979, he announced his intention to enter into a multilateral trade agreement. Except for cuts in tariffs, the entire agreement must be ratified by the Congress. Before final agreement on this trade agreement can be reached, however, the president must successfully steer through the Congress a renewal of the Treasury's authority to waive application of the countervailing duty law, which expired at the end of 1978 and which the EEC is very anxious to have renewed. Also, the president is unlikely to encounter any diminution in the attempts of individual industries to restrict imports; for example, there still may be an attempt to exempt the textile interests entirely from the purview of the multilateral trade agreement.

THE NIXON YEARS

Administration policy during this period was not focused just on external events. The Nixon administration also kept a clear eye on the Congress. In fact, a reasonable case can be made that support for the Burke-Hartke approach was steadily isolated and accommodated before the administration introduced its own Trade Reform Act in April 1973. Many administration policies were clear responses to interest group demands, while others reflected the changing economic circumstances or the pressures of foreign governments.

The Nixon administration must have been rudely shocked by the fate of its Trade Act of 1969. A modest, essentially housekeeping measure, the Trade Act was radically changed by the Ways and Means Committee. Administration attempts to negotiate voluntary export quotas for man-made fibers and woolens were swept aside by Ways and Means in favor of strict quotas. Similar treatment was extended to shoes. In addition, the Ways-and-Means-written Trade Act of 1970 contained the "Byrnes basket."* If a series of tests related to the increase and level of imports was met, under the Byrnes-basket proposal the Tariff Commission could recommend either tariff or import quota relief for an affected industry. The Byrnes-basket approach differed from the existing escape-clause provisions in a number of ways, most noticeably in the ability of Congress to limit presidential discretion. First, the president could not modify the findings of the Tariff Commission, he could only accept or reject them. Second, unless the president specifically found that the tariff or quotas would be contrary to the national interest, the Congress could override a presidential decision to reject the Tariff Commission recommendations.[2]

Although the Trade Act of 1970 eventually died on the Senate floor, it revealed a good deal about the flexibility of the administration in the trade field. The administration demonstrated a willingness to use its influence with business to advance trade legislation. Nixon threatened to veto the Trade Act of 1970, which contained quotas on the importation of man-made fibers and textiles, if support from the chemical, oil, and textile industries did not emerge for the repeal of the American Selling Price system.[3] Following lengthy and initially unsuccessful negotiations with the Japanese on voluntary textile quotas, the administration finally supported the inclusion of actual textile quotas in the Trade Act of 1970. Previous administrations had instituted quotas on agricultural products and oil, but not since before the first Reciprocal Tariff Act in 1934 had an administration actually advocated legislative quotas on industrial products.

---

*The Byrnes of the "Byrnes basket" was Congressman John W. Byrnes (R-Wis.), the ranking Republican member of the House Ways and Means Committee.

Textile quotas opened the door to the pleas of other industries. Shoes were explicitly added to the list and the Byrnes basket promised some relief to the remainder. To all appearances the Nixon White House emerged somewhat chastened by the whole experience. However, the administration was still faced with an unfulfilled 1968 campaign pledge to provide relief for the textile industry. That promise and still-existing protectionist pressures pushed the administration to continue to pursue attempts at voluntary negotiations. A combination of Nixon's New Economic Policy and some rather blunt intimations of impending import quotas led to the signing of voluntary textile agreements with Japan, Korea, Taiwan, and Hong Kong.[4]

The administration followed a somewhat similar course with regard to steel, another domestic industry suffering from import competition. In the case of steel, however, the Nixon administration could build on a voluntary restraint agreement negotiated by the Johnson administration. The first agreement, however, had not been an unqualified success. Not all foreign producers were covered by the agreement and even those that were exceeded the established limits contemplated for 1971. In addition, there was a tendency for foreign firms to concentrate their exports in certain specialty steels and in particular geographic areas. The Nixon administration succeeded in negotiating a new three-year agreement that encompassed more producers, allowed for a slower rate of growth in imports, specifically limited certain categories of steel imports, and included a pledge that importers would attempt to maintain the past geographic distribution of imports. The agreement had the effect of essentially neutralizing the steel industry in the Burke-Hartke debate.[5]

In retrospect, it is interesting to note that the administration concentrated its attention on instances where a large existing domestic industry might easily become allied with labor in a protectionist push. Neither the steel industry nor the textile industry were dominated by multinational firms, so the tax provisions of Burke-Hartke could not have been counted on to limit support for the bill. In industries such as electronics, where many firms had already relocated abroad, the Nixon administration made no effort at a voluntary restraint approach.

Throughout the 92nd Congress, the Nixon White House also moved to increase the use of a series of administrative actions that brought relief to firms and workers hit by imports. The movement actually started with the activities of a Johnson appointee to the Tariff Commission, Bruce E. Clubb. Based on a reading of the legislative history to the Trade Expansion Act of 1962, Clubb changed the escape clause and adjustment assistance test for injuries caused in "major part" by imports to a "but for" test: "The questions which they (Clubb and fellow commissioner Penelope H. Thunberg) asked themselves in deciding whether or not to grant relief became But for a tariff concession, would imports stand at this level? But for the current level of imports would the domestic producer have suffered injury?"[6]

The result of adopting the "but for" test and a further change in commission personnel led to a marked turnabout in Tariff Commission policy. Prior to 1969 the commission had not approved a single escape-clause or adjustment-assistance petition. From that time until mid 1971, however, the commission approved 15 petitions and recorded 38 tie votes on other petitions. Ties are broken by presidential decision.[7] The administration also moved to speed and tighten the application of the antidumping law. An existing trend toward more use of the countervailing duty law was continued during the Nixon years.

During much of the Burke-Hartke period the administration also put renewed emphasis on the stimulation of exports. Early in the Nixon presidency the administration turned to tax incentives. Whatever its actual impact on exports or capital flows, the then current U.S. law favored direct foreign investment over export earnings by taxing the profits of foreign subsidiaries only when repatriated. At the same time, U.S. membership in GATT prevented most forms of export subsidies. To slip between this particular Scylla and Charybdis of tax law and treaty commitments, the Nixon administration proposed the creation of Domestic International Sales Corporations. If U.S. companies conducted their export business through a DISC (which could be wholly owned by the exporting country), a portion of their export earnings would be subject to a permanent tax deferral. Although devaluation itself could be expected to act as a stimulus to U.S. exports, the Nixon administration did not alter its stance in favor of the DISC. Included in the House-passed version of the eventually unsuccessful Trade Act of 1970, the DISC provision finally entered the tax law as part of the Revenue Act of 1971.

Following a second devaluation in February 1973, the administration launched a governmentwide effort to increase exports. Studies covered a wide range of subjects, including expanded direct promotion abroad and various tax incentives.[8] Again, the Nixon administration was willing to use its considerable powers to push industry in a desired direction. The National Journal recounts an incident in which the administration used its influence with a foreign government to help secure a contract for a U.S. multinational in return for a pledge that the equipment for the project would be exported from the United States.[9]

Voluntary agreements, administrative practices, and even export promotion were fraught with difficulties. Voluntary agreements were constantly subject to pressure from new producers or the economic discontent of foreign signators. In the case of administrative practices, much of the renewed activity depended on the then current membership of the Tariff Commission. In any case, the bulk of the Tariff Commission findings were in the area of adjustment assistance rather than actual protection. Many workers and firms viewed government training and funds as burial, not adjustment, assistance. Export promotion proved to be a lengthy process and the advent of flexible exchange rates made the use of various export subsidies somewhat problematic.

Perhaps the most daring and certainly the most important of the Nixon initiatives in trade was involved with international monetary affairs. Faced with the prospect of massive balance of payments deficits and a rapidly eroding trade position, in August 1971 the Nixon administration had taken the almost-never-discussed step of closing the gold window. The Bretton Woods system built on the fixed value of the dollar was swept aside in favor of devaluation. By joining an import surtax to a floating dollar and a determination not to return too quickly to the old monetary order, the Nixon administration set in motion forces that were almost sure to undercut the Burke-Hartke Bill. And they did it all a month before labor had crystallized its position into final legislative form.

Conventional wisdom suggests it takes between one and two years for a devaluation to have its full impact. It demands a certain period of time for new contracts to replace the old, for purchasers to turn to domestic sources of supply, and for foreign consumers to accept a new source of cheaper goods. Interestingly, the Nixon administration waited for one year and nine months before introducing its Trade Reform Act in April 1973. Although it is tempting to conclude that the initial devaluation in 1971 was carefully tailored to the administration's timetable for trade legislation, immediate financial pressures seem to have been the principal cause.*

During much of 1971 and all of 1972 there was continual speculation about the state of the administration's trade bill. The administration engaged in a series of negotiations with key members of Capitol Hill and provided a number of briefings for congressional staffers. Nixon made Secretary of the Treasury George Shultz chairman of the cabinet-level Council on Economic Policy at the close of 1972. Almost immediately Shultz began to press for trade legislation. Again the administration turned to financial policy, this time with trade matters very clearly in mind.

---

*In a June 1976 interview with a former administration official who was central to the formulation of the administration's trade policy, financial matters rather than long-range trade strategy were cited as the basis for the first devaluation.

On February 12, 1973, Shultz announced a further 10 percent devaluation of the dollar against major foreign currencies and made public the administration's intention to seek broad trade negotiating authority. At the same time, Shultz indicated the administration's intention to end controls on U.S. investments abroad by December 31, 1974.[10] The plan was to reduce the U.S. trade deficit "without touching off a trade war or opening the protectionist floodgates at home."[11] At the time, the U.S. trade deficit was again mounting. The administration trade people hoped that the second devaluation would at least have the numbers moving in the right direction by the fall when House consideration was likely.[12] By the time the House finished its deliberations in December 1973, the U.S. merchandise trade account had registered a welcome $578 million surplus in the previous quarter. The trade group got all it hoped for and a good deal more.

The Nixon administration was feeling considerably more sanguine about the prospects for trade legislation. President Nixon had been reelected in a landslide of historic proportions. The Democratic party had emerged from its Miami convention with a number of serious divisions. The remnants of the old-line party bosses, much of the new South, and a good part of big labor were anything but enamoured of Democratic candidate George McGovern. These divisions persisted in the bitter wake of the electoral debacle. George Meany had broken with long-standing precedent and refused to endorse the Democratic candidate. He instructed the constituent unions to take a similar stance of aggressive neutrality. Following the election results, Meany was frequently reported to be in the company of either the president or Secretary of the Treasury Shultz. Formerly a secretary of labor, Shultz was widely reported to have a special rapport with labor's principal spokesman, George Meany. Press reports of a Nixon administration honeymoon with labor received wide circulation.

Shortly after the announcement of the second devaluation, Nixon met the AFL-CIO Executive Council "during the council's regular midwinter meeting in Bal Harbour, Florida."[13] At a press conference following the meeting, Meany "spoke favorably of the President's ideas on trade but . . . stopped short of endorsing the Administration's approach, since the White House still had not disclosed details."[14] Meany indicated that the AFL-CIO still backed Burke-Hartke but would be willing "to negotiate on specific details." Nixon termed the meeting "very constructive. . . ."[15] It began to look as though the president had just belled a very important labor cat.

Even before the second devaluation and the Nixon-Meany meeting, Senator Hartke had indicated a willingness to compromise. In a January 26, 1973, speech before the Electronic Industries Association, Hartke suggested that both the quota and tax provisions were subject to discussion. In this atmosphere the administration moved to introduce its long-awaited trade package. It included a few surprises.16 The president sought broad tariff-cutting authority for the upcoming round of international trade negotiations, asked for new authority to deal with nontariff barriers, and requested a general loosening of requirements to qualify for relief in the face of increased imports.

When the Nixon team did finally move to introduce trade legislation, there was some attempt to cement the relationship with labor. Instead of introducing a trade bill in isolation, the administration presented it as a package that included tax, unemployment, and pension reform. Somewhat surprisingly, the administration sought to move away from one of the principal innovations of the Trade Expansion Act of 1962: trade adjustment assistance. Instead, they adopted the Shultz view that jobless benefits should be improved regardless of whether the particular job was lost because of increased imports, technological innovation, or a change of tastes. In place of adjustment assistance the administration proposed federal standards for unemployment insurance (a long-time labor goal).

As it turned out, the package proved to be unpalatable to big labor. The tax reform elements were dismissed as being extremely modest proposals to limit the deferral privilege on foreign-source income.17 Labor roundly criticized the pension reform as being nothing more than a mild reworking of the administration's "rule of 50" proposal that had been presented in the last Congress.* Even the proposals for improved unemployment compensation were found seriously wanting.

Whether it was a serious miscalculation on the part of the Nixon administration or an exercise in postelection hubris, the much-rumored alliance with labor had foundered very early in the game. As far as big labor was concerned, it remained Burke-Hartke or nothing.18

But a number of tides were beginning to turn against the Burke-Hartke advocates. A variety of administrative initiatives, ranging from a beefed-up Treasury staff to process antidumping complaints to devaluation, had acted to erode support for Burke-Hartke. By mid 1973 congressional interest in the economic issues raised by Burke-Hartke had begun to wane. In part this shift in congressional

---

*The "rule of 50" required that a combination of an employee's years of service and age be equal to 50 before the vesting of pension rights became mandatory.

interest dated from another of the administration's trade initiatives.
Trade was to be one of the many specific areas in which detente was
to bear mutually acceptable fruit. Congress was quick to respond
to the generally warmer climate with a number of proposals to limit
or amend the existing ban on extending most-favored-nation (MFN)
status to the Soviet Union.[19] Some bills would have granted the
president authority to extend MFN to any country with which we had
diplomatic relations. Others focused on specific communist countries.

The entire picture for East-West trade in general and trade
with the Soviet Union in particular was clouded, however, with a
growing controversy over emigration by Soviet Jewry. The long-
standing Soviet restrictions on immigration were suddenly supple-
mented by an extremely high exit tax that allegedly reflected the costs
incurred by the state in educating the emigre. The combination of
the new exit tax and the MFN proposal virtually invited attack from
an increasingly militant Jewish movement in the United States. In
October 1972, Senator Jackson proposed an amendment that would
prohibit the extension of MFN to any country applying other than
nominal fees for the exit of its citizens.* The Jackson amendment
eventually garnered some 73 cosponsors, a rare display of Senate
support. A similar measure was introduced as a separate bill by
Ways and Means Chairman Wilbur Mills at the start of the 93rd Congress.† Despite administration protestations and extensive lobbying,
the free-emigration provision for MFN status became a part of the
trade law that eventually passed Congress in December 1974.‡

The importance of all this for the AFL-CIO and other supporters
of Burke-Hartke was that congressional attention was now focused
on an issue that was largely peripheral to questions of foreign trade
and investment. Although labor became a strong supporter of the
amendment—both on the merits and for tactical reasons—there was
little opportunity to recapture the trade and investment initiative.
The shift in emphasis was so intense that the two days of House
debate on the Ways and Means version of the Trade Reform Act of
1973 dealt almost entirely with the emigration question.[20]

---

*The amendment was proposed to the East-West Trade Exchange
Act of 1971 (S. 2620 of the 92nd Congress).

†The first of a number of House bills was actually introduced
by Congressman Daniels (H.R. 151, 93rd Congress).

‡In the Ways and Means Committee, Congressman Vanik introduced the MFN restriction as an amendment to the administration's
proposed Trade Reform Act of 1973. The policy became widely known
on Capitol Hill as the Jackson-Vanik amendment.

Equally important to the consideration of the trade and many other types of legislation was the Watergate scandal. For much of the period, official and unofficial Washington alike were caught up in a political soap opera of near epic proportions. The pace of legislation was slowed, the opportunities to garner national attention for even major proposals were severely limited. Space in the national press was virtually devoured by Watergate. By comparison, the trade and investment problems of organized labor lacked both novelty and urgency. Almost as demanding of congressional time and attention was the sudden success of the Organization of Petroleum Exporting Countries in raising the price of oil and the subsequent oil embargo by most of the Arab members of OPEC.

This is not to say that labor did not attempt to adapt its strategy to changed conditions.[21] They became strong supporters of the Jackson-Vanik amendment and joined those who questioned the desirability of delegating new trade-negotiating authority to an already bloated Executive Branch. But in making this leap, labor left its economic case to one side. In the end, the administration, under the tutelage of President Ford, got much of what the Nixon White House had sought.

With the passage of the Trade Act of 1974 at the very close of the 93rd Congress, the debate on trade and investment was focused on quite different issues. International monetary reform, the recycling of petrodollars, the question of foreign direct investment in the United States, and the possibility of a multiplying number of commodity cartels captured the lion's share of that part of congressional attention devoted to international economic questions.

Following his success with the Trade Act of 1974, President Ford prepared no major legislative initiatives in the trade and investment field. Some progress was made at the multilateral trade negotiations in Geneva and in trade discussions with the developing world. Amendments to the Articles of Agreement of the International Monetary Fund did include new surveillance powers for the IMF over exchange rate manipulations for trade purposes. But for the most part the Ford administration's attention was focused on the difficult economic job of bringing the United States out of the 1974-75 recession.

THE CARTER YEARS

President Carter entered the White House committed to reorganize the government, reform the tax code, develop a new energy policy, and present a host of other programs. In the early days of his administration the Congress was presented with a virtual flood of legislative proposals.

In terms of the economy, the president continued to emphasize management of the recovery from the 1974-75 recession and then gradually shifted his focus to controlling inflationary pressures. Record trade deficits in 1977 and 1978 and the unsteady condition of the dollar on foreign exchange markets began to preoccupy the administration. With regard to trade questions, the administration pushed for completion of the multilateral trade negotiations, continued discussions with developing countries over commodity agreements, and announced a new export policy.

The liberalized import relief provisions of the Trade Act of 1974 have forced the Carter administration to make a number of individual decisions on trade restraint cases. Much of the pressure has appeared in the guise of escape-(from import competition) clause cases.[22] Petitions for relief are filed with the International Trade Commission, which conducts an investigation to determine whether or not imports have been a "substantial cause" of injury to the workers or firms in question. If the ITC finds that imports have in fact been a substantial cause of injury and recommends import relief, the president must implement the recommendation within 60 days or explain to the Congress why he has taken some alternative action (or no action at all).

For the most part the administration has adopted a strategy of selective accommodation of protectionist pressures. For instance, in the case of shoes (nonrubber footwear), the ITC found injury and recommended higher tariffs on imported shoes once imports reached a certain level (a tariff quota). Instead, the president chose to negotiate quotas (orderly marketing agreements) with South Korea and Taiwan. Together, Korea and Taiwan had accounted for almost the entire increase in import penetration that took place between 1974 and 1976. In addition, the president provided the shoe industry with an expanded form of trade adjustment assistance.

The question of color television sets was also the subject of considerable congressional pressure[23] and of an ITC recommendation for a 20 percent increase in import duties that would be gradually phased down over a five-year period. The president, however, chose to negotiate an orderly marketing agreement with Japan, which accounted for about 80 percent of all imports. This agreement with Japan, however, did not provide as much import relief as hoped. Imports of color televisions from Korea and Taiwan started to take the place of Japanese imports. Subsequently the president negotiated orderly marketing agreements with Taiwan and Korea as well.[24]

The orderly marketing approach to trade restraint had several aspects that may have appealed to President Carter. First, it allowed him to target his response to domestic pressures for import relief. In some cases only one country need be involved. Second, because these agreements were voluntary rather than unilateral actions, the president avoided the GATT requirement to "pay compensation" to affected parties when tariffs are raised or mandatory quotas imposed. Compensation ordinarily takes the form of lowered tariffs on other imports from the affected countries and could result in triggering more domestic pressures for import restraint. Third, by not raising tariff levels, the president avoided an immediate increase in the price level.

President Carter also encouraged domestic industries to use existing law with regard to dumping and other unfair trade practices. Again in response to steel industry complaints, the administration first established a task force to study the administration of the antidumping law and then adopted a system of reference prices geared to the most efficient Japanese steel producers. Imports priced below the reference prices would automatically trigger a dumping investigation by the Treasury.

The policy of selective accommodation has also extended to the multilateral trade negotiations. The administration has emphasized its intent to open new doors for U.S. agricultural exports, and there is some evidence that they have done so.[25] Steel is another industry that has sought extensive import relief. Legislation had been introduced to exempt steel from any tariff reductions in the multilateral trade negotiations unless there was some type of international steel agreement.[26] Perhaps as a result of the congressional pressure, the administration worked to establish an international steel committee as part of the Organization for Economic Cooperation and Development. A section on this steel committee was included in the outline of a tentative trade agreement that the president sent to the Congress on January 4, 1979.[27]

There had also been a serious attempt to exempt the textile and apparel industries from any tariff reductions in the multilateral trade talks. In fact, the attempt was serious enough to reach the president's desk, where it was vetoed.[28] Press reports in early 1979, however, suggested that the president had been able to reach some understanding with the textile and apparel groups.[29]

The preceding sections suggest the range of powers an administration has in influencing legislation in the trade and investment field. From the decision to improve enforcement of existing laws to the sweeping alteration of an international financial system, the administration can act to create an economic climate favorable to its various ends. Its powers, however, are often constrained by the very number of goals an administration must pursue and are mitigated by the chance occurrences of events often beyond its control. But despite the political battles over detente, the tumult created by the Watergate scandal, or the need of a former governor of Georgia to feel his way with

Congress, the Executive Branch seems to have gotten most of what it wanted in terms of trade legislation and thus far to have blunted the labor drive to control the flow of goods, capital, and technology.

NOTES

1. The Ford administration later admitted that the embargo "undermined the confidence of our foreign customers." See International Economic Report of the President (Washington, D.C.: U.S. Government Printing Office, 1975), p. 20.
2. For more details on the Byrnes basket, see Frank V. Fowlkes, "Business Report/House Turns to Protectionism Despite Arm-twisting by Nixon Trade Experts," National Journal, August 22, 1970, pp. 1818 and 1850.
3. Ibid., p. 1816.
4. For a brief discussion of the evolution of voluntary quotas from campaign pledge to final signing, see Gerald M. Meir, Problems of Trade Policy (New York: Oxford University Press, 1973), pp. 92-179.
5. For a more detailed discussion of the voluntary steel agreement, see Richard S. Frank, "Trade Report/Consumers Union Attack on Steel Quotas Could Release Protectionist Pressures," National Journal, July 7, 1972, pp. 1229-1326.
6. Frank V. Fowlkes, "Economic Report/Administrative Escape Valves Relieve Pressures of Imports on Domestic Industries," National Journal, July 24, 1971, p. 1547.
7. Ibid.
8. Richard S. Frank, "Trade Report/Administration Seeks Incentives to Spur Exports in Drive to Correct Huge Trade Deficit," National Journal, April 21, 1973, p. 566.
9. Ibid., p. 561.
10. Richard S. Frank, "Economic Report/Shultz Takes Charge as United States Presses for Monetary, Trade Reforms," National Journal, March 10, 1973, pp. 352-58.
11. Frank, "Trade Report/Administration Seeks Incentives," op. cit., p. 557.
12. June 1976 interview with a former administration official actively involved in trade strategy.
13. Charles Culhane, "Trade Report/Labor Shifts Tactics on Administration Bill, Seeks Concessions on Imports, Multinationals," National Journal, July 28, 1973, p. 1092.
14. Ibid.
15. Ibid.

16. The text of administration bill, H.R. 6767, can be found in Hearings before the Committee on Ways and Means, U.S. House of Representatives, 93d Cong., 1st sess., on H.R. 6767, The Trade Reform Act of 1973, Part 1 (Washington, D.C.: U.S. Government Printing Office, 1973), pp. 4-100.

17. According to the National Journal, at one time the administration actually considered a provision for full repeal of the deferral of tax liability on foreign source income but chose not to. Richard S. Frank, "Trade Report/Administration Asks for Trade Sanctions Against Balance of Payments Offenders," National Journal, March 31, 1973, p. 472.

18. See Charles Culhane, "Labor Report/Labor Readies Stronger Jobless-Pay Plan, Rejects Version Offered With Nixon Trade Bill," National Journal, June 9, 1973, pp. 821-30.

19. The ban was contained in Section 231 of the Trade Expansion Act of 1962, 19 U.S.C. 1861.

20. See Congressional Record, December 10, 1973, H10915-H11002 and December 11, 1973, H11027-72.

21. See, for instance, Charles Culhane, "Trade Report/Labor Shifts Tactics on Administration Bill, Seeks Concessions on Imports, Multinationals," National Journal, July 28, 1973, pp. 1091-98.

22. The Trade Act of 1974, 93-618, Sec. 201.

23. See, for instance, "The Implications of Our International Trade Policy for American Business and Consumers," U.S. Congress, House Committee on Banking, Finance, and Urban Affairs, "The Implications of our International Trade Policy for American Business Consumers," Hearings, before the Subcommittee on International Trade, Investment, and Monetary Policy of the Committee on Banking, Finance, and Urban Affairs, 95th Cong., 1st sess. (Washington, D.C.: U.S. Government Printing Office, 1977).

24. The president did not always reject the higher tariff approach. In the case of high-carbon ferrochromium, he adopted a minimum import price approach under which a tariff of 4 cents a pound is imposed when imports enter for less than 38 cents a pound. There was congressional interest in this case, but it appeared to be as much directed toward the political and racial situation in South Africa, the principal foreign supplier, as it was to the impact on the domestic industry. See "Import Relief to the U.S. High-Carbon Ferrochromium Industry," Hearing before the Subcommittee on Trade of the Committee on Ways and Means, U.S. House of Representatives, 95th Cong., 2d sess., March 22, 1978 (Washington, D.C.: U.S. Government Printing Office, 1978).

25. See "International Trade Agreements," Federal Register 44, no. 5 (January 8, 1979):1950-54. Bilateral negotiations with

202 / TRADE, TAXES, & TRANSNATIONALS

Japan have also yielded some benefits to U.S. citrus and beef exporters. See the testimony of Robert Strauss before the Joint Economic Committee, January 25, 1979.

26. See the Steel Trade Negotiations Act (S. 3058), introduced by Senator John Heinz on May 11, 1978. Representative Charles Carney introduced a similar measure (H.R. 10039).

27. See "International Trade Agreements," op. cit.

28. See discussion in Chapter 2.

29. See "Strauss, Textiles Reach Agreement," Washington Post, January 19, 1979, p. A2.

CHAPTER 10

SOME TENTATIVE CONCLUSIONS
AND A LOOK AT THE MAKING
OF FUTURE FOREIGN
ECONOMIC POLICY

SCOPE OF THE STUDY

The early part of this foreign trade and investment study was devoted to contrasting the relative importance of economic events and economic theory in predicting the behavior of major interest groups. The positions and actions of both big labor and big business were tied to the nature of the Bretton Woods system, the principal changes in the world economy, and a series of specific indexes, including the rate of unemployment and the balance of merchandise trade.

The study also encompassed a selective review of foreign trade and investment theory. The legislative battles over trade and investment issues provide a rich opportunity to assess both the descriptive and predictive powers of economic theory with regard to big business and big labor. Although economic theory proved to be a useful and insightful guide to major interest group behavior, there were still a number of apparent anomalies. And there remained the possibility that the theory could be used to rationalize a position taken for a variety of other reasons rather than as a guide to economic self-interest. The study of how Congress deals with trade, taxes, and the transnationals is also rich in suggesting how international economic issues are raised before the Congress, what economics are brought to bear on the debate, and how Congress moves to a decision on a major issue.

In focusing on the clash of major interest groups in the congressional forum, the study contains a number of tentative lessons about the influence of the national press, the continuing power of administrative initiative, and the impact of congressional structure and personalities.

Despite the richness of the ongoing congressional debate over foreign trade and investment, a final summing up must stress the tenuousness of any results. For from the start, the study had been subjected to the liabilities of the case approach. Generalizations are perforce more in the nature of hypotheses for further testing rather than firm conclusions within well-defined confidence limits. To the admitted limitations of the case approach, one must add the complexities of the Congress, 535 distinct individuals, subject to a host of political and economic pressures.

Finally, this study of congressional behavior has kept its focus more on issues—how they were raised and how they were considered—rather than on the exercise of power in a final decision. The stress is more on the rationales of the interest groups and the ratiocination of the Congress—Congress weighing the evidence rather than the political advantage. Even with all these limitations, the conclusions are there. Tentative and yet suggestive, the congressional debate on foreign trade and investment does provide a number of lessons.

ECONOMIC EVENTS AND THE INTEREST GROUPS

The structure of the Bretton Woods system certainly held the seeds of difficulty for the U.S. economy. As possessor of the key currency in what became the dollar-gold standard, the United States was under constant and considerable pressure to maintain the value of the dollar. At the same time, the initial need for increased world liquidity reduced the importance of the United States maintaining a balance in its international payments position. The specific rules for international trading also favored the recovering economies of Western Europe and Japan. For long periods of time, the West European nations were allowed to maintain a series of restrictions on trade that were designed to preserve their payments position. When Japan acceded to GATT, a number of European nations maintained quotas against many Japanese products. The United States did not and became the natural focus of Japanese exporters.

During the late 1950s and early 1960s, the world economy underwent a major transformation. Western Europe and Japan emerged as important industrial competitors of the United States. The steady increase in U.S. foreign direct investment tended to quicken. The multinational enterprise—more often than not a U.S.-based firm—posed particular problems for the national labor movements in the industrial countries. By the late 1960s the trade pressures on U.S. labor were reflected in a number of specific indexes. The persistent U.S. payments deficits were now accompanied by a steady decline in the U.S. merchandise trade account.

For specific products, imports actually came to dominate markets formerly supplied by domestic producers.

It is tempting to see the labor break with the free trade coalition as solely a response to a series of economic pressures. But the stance adopted by the AFL-CIO also indicated a new perception of economic self-interest that rested on far more than a year or two of bad trade figures and a sharp increase in the level of unemployment among manufacturing workers. An alternative explanation for labor's break and the business response to it could lie in economic theory.

ECONOMIC THEORY AND THE INTEREST GROUPS

An opening look at the Heckscher-Ohlin theory did suggest a possible divergence of interest between capital and labor. Both the factor equalization theorem and the Stolper-Samuelson theorem would provide possible grounds for labor either to resist an increase in free trade or to seek a reduction in the current level of trade.

Despite the rather large leap from a two-factor world to a legislative contest between the AFL-CIO and the bulk of big (and usually multinational) business, the implications of the HO theory do seem roughly consistent with current interest group behavior. However, a look at the post-World War II era reveals that the divergence of labor and business in the international sphere is of relatively recent vintage. Why the change? No doubt part of the answer can be found in the fact that the industrially intact United States had a favorable balance of trade in almost all sectors of production. As industrial competitors began to appear on the scene there was a steady change in the U.S. comparative advantage that was exaggerated by the rigidities of the Bretton Woods system.

Relaxing the usual factor mobility assumptions that accompany a HO approach adds considerable explanatory and descriptive power. The domestic immobility of labor implied the potential loss of human capital and certainly was a partial motivation for the AFL-CIO. In addition, geographic immobility could entail not only the loss of a job but also a considerable loss of actual and potential wealth. The closing of a factory in a small company town could lead to a severe drop in property values, the elimination or reduction of pension rights, and the loss of seniority standing. Even for the mobile, non-property owning, unskilled worker, the loss of a job may be a tremendous burden if there are no alternative opportunities available. One must also keep in mind that some labor will be heavily dependent on the industries with a comparative advantage. In part, this may account for the differing positions of the United Auto Workers and the AFL-CIO.

Allowing for the international mobility of capital, also excluded in the usual formulation of the HO theory, is just as productive as admitting the domestic immobility of labor. Throughout the post-World War II era, large international flows of capital, technology, and organizational skills were the order of the day. The classical substitution assumptions advanced by Hufbauer and Adler certainly contain the seeds for economic disagreements between labor and capital in terms of growth, stabilization policy, and income distribution.

It is also important to keep in mind the apparent differential mobility of capital between industries. The electronics industry adapted to foreign imports by investing abroad, while the shoe industry bent its efforts to obtaining some sort of administrative or legislative protection against imports. The much smaller size and therefore more limited financial resources of the average shoe producer no doubt played an important role in the import strategy adopted by the industry.

Further explanatory power can be garnered by admitting a variety of market imperfections, particularly government intrusion and the widespread existence of oligopoly. Vernon's product cycle theory and Caves's emphasis on sector-specific expertise do much to describe the economic interests of the multinationals.

With all the evident insight accumulated from existing economic theory, there remain some serious difficulties in the use of theory to explain economic behavior. First, the entire foreign trade and investment study takes place within the confines of interest group analysis. But the two-factor world that provides such a nice fit with the business-labor confrontation would also provide an adequate framework for a class-based approach. Second, there is the contrasting behavior of the United Auto Workers and the International Association of Machinists. Although the differences between the two can be explained by differing traditions, distinct institutional loyalties, and the varying importance of Canadian members, none of these factors is implicit in the economic theory of trade and investment. Third, the long-standing unity of labor and business as major components of the free trade alliance does not flow clearly from the HO theory. Fourth, labor's very definite opposition to the export of technology was not obviously consistent with the otherwise very helpful product cycle theory. Fifth, the persistent silence of both major interest groups with regard to devaluation remains rather startling, although possible explanations do exist in labor's search for stability and a widespread acceptance of the Bretton Woods structure by business. Sixth, the two-sector approach ignores the importance of agriculture and does not account for the fact that major agricultural organizations were not active in the Burke-Hartke dispute. And seventh, theory itself cannot readily determine whether theory was used to rationalize, to explain, or to actually determine a course of action.

As one moves closer to the specifics of a legislative battle, the predictive powers of economic theory decline even more. Economic theory rather definitely abstracted from the questions of intrainterest-group policies and the manner in which economic positions were first formed and then presented to the Congress. Interest groups made their case in a variety of ways. Both labor and business commissioned studies and made economic analyses. Business was particularly effective at presenting its case in the national daily press. Although big labor put business on the defensive, a series of business-funded studies seemed to have put the "burden of going forward" back on the labor movement.

In building support for a position on foreign trade and investment legislation, the AFL-CIO was faced with a number of conflicting pressures. On the one hand, they had to forge a policy that was acceptable to the bulk of constituent unions and would still meet the needs of unions that had felt the brunt of import competition. On the other hand, they had to craft a piece of legislation that would find some degree of acceptance on Capitol Hill. Burke-Hartke went a fair distance to garner union support, but it never met the expected success in the Congress.

No doubt labor faced a host of obstacles in pressing its case. The general climate of the times still favored free trade and a post-war vision that had grown out of U.S. economic hegemony. Protectionism was still an ugly word to many policy makers, and despite labor's efforts it was never able to shake the label. Stock phrases such as "fair trade" and the "sliding door" were never enough to avoid the nagging charge of protectionism.

The business counteroffensive was launched by a number of separate groups with overlapping memberships. The single major advocate of broad-based restrictions on trade and investment was the AFL-CIO. Although the UAW was even more stringent in its proposals for controlling capital flows, until the 1973 debacle in domestic auto sales the UAW remained opposed to import quotas.

A series of studies that sought to rebut the charges against the multinationals generally received favorable comment in the press. They raised doubt in the minds of the congressional jury. Labor never succeeded in adequately rebutting the studies nor in presenting its own data. Therefore, economic events were central to labor's change of position on foreign trade and investment questions. The pinching shoe had affected the rank and file and the AFL-CIO leadership was warned of rising imports, plant closings, and the growth of investment abroad. But the individual economic events

did not determine the contours of the Burke-Hartke Bill. Nor did
the events themselves provide a theory to guide labor in a new direction.

With all its limitations—the inability to explain all facets of
interest group behavior and the abstraction from often vital legislative detail—economic theory proved to be a useful tool. Existing
economic theory demonstrated the likelihood that there will be enduring differences between labor and business in the field of trade and
investment. It also provided a framework with which to assess the
differing positions of big labor and big business.

Economic events seem most important in focusing a group's
or an organization's attention on a particular set of problems. They
are often an acute predictor of how intensely a group will pursue a
particular issue. Theory may not adequately explain the timing of
events or the weighting of a group's priorities, but it can provide
real insight into the nature of an interest group battle. Although
theory can be used simply to rationalize behavior, it can also guide
it. To some extent the labor case also acted as a challenge to the
current state of the economic art. The impact of the multinational
corporation on the nature of comparative advantage is not a settled
question. The immediate foreign sale of new technology may change
the implications of the product cycle theory for domestic production
and employment. But the existing theory proved to be useful in both
explaining interest group behavior and in clarifying avenues that
demanded further research.

THE USE OF ECONOMICS IN THE CONGRESSIONAL
CONSIDERATION OF FOREIGN TRADE AND
INVESTMENT ISSUES

In considering any piece of legislation, Congress listens with
many ears. Angry constituents, old friends, personal and committee
staffs, party leaders, advocates for the major interest groups, leading economic columnists, various representatives of the administration, and the occasional voice of the national press. With regard to
the Burke-Hartke Bill, certain segments of the Congress took some
initiatives of their own. For instance, Senator Ribicoff's subcommittee asked the Tariff Commission for a lengthy study on many of
the issues raised by Burke-Hartke and solicited papers from interested parties. Although it came rather late in the Burke-Hartke
game, the Senate Labor and Public Welfare Committee did commission a study on the relationship of the multinational firm to the national
interest.

And there were the hearings, volumes and volumes of hearings in both the House and the Senate. A quick look at the index for the Ways and Means Committee hearings on the Trade Reform Act of 1973 reveals the range of interests that were heard. The hearings did constitute an extensive opportunity for the committees with the actual legislative responsibility to receive testimony and question witnesses. But with all the pages of testimony, with the sometimes lengthy, often barbed, interchange between witnesses and individual congressmen, there seems to be so much missing. Nothing is so striking as the relative disuse of economics, even in the formal evaluation of a bill that was fraught with economic complexities. Devaluation, the aspect of President Nixon's New Economic Policy that did the most to change the complexion of our foreign economic policy, was virtually unmentioned. For every economist of note who received a hearing before the committee, there were 20 advocates of special interests mingled with pages of desultory talk about the death of the theory of comparative advantage.

In the years since the passage of the Trade Act of 1974, there has been a growing awareness of and interest in the international economy. The advent of flexible exchange rates and the emergence of a persistent inflation have brought every constituent into contact with the rising prices of foreign goods. The arcane workings of the foreign exchange markets have rudely intruded into the family budget.

The creation of an active trade subcommittee in the House and the larger trade staffs on both the Senate Finance Committee and the House Ways and Means Committee have resulted in more congressionally inspired analyses of trade problems. The role of economics has begun to grow, but at a slow pace. In noting the neglect of economics, the author does not mean to suggest that "facts and figures" do not appear in committee deliberations, floor debate, or the occasional speech, for they do. But the figures cited are more often those chosen to buttress a position, not those used to reach a conclusion.

The basic source of much foreign trade data is the government. But the statistics are often dated. For instance, the most recent figures for U.S. direct foreign investment date from 1966. Even worse, government statistics are often nonexistent. Any attempt to relate foreign trade to domestic employment is compounded by the fact that data on exports, imports, and domestic production are not strictly comparable.[1] Various private groups may attempt to fill a void left by the government statisticians, but their efforts must be discounted for a number of reasons. The private data-gathering surveys are frequently careless of statistical bias; they may in fact be structured with political bias in mind. Only some questions are

asked and the answers are neither thoroughly analyzed or clearly
reported. Finally, the form in which the data reach the individual
member or the congressional committee often make them unusable.
The data are seldom related to the major decisions each committee
member must make.

Despite the disuse and misuse of data, one would expect that
economic analysis would play a large role in congressional deliberations. Certainly the conventional wisdom suggests that when "political" considerations force a particular decision, at least the policy
maker knows full well what he or she is doing. The textbook view
of political reality portrays a host of interventions with the market
system. Some are portrayed as rational, others as politically motivated, but the interventions are always made with wide open, economic eyes. In sum, analysis precedes action. Whether or not this
reflects reality as seen in the Treasury or Commerce Departments,
it has little place in a description of international economic decision
making on Capitol Hill. Economic analysis is little used and frequently not sought.

What might explain this dismal neglect of the dismal science?
The author has no definitive answers but can suggest a number of
hypotheses that may provide partial illumination and precipitate
further research. First, neither of the principal parties to the battle
over foreign trade and investment stated their case in clear, economic terms. In both instances, considerable "intellectual reconstruction" is required to put the dispute in an economic perspective.
In part this reflected the need to communicate with their own membership and in part it was a product of their need to communicate with
the Congress.

Second, economic analysis frequently follows events. At the
time, much of the economic commentary on Burke-Hartke consisted
of poorly done surveys, editorials filled with aphorisms for or against
comparative advantage, essays on the political implications of protectionism, or vague exhortations to increase the level of productivity.
Although existing economic theory could lend considerable insight
into the debate on direct foreign investment and the changing nature
of U.S. trade, there were few attempts to treat either labor or business in this light.[2] In a 1973 volume delimiting areas of needed
research, C. Fred Bergsten called for detailed studies on many of
the issues that were raised by the Burke-Hartke Bill.[3] But Congress
had long since set Burke-Hartke aside for more pressing problems.

Third, economic policy analysis comes in a bewildering range
of qualities. A particular problem may be treated in everything from
the American Economic Review to the editorial pages of the New York
Daily News. Except for the rare congressman who holds a doctorate
in economics, separating the wheat from the chaff—or even the wheat

from the rye—can be an impossible task. The mix of value judgments
and theoretical assumptions that make up most analyses often leaves
the lay reader with nothing but growing skepticism for the dismal
science. Congressional debate over foreign trade and investment
issues did stimulate a good deal of research on the impact of current
trade and investment policies on the U.S. economy, but with results
that would buttress both labor's and the multinational's position.
The new research findings could hardly be called conclusive. Reflecting the complexity of the questions involved, the fatal flaw of much
academic advice to policy makers is that it so often ends in a call
for yet more research.

Fourth, Congressmen do not always find economic analysis
responsive to their own needs and preoccupations. Congressmen
are not economists by profession. Senator Paul Douglas was a noted
exception to this rule. Clarence Long (D-Md.), Les Aspin (D-Md.),
and Joseph Fisher (D-Va.) are among the small group of professional
economists currently serving in the House. In fact, professional
academics are few and far between in the halls of Congress. It is
men of affairs, particularly lawyers, who dominate congressional
circles. Trained as advocates, schooled in an ancient method of
ferreting out the truth, taught to see themselves as competent general-
ists, lawyers tend to view economists with a mix of wary diffidence
and smoldering skepticism. Congressmen, after all, are vitally
concerned with who wins and loses. They may talk about the national
interest, but there is little concern for a "national welfare function."
The time horizon of economists and congressmen is often quite different. For most congressmen the long run is almost always somewhere
before the next election. The lawyer/congressman is accustomed to
adversaries having their own expert witnesses. And congressmen
will frequently cite economic arguments or economic data to support
an adversary position—a position that may actually have been taken
because of political pressure, loyalty, or some other reasons. Nor
can it be forgotten that for many congressmen politics is a career.
Their ambitions for higher political office or more power within
Congress itself depend upon their satisfying a majority of voters
every two or every six years. They are not primarily rewarded or
punished for correctly applying economic theory to a particular problem.

Finally, the perception of an economic problem is often in
inverse proportion to one's degree of formal economic training.
Shoe imports rise and a low-paid worker in Massachusetts loses his
job. He complains to the union and the union drops by to see the
congressman. As far as the economics profession is concerned,
there may yet be no problem. The overall merchandise trade account
may be running a healthy surplus, suggesting that the foreign trade

sector is not forcing any adjustments on the domestic economy.
But the congressman is faced with a decision on which even the political economists are not offering any advice.

All of this is not to say that economics plays no role in the
final disposition of trade and investment issues. The economists
who shaped the Bretton Woods system and those who advocated de-
struction of that system to allow dollar devaluation certainly influenced
the consideration of Burke-Hartke, the Trade Act of 1974, and subsequent legislation. The economists had helped create a climate of
opinion that favored free trade. But what this does suggest is that
the economics profession must increase its awareness of Congress
and the timeliness of public issues if it is to have a larger role in
determining congressional policy.

THE INFLUENCE OF OTHER EVENTS

The legislative course of various trade and investment proposals clearly shows the impact of nontrade-related events on the
congressional consideration of trade legislation. Consideration of
both Burke-Hartke and the proposed Trade Reform Act of 1973 was
colored by the course of economic and political happenings beyond
the halls of Congress. At first it was the growing concern with the
emigration of Soviet Jewry. Tied to an administration proposal to
extend most-favored-nation status to a number of nonmarket economies, the Jackson-Vanik amendment increasingly overshadowed the
debate on the economic questions raised by Burke-Hartke.

The advent of Watergate further deflected congressional attention from the intricacies of foreign trade legislation. To the extent
that concern remained, Watergate tended to focus attention on the
question of delegating powers to the president rather than the gains
or losses to be found in freer trade.

Nor were these the only public issues of considerable note.
The Soviet grain sale aroused considerable consumer ire. The Arab
oil embargo and the continuing economic successes of the OPEC
cartel presented Congress with a series of economic challenges.
Recycling, safety nets, and the possibility of foreign takeovers of
U.S. business all clamored for a spot on Congress's always busy
schedule. The study of foreign trade and investment proposals is
a constant reminder that public concern and congressional attention
are two of the scarcest national commodities.

In 1977 and 1978, continuing inflation, trade deficits, and a
declining international value of the dollar have added to the already
quickening congressional interest in trade issues. President Carter's
decision to push for a new export policy and the prospect of debating

the multilateral trade agreement are sure to make 1979 a major
trade year on Capitol Hill.

ADMINISTRATION INITIATIVES

Although external events played an important role in the consideration of Burke-Hartke, administration initiatives were even
more important. Ranging from an increase in staff for antidumping
problems to a full devaluation, the Nixon administration was a constant reminder of the flexibility and reach of the Executive Branch.
Burke-Hartke certainly had some impact on both the content and the
timing of the administration bill, but the administration appears to
have been more than able to meet most of the protectionist thrusts
by both industry and labor. Where industry was likely to be a major
protectionist force—for instance in textiles or steel—the administration met their needs with voluntary agreements or other special
considerations. Where industry was weak, fragmented, or already
international in character, the administration felt free to ignore
their particular pleadings.

Having once decided on a devaluation, the administration had
immense flexibility in when to proceed with a new legislative proposal. They waited so that devaluation would have a chance to eliminate a merchandise trade deficit by the time the Ways and Means
Committee would move to serious consideration of the trade bill.
As it turned out, devaluation and worldwide agricultural shortages
combined to do just that. Perhaps labor's greatest triumph was in
acting as one of the forces that led to devaluation and a tougher U.S.
posture on international economic matters.

In a similar fashion, the Carter administration has been able
to dull the drive for import restrictions by adopting a strategy of
selective accommodation and by attempting to tailor the multilateral
trade agreement to the most active export-oriented and import-
competing groups.

CONGRESSIONAL STRUCTURE AND PERSONALITIES

Despite recent reforms in the Senate and the House of Representatives, the structure for international economic decision making
in Congress remains a hodgepodge. In the early 1970s debate over
foreign trade and investment policy, however, jurisdictional problems
do not seem to have raised much difficulty. The Ways and Means
Committee clearly had jurisdiction of the basic parts of the Burke-
Hartke Bill and serious alternatives never really surfaced. The

administration's proposed Trade Reform Act of 1973 also clearly
fell within the purview of the Ways and Means Committee.

The structure of both the Ways and Means and Finance Committees, however, may have had a substantial effect on trade and
investment legislation. In neither committee were there legislative
subcommittees—all legislation was written and considered by the
full committee. This kept control much more tightly in the hands
of the particular chairman and prevented an aggressive and different-
minded subcommittee chairman from pushing a variant point of view.
In fact, at the time of Burke-Hartke, Ways and Means did not even
have investigative subcommittees that could at least serve as a forum
for interested parties.

Since the time of Burke-Hartke, real change has come to the
Ways and Means Committee. The committee's role as committee
on committees for the Democratic majority has been taken over by
the Democratic Caucus. A larger, more liberal membership has
altered the political balance on the committee. In other words, the
AFL-CIO might now find more indebted if not more sympathetic ears
on the new Ways and Means Committee. The committee also now
has a number of legislative subcommittees, including one on international trade. Burke-Hartke certainly might have fared better
before an international trade subcommittee chaired by Congressman
Burke.

Congressman Charles Vanik, chairman of the still relatively
new Trade Subcommittee of the House Ways and Means Committee,
has demonstrated how active a chairman of a legislative subcommittee might have been in the deliberations leading up to passage
of the Trade Act of 1974. In addition to following the progress of
the multilateral trade negotiations, Vanik has held hearings on a
wide variety of trade proposals; at one point he urged the president
to impose a unilateral surcharge on imports from Japan.

The study also suggests what has by now become commonplace:
personalities do count. Neither Senator Hartke nor Congressman
Burke were chairmen of their respective committees. Differently
placed legislators might have made Burke-Hartke a more serious
contender. Certainly the commanding role of Congressman Mills
had an impact, as did the no less formidable personage of Finance
Chairman Russell Long.

THE PRESS

Economics reaches the congressman through a host of channels.
An influential constituent, a favorite source, personal and committee

staffs all play a part in getting economic information and analyses to the congressman. As noted above, the interest groups are also active in getting their views to the congressman. And, of course, the congressman's individual background conditions his interest and tempers his views on every matter of public policy.

Then there is the press. An evaluation of the importance of the press in the congressional debate on foreign trade and investment policy does not flow so readily from the preceding material and therefore must be treated as largely personal speculation. However, the congressional debate over foreign trade and investment strongly suggest that the national press plays a major role in determining the flow of economic information and analysis to the Congress. Foreign trade, after all, is not generally a matter for the evening news or the wire services. In fact, the congressman relies on four main sources for the press debate on foreign trade policy: the New York Times, the Wall Street Journal, the Washington Post, and the Journal of Commerce.

Particularly during the period leading up to passage of the Trade Act of 1974, labor had great difficulties in getting adequate coverage of its case. Hostile editorial opinion and an overall acceptance of the virtues of free trade made it virtually impossible for labor to move beyond the protectionist label. Business groups, on the other hand, benefited from a largely hospitable editorial page and rather extensive coverage of their individual studies on some of the Burke-Hartke issues.

In addition to general reportage, the importance of economic columnists is generally underrated. Hobart Rowan of the Washington Post and Edwin Dale of the New York Times had a tremendous influence on the flow of economics to the Congress. Dale has since moved to a staff position with the Congress. But Rowan and other economic columnists on the leading national papers continue to have an impact on congressional deliberations.

Why might the national daily press be so powerful in this area? First, because the information is usually stated in simple straightforward terms. Second, because a limited number of papers are read by all the participants in a foreign trade debate. And finally, because congressmen use the national press in the same way businessmen often use the stock market: as a measure of their own performance. A senator is up for election every six years; even a congressman is tested only every two years. In any case, an election is at best only a very general measure of overall performance. The press can help to measure how one did on a particular issue in a particular week.

THE LABOR VIEW AND THE FUTURE OF
FOREIGN ECONOMIC POLICY

The labor break with the free trade coalition has changed the
political equation for foreign trade legislation. That change may or
may not be reflected in trade legislation itself. For instance, the
Nixon administration sought to obtain AFL-CIO support for the Trade
Reform Act of 1973 by proposing to change the law governing unemployment compensation.

How much, then, did the labor drive to the early 1970s affect
the final outcome of the legislative debate over trade and investment
issues? What of the Burke-Hartke Bill? Did a proposal that engendered so much apprehension and precipitated so much activity have,
in the end, very little impact at all? The evidence suggests a much
more sizable role for Burke-Hartke and the interests it represented.

First, the international aspects of Nixon's New Economic Policy
were almost surely colored by protectionist pressures that were so
prominent in the writing of the Trade Act of 1970. The Burke-Hartke
Bill was a product of some of those same forces.

Second, much of the administrative initiatives in the trade
relief area were quite explicit attempts to meet specific import
penetration problems without moving to any overall pattern of restriction. Most of these moves also anticipated the introduction of Burke-
Hartke.

Third, Burke-Hartke played an important part in delaying the
introduction of the administration's trade legislation. No doubt the
lags and uncertainties involved in devaluation and the vagaries of
presidential politics were also major factors.

Fourth, for the first time Burke-Hartke challenged the multinational firm on explicitly economic grounds. Although unsuccessful
in its first attempt, labor did succeed in posing a series of questions
that are not yet answered. And many of the Burke-Hartke proposals
with regard to the multinationals are still very much alive.

Fifth, Burke-Hartke forced the Congress and the foreign trade
policy community in Washington to take more seriously the trade
and investment pressures on specific industries or communities.
Burke-Hartke acted as something of an intellectual lightening rod:
as long as one was against Burke-Hartke one's free trade credentials
were preserved. In many ways Burke-Hartke made "safeguards"
an acceptable part of the free trader's lexicon.

But what about the trade bill itself? Are there traces of Burke-
Hartke thought that actually passed into law? The Trade Act of 1974
did contain a number of changes in the way an increase in imports
was to be treated. Many of these new methods reflected specific
proposals contained in the Burke-Hartke Bill. But then, many of

those proposals had been made by past administrations and received broad support throughout both the labor and the business communities. The far ranging policies contained in Burke-Hartke seem to have made temporary import restraints more acceptable.

Only in a series of limitations imposed on the Generalized System of Preferences (GSP) did labor have an obvious influence in the actual language of the bill.[4] Originally conceived as a means to spur exports from the developing to the developed countries, labor was quick to see the proposal as nothing more than a further opportunity for the multinationals to shift production to low-wage countries. Instead of viewing GSP as a trade, not aid, type of proposal, labor saw it as an extension of the Item 807 type loophole that encouraged production of labor-intensive activities in low-wage areas.

In place of the admittedly restricted proposal made by the administration, GSP emerged heavily burdened by a number of limitations. The law specifically declares certain articles and categories of articles ineligible for GSP treatment. Watches and "textile and apparel articles which are subject to textile agreements" are two of the banned items.[5] A number of footwear items are also ineligible. The president is constrained from designating for GSP treatment any steel, electronic, or semimanufactured and manufactured glass products that are import-sensitive. In addition, "any other articles which the President determines to be import-sensitive in the context of the Generalized System of Preferences" will be denied GSP status.[6] Goods that are the subject of an escape clause or certain other administrative actions are also ineligible. Why such a tide of restrictions in a relatively unimportant section of the law? Aside from the "finger in the dike" argument, the AFL-CIO could show concrete results for every constituent union that had suffered severe import competition.

Labor did succeed in raising many of the issues that have dominated the congressional debate over foreign economic policy throughout the 1970s: the impact of the multinational corporation on domestic employment and production; the impact of technology flows on the U.S. changing comparative advantage; and the question of how best to protect individual import-competing industries. Gradually the labor fear about the U.S. changing place in the world economy has crept into the national mind. There has been a slow shift in opinion that has touched the academic community as well as the world of Washington. Suddenly there is greater recognition of the pains of adjustment that may accompany rising imports and other economic change.[7] In the Congress and elsewhere throughout the country there is also a growing perception that the rest of the world plays by a different, less liberal set of trade rules.

218 / TRADE, TAXES, & TRANSNATIONALS

All this has not come about solely as a result of labor's initiatives in the field of foreign trade and investment. The record trade deficits and sharp fall in the international value of the dollar have brought international economics from the financial page to front page headlines. The Carter administration's decision to intervene massively in foreign exchange markets to support the dollar was a tacit admission that the country could not rely on flexible exchange rates to solve all our trade problems. A dollar value low enough to balance our trade accounts in a slow-growth world implied international financial instability and considerable domestic inflation.

Prominent economists and politicians have suggested a surcharge on imports as the best way to stabilize the dollar and an effective device to open up new markets for U.S. exports. In effect, they are questioning whether the United States can simultaneously meet its international monetary responsibilities and still maintain its position of leadership in fostering a world economy open to the free flow of goods and capital.

The early 1970s were marked by a national struggle to adjust to a changed international economy. An "arrogance of economic power" was finally taking its toll. Caught between the success of postwar reconstruction and the rigidities of the Bretton Woods system, it was hardly surprising that the Congress was subjected to a rising tide of protectionist sentiment. The democratic shoe (perhaps an imported one) was beginning to pinch rather badly. In this context, Burke-Hartke appears as the fullest flower of much of the protectionist effort. In part, Burke-Hartke was the AFL-CIO's comprehensive attempt to slow the pace of change brought on by the workings of the international economy.

The rapid growth of the multinational enterprise, the U.S. growing vulnerability to international competition, and the limitations of the Trade Expansion Act of 1962 had combined to bring big labor and big business into very direct confrontation. And if their battle over Burke-Hartke is in the least bit representative, it suggests that in all but national controversies—such as Vietnam or busing to achieve racial balance—major interest groups may determine the content and direction of a congressional debate.

Interest group behavior in the Burke-Hartke controversy marked a sharp change from previous foreign trade disputes. In the past, much of American business has opposed foreign trade liberalization, or had been so divided as to greatly weaken its influence. Although labor had not made foreign trade a top priority in the past, it had generally supported the free trade position. Burke-Hartke represented a new set of labor priorities and an apparent reversal of labor's position in support of the Trade Expansion Act of 1962.

Just as striking as the predominance of big labor and big business was the relative inactivity of a variety of other interests. Mingled with a series of special pleaders were a few public interest groups that generally praised free trade and world economic order. There is no indication that any of these groups had a major impact on the Burke-Hartke-inspired debate on foreign trade and investment policy.

Any alternative to the current pattern of foreign economic policy making must add some other forces to the equation. Although vitally affected by both trade and investment, consumer groups were relatively inactive throughout the debate. Groups that focused on the domestic problems of the environment or occupational safety and health seemed unaware of the foreign economic policy implications of their positions. And finally, there were few technical specialists acting in a reform capacity. The complicated world of congressional tax policy is currently watched by both a Nader organization and the Washington-based Tax Analysts and Advocates. There is nothing comparable in the foreign trade and investment fields.

Since the introduction of Burke-Hartke, new circumstances have brought other international economic issues to the fore. Devaluation of the dollar and the regime of flexible exchange rates have had an important role in correcting the imbalances of the Bretton Woods system. Flexible rates have also tended to retard the flow of U.S. capital abroad both by allowing the value of foreign currencies to move upward in response to capital flows and by improving the competitive position of many U.S. manufacturers.

The steady stream of new problems and the ameliorating effects of flexible exchange rates have not, however, restored the old free trade alliance. There was really no reason to suspect that flexible rates would remove all sources of friction from the trade field. After all, flexible rates do not assure protection to any particular line of products. Differential rates of productivity growth or increases in costs will continue to alter the nature of comparative advantage in various countries.

The current system of flexible exchange rates is far from a perfect float. There is ample evidence that the central banks of a number of industrial countries have intervened to limit the appreciation of their currencies. The intervention is almost always made to preserve an existing export market or to prevent too precipitous a fall in the cost of competing imports.

It is interesting to note that the leading OECD countries have maintained the existing structure of export subsidies despite the advent of flexible exchange rates. The maintenance of these subsidies may reflect the fact that they are subject to discussion at the multilateral trade negotiations in Geneva. They may also indicate a desire by the industrial countries to maintain their export-oriented industries. Under flexible exchange rates a U.S. export subsidy will still tend to increase exports, although the subsidy-induced increase in the value of dollars will mitigate the impact of the subsidy and tend to increase the level of imports. Trade grows, export-oriented industries prosper, and import-competing industries are subjected to added pressure. To the AFL-CIO leadership, that particular path looks much like the one that precipitated the same type of pressures that spawned Burke-Hartke. Nor has devaluation reduced labor's concern about the international mobility of capital. The U.S.-based multinational companies are continuing to expand their international operations, albeit at a somewhat slower pace than occurred in the 1960s.

There is every indication that big labor and big business will continue to take different positions on foreign trade and investment issues. The continuing growth of the U.S.-based multinationals promises to increase their importance to the world economy. The gradual movement to international codes of conduct for multinationals and the increasingly forceful policies of host countries should make the U.S. multinational somewhat more dependent on the actions of the U.S. government. That in turn will invite more evaluation of their policies in a public forum. For its part, the AFL-CIO has remained adamant in its support of policies contained in the Burke-Hartke Bill. If anything, there has been even more emphasis on the provisions that would strike most directly at the multinational corporation.

The tax aspects of Burke-Hartke have a potentially broader base of support because they can be related to tax reform as well as to trade and investment issues. Not surprisingly, the AFL-CIO has concentrated its attention on the practice of taxing the foreign-source income of U.S. subsidiaries only when repatriated. Repeal of the deferral provision has attracted considerable academic support and is generally accepted by the liberal tax reform elements of the Congress. Also, deferral is not nearly as important to the multinational firms as is the foreign tax credit. Business opposition might be somewhat muted.

Senator Hartke again led the way in the Senate. He succeeded in securing Senate agreement to a repeal of the deferral privilege. [8] Added as an amendment to the Tax Reduction Act of 1975, the Hartke provision was eventually dropped in conference. [9] The AFL-CIO remained very active in the effort to repeal deferral during Senate consideration of H.R. 10612, the Tax Reform Act of 1976. Although the vote was extremely close, the combination of labor and liberal tax reformers was unable to secure full repeal of the deferral provisions. [10]

The high-water mark for tax reform in the international economic sphere may now have passed. Despite presidential backing, attempts to repeal deferral were unsuccessful in the 95th Congress. In addition, the 95th Congress restored liberal treatment to the overseas earnings of Americans working abroad.

In many ways, the current labor view of foreign trade and investment dates to union-backed attempts to repeal Item 807.00 of the Tariff Schedules of the United States. Under the 807 system, components could be manufactured domestically, shipped abroad for assembly, reimported, and a duty would be applied only to the value added abroad. In early 1976 the International Ladies Garment Workers Union led a concerted drive to secure the elimination of Item 807. Although they had the active support of the AFL-CIO, the effort to repeal Item 807 has not yet met with any success. Union interest, however, is still very much alive.

The AFL-CIO continues to be concerned about the future implications of the Generalized System of Preferences. To many in the union movement, GSP will act principally as another means by which the multinational companies will use the developing world as an export platform directed at the United States and other developed economies. Interestingly, the more traditionally free-trade-oriented UAW has begun to express a similar concern. The UAW has opposed the extension of GSP status to Mercedes Benz truck chassis from Brazil and to ball bearings from Singapore. In the case of Singapore, the local firm was a subsidiary of a Japanese multinational.[11]

There are still substantial differences between the trade posture of the UAW and that of the AFL-CIO. But the UAW has begun to feel the pressure of foreign sourcing decisions made in Detroit. Ford decided to ship engines from Brazil to an Ontario, Canada, plant that replaced exports from Lima, Ohio, and displaced some UAW members. Chrysler's decision to purchase major components from Volkswagen (drive trains and engines) has direct implications for UAW members. Trade adjustment assistance has already been awarded in response to export of automotive components from Mexico.[12] At the March 1976 collective bargaining session of the UAW, a motion from the floor made the importation of component parts part of the collective bargaining package with Ford.[13] One UAW staff person thought the foreign sourcing problem could become so severe that it might force a change in the UAW's all but unbroken commitment to free trade.

The broad spectrum of trade and investment issues did not constitute a top labor priority in either the 94th or the 95th Congress. The economic recession of 1974-75 and the presidential election of 1976 occupied a considerable share of the AFL-CIO's resources. With a Democrat in the White House for the first time in eight years, labor pushed for labor law reform and broad social measures such as the Humphrey-Hawkins Bill. And a full legislative program ranging from health care to more narrowly defined labor issues put considerable demands on the AFL-CIO's small but talented legislative and research staffs.

But the concern about trade and investment issues remains very much alive. And the groundwork has been laid for a future effort. The time-consuming process of internal education to the Burke-Hartke issues is largely complete. There has even been a shift in the attitude of some of the service unions. The point has been made that the whole community can suffer when local industry has been shifted abroad or severely injured by import competition. [14] Current changes in the UAW posture might eventually lead to a unified labor movement in the next major trade or investment battle.

In the 95th Congress there was a discernible trend toward a united front between business and labor in particular industries (such as steel and textiles) and on certain issues (opposition to the extension of the countervailing duty waiver). Broader links with various parts of the business community could put labor in a stronger position in future legislative contests over trade and investment.

Although the last decade has seen multinational firms on the defensive both at home and abroad, they are not without considerable resources. Their adaptability shows clearly in the response of the multinational corporations to reform efforts in the tax area. In the battles over deferral and the Domestic International Sales Corporation the multinational firms have shown considerable ability to mobilize the support of workers in export-oriented industries, a tactic that was initiated in the midst of the Burke-Hartke struggle. Their success suggests that although some forces are working for labor unity on trade and investment issues, there is also a tendency for workers to split along export-oriented or import-competing lines.

The future of foreign economic policy in the trade and investment field will surely depend on a variety of imponderables. Dollar devaluation and a regime of flexible exchange rates have prevented some of the major trade distortions that occurred during the 1960s, but they have not brought the United States the hoped-for stability in its trade accounts. The size of the future trade deficits, the strength of the dollar in international markets, and the general health of the domestic economy are important but uncertain factors in determining the course of future foreign economic policy.

In addition, the changing climate of U.S. opinion has probably made trade restrictions a little more respectable than they were in the early 1970s. Labor now has a friend at the head of an active trade subcommittee where once there was no subcommittee at all. With new procedures and more power at the command of both individ-

ual senators and congressmen, any popular swing toward protectionism might be more readily translated into legislation. The very
newness of the Congress in the sense of membership turnover may
put the Congress much closer to grass roots economic questions,
rather than to broader matters of international economic policy.

Clearly, the seeds for further discord in this area of economic
policy making are still present. Economic theory suggests persistent
differences of interest between big labor and big business. The continuing power of the multinational firm constitutes a constant challenge
to the far less mobile resources of big labor. And the pressure of
the developing world for greater access to the industrial markets of
the developed world could bring further dislocations in the domestic
job market. The 1980s will be a troubled and tumultuous period for
international economic policy.

NOTES

1. In passing the Trade Act of 1974, the Congress sought to
make some headway in achieving comparability in export, import,
and production data. See Trade Act of 1974, 93-618, Title VI,
Sec. 608.

2. McGee's analysis of the potential costs of the Burke-
Hartke quota provisions was one of the few timely evaluations of
the bill. See Stephen McGee, "The Welfare Effects of Restrictions
on U.S. Trade," Brookings Papers on Economic Activity, No. 3
(Washington, D.C.: Brookings Institution, 1973), pp. 686-707.

3. C. Fred Bergsten, ed., The Future of the International
Order: An Agenda for Research (Lexington, Mass.: Lexington Books,
1973). See especially Chapter I, pp. 17-30.

4. Trade Act of 1974, Title V., P.L. 93-618.

5. Trade Act of 1974, Sec. 503(c)(1)(A) and (B), P.L. 93-618.
The original administration bill had contained only certain general
prohibitions. The specific limitations were added in the Senate.

6. Trade Act of 1974, Sec. 503(c)(g), P.L. 93-618.

7. For instance, see testimony of David Richardson before
the Joint Economic Committee, The 1978 Midyear Review of the
Economy, Hearings before the Joint Economic Committee, 95th
Cong., 2d sess., Part 2 (Washington, D.C.: U.S. Government
Printing Office, 1978).

8. See Congressional Record, March 19, 1975, S4361-70.
Somewhat surprisingly, the Hartke amendment no. 161 passed 73 to
34 (S4370).

9. The Tax Reduction Act of 1975 (P.L. 94-12) did include
some new limitations on the use of deferral by changing the Subpart

F rules. The act repealed the minimum distribution rule and the developing country provision. The 30 percent rule was reduced to 10 percent and the deferral of tax on shipping profits was removed unless the income is actually invested in shipping operations. See Susan Drake, Jane G. Gravelle, and Harold A. Kohnen, "The Tax Reduction Act of 1975, P.L. 94-12 (H.R. 2166); The Legislative Development of Each Provision, Including Those Items Not Adopted," Congressional Research Service, April 11, 1975, p. 56.

10. The debate on the Hartke amendment can be found in the Congressional Record for June 29, 1976, pp. S10987-S11018. The Hartke amendment was eventually tabled by a vote of 47 to 43. The motion to reconsider the vote to table was defeated by 45 to 44. An AFL-CIO staff person actively involved in the deferral fight suggested that the vote was not quite as close as it appeared. According to this staffer, Senator Long called in only enough votes to secure a victory.

11. June 1976 interview at the UAW.

12. Ibid.

13. Ibid. See also "UAW Special Collective Bargaining Convention: Collective Bargaining Program" (Detroit: UAW, March 1976), pp. 29-31.

14. June 1976 interview at the AFL-CIO.

BIBLIOGRAPHY

Abel, I. W. Statement before the Committee on Ways and Means, U.S. House of Representatives, 93d Cong., 1st sess. on H.R. 6767, The Trade Reform Act of 1973, Part 4. Washington, D.C.: U.S. Government Printing Office, p. 1209.

Abel, I. W., and Floyd E. Smith. In United States International Economic Policy in an Interdependent World. Commission on International Trade and Investment Policy. Washington, D.C.: U.S. Government Printing Office, 1971, pp. 338-42.

AFL-CIO Executive Council. "The Critical Need for New International Trade and Investment Legislation." Atlanta, May 12, 1971.

Auerbach, Stuart. "'Sore Throat' Gives AMA High Fever." Washington Post, July 13, 1975, pp. C1 and C5.

Aufricht, Hans. The International Monetary Fund: Legal Bases, Structure, Functions. New York: Frederick A. Praeger, 1964, pp. 23-24.

Baerresen, Donald W. The Border Industrialization Program of Mexico. Lexington, Mass.: D. C. Heath, 1971.

Baranson, Jack. "Technology Transfer: Effects on U.S. Competitiveness and Employment." In U.S. Department of Labor, The Impact of International Trade and Investment on Employment. Washington, D.C.: U.S. Government Printing Office, 1978, pp. 177-203.

Bailey, Stephen K. Congress Makes A Law. New York: Columbia University Press, 1950.

Bauer, Raymond A., Ithiel de Sola Pool, and Lewis Anthony Dexter. American Business and Public Policy: The Politics of Foreign Trade. Chicago: Aldine, Atherton, 1972 (first published in 1963).

Bell, Philip W. "Private Capital Movements and the U.S. Balance of Payments Position." Factors Affecting the United States Balance of Payments. Joint Economic Committee, 87th Cong., 2d sess. Washington, D.C.: U.S. Government Printing Office, 1962.

Bergsten, C. Fred. "The Cost of Import Restrictions to the American Consumer." New York: American Importers Association, 1972.

____. "Crisis in U.S. Trade Policy." Foreign Affairs 49 (June 1971):619-35.

____. The Future of the International Order: An Agenda for Research. Lexington, Mass.: Lexington Books, 1973.

Bergsten, C. Fred, Thomas Horst, and Theodore H. Moran. American Multinationals and American Interests. Washington, D.C.: Brookings Institution, 1978.

Bhagwati, Jagdish. "The Pure Theory of International Trade: A Survey." In Jagdish Bhagwati, Trade Tariffs and Growth. Cambridge, Mass.: The MIT Press, 1969.

Biemiller, Andrew J. Statement before the Committee on Ways and Means, U.S. House of Representatives. Tariff and Trade Proposals, Hearings, Part 4, May 1970. Washington, D.C.: U.S. Government Printing Office, 1970, p. 1001.

____. Statement before the Committee on Ways and Means, U.S. House of Representatives. Foreign Trade and Tariff Proposals, Hearings, Part 3, Washington, D.C.: U.S. Government Printing Office, 1968, pp. 1091-1109.

Bronfenbrenner, Martin. "Japanese-American Economic War? Some Further Reflections," Quarterly Review of Economics and Business 13 (Autumn 1973).

Business International. The Effects of U.S. Corporate Foreign Investment 1960 to 1970. New York, 1972.

Caves, Richard E. "International Corporations: The Industrial Economics of Foreign Investment," Economica 38 (February 1971):1-27.

____. International Trade, International Investment, and Imperfect Markets. Special Papers in International Economics, No. 10, International Finance Section, Department of Economics, Princeton University, 1974.

____. "Multinational Firms, Competition, and Productivity in Host Country Markets," Economica 41 (1974).

____. Trade and Economic Structure. Cambridge, Mass.: Harvard University Press, 1960.

Caves, Richard E., and Ronald W. Jones. World Trade and Payments: An Introduction. Boston: Little, Brown, 1973.

Chamber of Commerce of the United States. Board Rules and Administrative Policies. Washington, D.C., 1975.

____. Bylaws of the Chamber of Commerce of the United States. Washington, D.C., 1975. Article VIII, Section I.

____. United States Multinational Enterprise: Report on a Multinational Enterprise Survey (1960-1970). Washington, D.C.:1972.

Chipman, John S. "A Survey of the Theory of International Trade: Part 1: The Classical Theory," Econometrica 33, no. 3 (July 1965).

____. "A Survey of the Theory of International Trade: Part 2, The Neo Classical Theory." Econometrica 33, no. 4 (October 1965).

____. "A Survey of the Theory of International Trade: Part 3, The Modern Theory," Econometrica 34, no. 1 (January 1966).

Christian Science Monitor. "Memories of Smoot-Hawley," Christian Science Monitor, March 15, 1972, p. 16.

____. "Protectionist Action Unlikely in First Trade-Bill Skirmish," Christian Science Monitor, January 27, 1972, p. 9.

Clayman, Jacob. Statement before the Committee on Ways and Means, U.S. House of Representatives. Tariff and Trade Proposals, Hearings, 91st Cong., 2d sess., Part 6 (May 22 and June 1, 1970). Washington, D.C.: U.S. Government Printing Office, 1970, pp. 1776-96.

Colvin, Terrence R., and Donald E. DeKieffer, "A Legal and Economic Analysis of the Quota Provisions of the Proposed Foreign Trade and Investment Act of 1972." International Lawyer 6, no. 4 (1972):771-95.

Corden, W. M. Recent Developments in the Theory of International Trade. Special Papers in International Economics, No. 7, International Finance Section, Department of Economics, Princeton University, 1965.

____. Trade Policy and Economic Welfare. Oxford: Clarendon Press, 1974.

Culhane, Charles. "Economic Report/Labor and Industry Gear for Major Battle over Bill to Curb Imports, Multinationals," National Journal, January 15, 1972, pp. 108-19.

____. "Labor Report/Labor Readies Stronger Jobless-Pay Plan, Rejects Version Offered With Nixon Trade Bill." National Journal, June 8, 1973, pp. 821-30.

____. "Trade Report/Labor Shifts Tactics on Administration Bill, Seeks Concessions on Imports, Multinationals." National Journal, July 28, 1973, pp. 1091-98.

____. "Washington Pressures/UAW Narrows Lobbying Focus, Stresses Issues Vital to Members." National Journal, July 3, 1971, pp. 1405-16.

Dahl, R. A., and C. E. Lindblom. Politics, Economics and Welfare. New York: Harper, 1953.

Dale, Edwin L., Jr. "Should We Forget About Trade," New York Times, March 18, 1973, Section 4, p. 3.

____. "'Situation Report' on an Import Bill," New York Times, January 23, 1972, Section 3, p. 5.

Dam, Kenneth W. The GATT: Law and International Economic Organization. Chicago: University of Chicago Press, 1970.

Denison, E. The Sources of Economic Growth in the United States and Alternatives Before Us. New York: Committee for Economic Development, 1962.

Dietsch, Robert W. "Maneuvering Around Tariff Barriers." New Republic, April 21, 1973, p. 10.

Dodd, Lawrence C., and Bruce I. Oppenheimer. "The House in Transition." In Lawrence C. Dodd and Bruce I. Oppenheimer,

<u>Congress Reconsidered</u>. New York: Praeger Publishers, 1977, pp. 21-53.

Downs, Anthony. <u>An Economic Theory of Democracy</u>. New York: Harper, 1957.

Drake, Susan, Jane G. Gravelle, and Harold A. Kohnen. "The Tax Reduction Act of 1975, P.L. 94-12 (H.R. 2166); The Legislative Development of Each Provision, Including Those Items Not Adopted." Washington, D.C.: Congressional Research Service, April 11, 1975.

Emergency Committee for American Trade. <u>The Role of the Multi-national Corporation (MNC) in the United States and World Economies</u>. Washington, D.C., 1972.

Evans, John W. <u>The Kennedy Round in American Trade Policy: The Twilight of the GATT?</u> Cambridge, Mass.: Harvard University Press, 1971.

Fenno, Richard F. <u>The Power of the Purse: Appropriations Politics in Congress</u>. Boston: Little, Brown, 1966.

Fowlkes, Frank V. "Business Report/House Turns to Protectionism Despite Arm-Twisting by Nixon Trade Experts." <u>National Journal</u>, August 8, 1970, pp. 1815-21.

____. "Economic Report/Administrative Escape Valves Relieve Pressures of Imports on Domestic Industries." <u>National Journal</u>, July 24, 1971, pp. 1544-50.

Frank, Richard S. "Economic Report/Improved Balance of Payments Prospect Prompts End to Controls on Foreign Investment." <u>National Journal</u>, June 2, 1973, pp. 809-15.

____. "Economic Report/Shultz Takes Charge as United States Presses for Monetary, Trade Reforms." <u>National Journal</u>, March 10, 1973, pp. 352-58.

____ "Trade Report/Administration Asks for Trade Sanctions Against Balance of Payments Offenders." <u>National Journal</u>, March 31, 1973, p. 472.

____. "Trade Report/Administration's Reform Bill Threatened by Dispute Over Relations With Russia." <u>National Journal</u>, December 24, 1973, pp. 1741-52.

____. "Trade Report/Administration Seeks Incentives to Spur Exports in Drive to Correct Huge Trade Deficit." National Journal, April 21, 1973, pp. 557-66.

____. "Trade Report/Administration Torn Between Domestic, Overseas Interests in Drafting Trade Bill." National Journal, January 13, 1973, pp. 44-53.

____. "Trade Report/Black Olives and Ball Bearings Lobby Groups Attempt to Restrict Competing Foreign Imports." National Journal, August 8, 1973, pp. 1224-25.

____. "Trade Report/Consumer Movement Shifts Tactics, Not Goals in Legal Attack on Steel Quotas." National Journal, August 5, 1972, pp. 1258-66.

____. "Trade Report/Consumers Union Attack on Steel Quotas Could Release Protectionist Pressures." National Journal, July 7, 1972, pp. 1229-1326.

____. "Trade Report/White House Assembles Trade Specialists to Guide Nixon Bill Through Congress." National Journal, May 5, 1973, pp. 692-97.

____. "Washington Pressures/Multinationals Mobilize to Preserve Favorable Tax Status on Overseas Income." National Journal, July 14, 1973, pp. 1019-28.

Frank, Robert H., and Richard T. Freeman. "The Distributional Consequences of Direct Foreign Investment." In U.S. Department of Labor, The Impact of International Trade and Investment on Employment. Washington, D.C.: U.S. Government Printing Office, 1978, pp. 139-51.

Frankel, Marvin. "Home Versus Foreign Investment: A Case Against Capital Export." Kyklos 18, no. 3 (1965):411-33.

Friedlin, J. N., and L. A. Lupo. "U.S. Direct Investment Abroad in 1973." Survey of Current Business 54, no. 8, Part II (August 1974):11-24.

Fulda, Carl H. "Adjustment to Hardship Caused by Imports: The New Decisions of the Tariff Commission and the Need for Legislative Clarification." Michigan Law Review 70, no. 5 (April 1972):791-830.

Gilpin, Robert. The Multinational Corporation and the National Interest. Prepared for the Committee on Labor and Public Welfare, U.S. Senate. Washington, D.C.: U.S. Government Printing Office, 1973.

____. Technology, Economic Growth and International Competitiveness. Subcommittee on Economic Growth of the Joint Economic Committee, Washington, D.C.: U.S. Government Printing Office, 1975.

____. U.S. Power and the Multinational Corporation. New York: Basic Books, 1975.

Goode, Richard. The Corporation Income Tax. New York: John Wiley, 1951.

Government Research Company. The Politics of Foreign Trade, Tax and Investment Policy. Washington, D.C., 1972.

Graduate Institute of International Studies (A Study Group). The European Free Trade Association and the Crisis of European Integration. New York: The Humanities Press, 1968.

Gravelle, Jane et al. "Tax Expenditures: Compendium of Background Material on Individual Provisions." Committee on the Budget, U.S. Senate. Washington, D.C.: U.S. Government Printing Office, March 17, 1976.

Habakkuk, H. J. American and British Technology in the Nineteenth Century: The Search for Labor-Saving Inventions. Cambridge: Cambridge University Press, 1962.

Haberler, Gottfried. A Survey of International Trade Theory. Special Papers in International Economics, No. 1, International Finance Section, Department of Economics, Princeton University, 1961.

Harberger, A. "The Incidence of the Corporation Income Tax." Journal of Political Economy, June 1962.

Hawkins, Robert G. "U.S. Multinational Investment in Manufacturing and Domestic Economic Performance." New York: International Economic Policy Association, 1972.

Hellawell, Robert. "The United States Income Taxation and Less Developed Countries: A Critical Appraisal." Columbia Law Review, December 1966, pp. 1393-1427.

Horst, Thomas. "The Impact of American Investments Abroad on U.S. Exports, Imports, and Employment." In U.S. Department of Labor, The Impact of International Trade and Investment on Employment. Washington, D.C.: U.S. Government Printing Office, 1978, pp. 139-51.

Hufbauer, G. C., and F. M. Adler. Overseas Manufacturing Investment and the Balance of Payments. Tax Policy Research Study No. 1. Washington, D.C.: U.S. Treasury Department, 1968.

Hughes, Kent. "Factor Prices, Capital Intensity, and Technological Adaptation in Brazil." In Contemporary Brazil: Issues in Economic and Political Development, edited by H. Jon Rosenbaum and William Tyler. New York: Praeger Publishers, 1972.

Hunt, Albert R. "Labor, Business Square Off in Trade Fight Even Though Key Bill Has No Chance in '72," Wall Street Journal, May 15, 1972, p. 34.

Jasey, A. E. "The Social Choice Between Home and Overseas Investment," Economic Journal 70, no. 277 (March 1960): 105-13.

Johnson, Harry G. "An Economic Theory of Protectionism, Tariff Bargaining and the Formation of Customs Unions." Journal of Political Economy 73, no. 3 (June 1965): 256-83.

____. International Trade and Economic Growth. London: George Allen and Unwin, 1958.

Jones, R. W. "Factor Proportions and the Heckscher-Ohlin Model." Review of Economic Studies 24 (1956-57).

Journal of Commerce. "Burke-Hartke Bill Seen Striking Hard Blow to State," Journal of Commerce, April 18, 1973, p. 11.

____. "'Hands Off' World Trade Urged." Journal of Commerce, August 17, 1972, p. 9.

____. "Hartke Bill's Tax Steps Scored." Journal of Commerce, June 28, 1972, p. 3.

Karlik, John R., and Stephen B. Watkins. Anticipating Disruptive Imports. U.S. Congress, Joint Economic Committee, 95th Cong., 2d sess. Washington, D.C.: U.S. Government Printing Office, 1978.

Kemp, Murray. "Foreign Investment and the National Advantage." Economic Record, March 1962.

____. "The Gain from International Trade and Investment: A Neo-Heckscher-Ohlin Approach." American Economic Review 6, no. 4, Part 1 (September 1966): 788–809.

Kenen, P. B. "Economic Aspects of Private Direct Investment." Taxation and Operations Abroad. Tax Institute of America, 1960.

Kindleberger, Charles P. Foreign Trade and the National Economy. New Haven, Conn.: Yale University Press, 1962.

Kravis, I. "Availability and Other Influences on the Commodity Composition of Trade." Journal of Political Economy 64 (April 1956).

Kreinin, Mordechai E. "Comparative Labor Effectiveness and the Leontief Scarce-Factor Paradox." American Economic Review, March 1965, pp. 131–40.

____. International Economics: A Policy Approach, 2d ed. New York: Harcourt Brace Jovanovich, 1975.

Kujawa, Duane, ed. American Labor and the Multinational Corporation. New York: Praeger Publishers, 1973.

Laing, N. "Factor Price Equalization in International Trade and Returns to Scale." Economic Record 37 (September 1961).

Leontief, Wassily. "Domestic Production and Foreign Trade: The American Capital Position Re-Examined." Economica Internazionale 7 (1954).

Linder, S. An Essay on Trade and Transformation. New York: John Wiley, 1961.

MacDougall, G. D. A. "The Benefits and Costs of Private Investments from Abroad: A Theoretical Approach." Bulletin of the Oxford University Institute of Statistics, August 1960.

McGee, Stephen P. "The Welfare Effects of Restrictions on U.S. Trade." Brookings Papers on Economic Activity, No. 3 (1972), pp. 669-74.

Manley, John F. The Politics of Finance: The House Committee on Ways and Means. Boston: Little, Brown, 1970.

Meany, George. Statement before the Committee on Ways and Means, U.S. House of Representatives, 87th Cong., 2d sess. on The Trade Expansion Act of 1962, Part 2. Washington, D.C.: U.S. Government Printing Office, pp. 1148, 1150, and 1160.

_____. Statement before the Subcommittee on International Trade of the Committee on Finance, 92d Cong., 1st sess. on World Trade and Investment Issues, Part 1. Washington, D.C.: U.S. Government Printing Office, 1971, pp. 167-213.

Meerhaeghe, M. A. G. van. International Economic Institutions. New York: St. Martins Press, 1971, pp. 90 et seq.

Meier, Gerald M. Problems of Trade Policy. Oxford: Oxford University Press, 1973.

Metzger, Stanley D. Trade Agreements and the Kennedy Round. Fairfax, Va.: Coiner Publications, 1963.

Minhas, B. S. "The Homohypallagic Production Function, Factor Intensity Reversals, and the Heckscher-Ohlin Theorem." Journal of Political Economy 70 (April 1962).

Mintz, Ilse. U.S. Import Quotas: Costs and Consequences. Washington, D.C.: American Enterprise Institute for Public Policy Research, 1973.

Monroe, Wilbur F. International Monetary Reconstruction: Problems and Issues. Lexington, Mass.: D. C. Heath, 1974.

Mundell, R. A. "International Trade and Factor Mobility." American Economic Review 47 (June 1957).

Musgrave, Peggy. Direct Investment Abroad and the Multinationals: Effects on the United States Economy. Subcommittee on Multinational Corporations, Committee on Foreign Relations, 94th Cong., 1st sess. Washington, D.C.: U.S. Government Printing Office, 1975.

____. "Tax Preferences to Foreign Investment." In The Economics of Federal Subsidy Programs, Part 2, Joint Economic Committee, 92d Cong., 2d sess. Washington, D.C.: U.S. Government Printing Office, 1972.

____. United States Taxation of Foreign Investment Income: Issues and Arguments. Cambridge, Mass.: The Law School of Harvard University, 1969.

Musgrave, Richard A., and Peggy B. Musgrave. Public Finance in Theory and Practice. New York: McGraw-Hill, 1973.

National Association of Manufacturers. The U.S. Stake in World Trade and Investment: The Role of the Multinational Corporation. New York, 1971.

Nenneman, Richard. "Jobs: Key Issue Behind Trade Talks." Christian Science Monitor, February 17, 1973, p. 4.

New Republic. "Economic Warfare." New Republic, December 4, 1971, p. 7.

New York Times. "Labor's Protectionist Swing." New York Times, March 4, 1973, Section 3, p. 2.

Ohlin, Bertil. Interregional and International Trade, Harvard Economic Studies, Vol. 39. Cambridge, Mass.: Harvard University Press, 1939.

Oppenheimer, Bruce Ian. Oil and the Congressional Process: The Limits of Symbolic Politics. Lexington, Mass.: D. C. Heath, 1974.

Ornstein, Norman J., Robert L. Peabody, and David W. Rohde. "The Changing Senate: From the 1950s to the 1970s." In Congress Reconsidered, edited by Lawrence C. Dodd and Bruce I. Oppenheimer. New York: Praeger Publishers, 1977, pp. 3-20.

Pechman, Joseph A., and Stanley S. Surrey. "Compendium of Papers on Tax Reform." Prepared at the Request of Individual Members of the U.S. Senate, Washington, D.C., June 7, 1976.

Peterson, Peter G. The United States in the Changing World Economy, Vol. II: Background Material. Washington, D.C.: U.S. Government Printing Office, 1972.

Pincus, J. J. "Pressure Groups and the Pattern of Tariffs." Journal of Political Economy 83, no. 4 (1975): 757-78.

Pizer, Samuel. "Capital Restraint Programs." In Commission on International Trade and Investment Policy, United States International Economic Policy in an Interdependent World. Washington, D.C.: U.S. Government Printing Office, 1971, pp. 87-112.

Pregelj, Vladimir. "Burke-Hartke Bill and Other Major Trade Legislation in the 93rd Congress." Washington, D.C., Congressional Research Service, Library of Congress, February 5, 1973.

____. "Item 807.00 of the Tariff Schedules of the United States: Selected Facts and Comments." Washington, D.C., Congressional Research Service, Library of Congress, 1976.

____. Multinational Firm and Its Implications for the United States Foreign Trade Policy. Washington, D.C., Congressional Research Service, Library of Congress, 1971, p. 10.

Reddaway, W. B. et al. Effects of U.K. Direct Investments Overseas: An Interim Report. Cambridge: Cambridge University Press, 1967.

Ricardo, David. The Principles of Political Economy and Taxation. New York: Penguin, 1971.

Ross, Irwin. "Labor's Big Push for Protectionism." Fortune, March 1973, pp. 92 et seq.

____. "We Must Stop This Isolationist Trade Bill." Readers Digest, August 1972, pp. 150-53.

Rowen, Hobart. "AFL-CIO Quota Drive Ignores Consumer." Washington Post, August 9, 1970, Section E, p. 1.

____. "Burke-Hartke Bill: Higher Prices, Fewer Jobs." Washington Post, March 5, 1972.

____. "Cost of Tariff Barriers Put Over $7.5 Million." Washington Post, March 5, 1973, p. D12.

____. "Proposals for Trade Quotas Could Harm All Consumers." Washington Post, January 23, 1972, Section E, p. 1.

_____. "UAW Points the Way." Washington Post, May 4, 1972, p. A27.

Ruttenberg, Stanley H. and Associates. Needed: A Constructive Foreign Trade Policy. Washington, D.C.: Industrial Union Department, AFL-CIO, 1971.

Scammell, W. M. International Monetary Policy: Bretton Woods and After. New York: John Wiley, 1975.

Schattschneider, E. D. Politics, Pressures and the Tariff. Englewood Cliffs, N.J.: Prentice-Hall, 1935.

Shultz, George. In Tariff and Trade Proposals. Hearings before the Committee on Ways and Means, U.S. House of Representatives, 91st Cong., 2d sess., Part 2 of 16 Parts. Washington, D.C.: U.S. Government Printing Office, 1970, pp. 608-13.

Stern, R. M. "Tariffs and Other Measures of Trade Control: A Survey of Recent Developments." Journal of Economic Literature 11, no. 3 (September 1973).

Smith, Adam. An Inquiry into the Nature and Causes of the Wealth of Nations. Middlesex: Penguin Books, 1971.

Stolper, W., and Paul A. Samuelson. "Protection and Real Wages." Review of Economic Studies 9 (November 1941).

Townsend, Ed. "Imports Nettle Labor." Christian Science Monitor, July 16, 1971, p. 7.

"UAW Special Collective Bargaining Convention: Collective Bargaining Program." Detroit: United Auto Workers, March 1976, pp. 29-31.

Uekawa, Yasua. "Generalization of the Stolper-Samuelson Theory." Econometrica 39 (March 1971):197-217.

Union Carbide. Union Carbide's International Investment Benefits the U.S. Economy. New York, 1972.

United States Commission on International Trade and Investment Policy. United States International Economic Policy in an Interdependent World. Report, Papers Vol. I and Papers Vol. II. Washington, D.C.: U.S. Government Printing Office, 1971.

U.S. Congress. House. Committee on Banking, Finance, and Urban Affairs. The Implications of our International Trade Policy for American Business and Consumers. Hearings before the Subcommittee on International Trade, Investment, and Monetary Policy of the Committee on Banking, Finance, and Urban Affairs, 95th Cong., 1st sess. Washington, D.C.: U.S. Government Printing Office, 1977.

_____. Trade Policy and Protectionism. Hearings before the Subcommittee on International Trade, Investment, and Monetary Policy of the Committee on Banking, Finance, and Urban Affairs, 95th Cong., 2d sess. Washington, D.C.: U.S. Government Printing Office, 1978.

_____. To Amend and Extend the Export-Import Bank Act of 1945. Hearings before the Subcommittee on International Trade, Investment, and Monetary Policy of the Committee on Banking, Finance, and Urban Affairs, 95th Cong., 2d sess. Washington, D.C.: U.S. Government Printing Office, 1978.

U.S. Congress. House. Committee on Foreign Affairs. Trade Adjustment Assistance. Hearings before the Subcommittee on Foreign Economic Policy. Washington, D.C.: U.S. Government Printing Office, 1972.

U.S. Congress. House. Committee on Ways and Means. Background Material on Selected Trade Legislation Introduced in Connection With Hearings on the Subject of Foreign Trade and Tariffs, by the staff. 93rd Cong., 1st sess., Committee print. Washington, D.C.: U.S. Government Printing Office, 1973.

_____. Briefing Materials Prepared in Connection with Hearings on the Subject of Foreign Trade and Tariffs. 93rd Cong., 1st sess., Committee print. Washington, D.C.: U.S. Government Printing Office, 1973.

_____. Causes and Consequences of the U.S. Trade Deficit and Developing Problems in U.S. Exports. Hearings before the Subcommittee on Trade of the Committee on Ways and Means, 95th Cong., 1st sess. Washington, D.C.: U.S. Government Printing Office, 1977.

_____. Countervailing Duty Waiver Extension. Hearing before the Subcommittee on Trade of the Committee on Ways and Means, 95th Cong., 2d sess. Washington, D.C.: U.S. Government Printing Office, 1978.

____. European Community Restrictions on Imports of United States Specialty Agricultural Products. Hearing before the Subcommittee on Trade of the Committee on Ways and Means, 95th Cong., 1st sess. Washington, D.C.: U.S. Government Printing Office, 1977.

____. Exemption of Certain Products from Tariff Reductions Negotiated in the Multilateral Trade Negotiations (MTN). Hearing before the Subcommittee on Trade of the Committee on Ways and Means, 95th Cong., 2d sess. Washington, D.C.: U.S. Government Printing Office, 1978.

____. Foreign Earned Income Act of 1978. Report, 95th Cong., 2d sess. Washington, D.C.: U.S. Government Printing Office, 1978.

____. Foreign Trade and Tariff Proposals. Hearings, Parts 1-11. Washington, D.C.: U.S. Government Printing Office, 1968.

____. General Tax Reform. Panel Discussions before the Committee on Ways and Means, 93rd Cong., 1st sess., Part 11. Washington, D.C.: U.S. Government Printing Office, 1973.

____. The Impact of International Trade on U.S. Employment—A Survey of Literature. Subcommittee on Trade of the Committee on Ways and Means, 95th Cong., 1st sess. Washington, D.C.: U.S. Government Printing Office, 1977.

____. Import Relief to the U.S. High-Carbon Ferrochromium Industry. Hearing before the Subcommittee on Trade of the Committee on Ways and Means, 95th Cong., 2d sess. Washington, D.C.: U.S. Government Printing Office, 1978.

____. Income Tax Revision. Panel Discussions before the Committee on Ways and Means, 86th Cong., 1st sess. Washington, D.C.: U.S. Government Printing Office, 1959.

____. Legislative History of H.R. 10650, 87th Congress, The Revenue Act of 1962. 90th Cong., 1st sess., Parts 1-4. Washington, D.C.: U.S. Government Printing Office, 1967.

____. Material Relating to Adjustment Assistance for Workers. Prepared in Connection with Hearings on the Subject of Foreign Trade and Tariffs. 93rd Cong., 1st sess., Briefing paper no. 5. Washington, D.C.: U.S. Government Printing Office, 1973.

____. Multilateral Trade Negotiations. Hearing before the Sub-committee on Trade of the Committee on Ways and Means, 95th Cong., 2d sess. Washington, D.C.: U.S. Government Printing Office, 1978.

____. Preliminary Listing of Amendments Proposed to H.R. 6767 The Proposed Trade Reform Act of 1973. Prepared in Connection with Hearings on the Subject of Foreign Trade and Tariffs. 93rd Cong., 1st sess., Briefing paper no. 6. Washington, D.C.: U.S. Government Printing Office, 1973.

____. Press Release and Other Materials Relating to the Administration Proposal Entitled the "Trade Reform Act of 1973," 93rd Cong., 1st sess. Washington, D.C.: U.S. Government Printing Office, 1973.

____. Press Release Summary of Provisions of H.R. 18970, "The Trade Act of 1970," 91st Cong., 2d sess. Washington, D.C.: U.S. Government Printing Office, 1970.

____. Special Duty Treatment of Repeal of Articles Assembled or Fabricated Abroad. Hearing before the Subcommittee on Trade of the Committee on Ways and Means, 94th Cong., 2d sess. Washington, D.C.: U.S. Government Printing Office, 1976.

____. Tariff and Trade Proposals, Parts 1-16. Washington, D.C.: U.S. Government Printing Office, 1970.

____. Trade Reform. Hearings before the Committee on Ways and Means, 93rd Cong., 1st sess., on H.R. 6767, The Trade Reform Act of 1973, Parts 1-15. Washington, D.C.: U.S. Government Printing Office, 1973.

U.S. Congress. Joint Economic Committee. Economic Indicators. Prepared by the Council of Economic Advisers. Various Years.

U.S. Congress. Joint Committee on the Economic Report. Federal Tax Policy for Economic Growth and Stability. Papers Submitted by Panelists Appearing before the Subcommittee on Tax Policy, 84th Cong., 1st sess. Washington, D.C.: U.S. Government Printing Office, 1955.

U.S. Congress, Senate, Committee on Commerce, Science, and Transportation. National Export Program. Hearing, 95th Cong., 2d sess. Washington, D.C.: U.S. Government Printing Office, 1978.

U.S. Congress. Senate. Committee on Finance. Analysis of the Trade Agreements Program and the Trade Reform Act of 1973: Staff Papers Provided by the U.S. Tariff Commission. Washington, D.C.: U.S. Government Printing Office, 1974.

_____. Comparative Analysis of Existing Trade Laws with H.R. 10710—The Trade Reform Act of 1973. Washington, D.C.: U.S. Government Printing Office, 1974.

_____. Executive Branch Organization for International Economic Policy; Material Submitted by the Council on International Economic Policy (CIEP) and the Office of Management and Budget (OMB), in Response to a Committee on Finance Request. Washington, D.C.: U.S. Government Printing Office, 1974.

_____. Foreign Trade. Hearings before the Subcommittee on International Trade, Parts 1 and 2. Washington, D.C.: U.S. Government Printing Office, 1971.

_____. Multinational Corporations: A Compendium of Papers. Submitted to the Subcommittee on International Trade of the Committee on Finance. Washington, D.C.: U.S. Government Printing Office, 1973.

_____. Multinational Corporations. Hearings before the Subcommittee on International Trade of the Committee on Finance, 93rd Cong., 1st sess. Washington, D.C.: U.S. Government Printing Office, 1973.

_____. The Multinational Corporation and the World Economy. 93rd Cong., 1st sess. Washington, D.C.: U.S. Government Printing Office, 1973.

_____. Staff Data and Materials on U.S. Trade and Balance of Payments. Washington, D.C.: U.S. Government Printing Office, 1974.

_____. Summary and Analysis of H.R. 10710—The Trade Reform Act of 1973. Washington, D.C.: U.S. Government Printing Office, 1974.

_____. "Tax Adjustments in International Trade: GATT Provisions and EEC Practices," Executive Branch GATT Studies, 93rd Cong., 2d sess. Washington, D.C.: U.S. Government Printing Office, March 1974, p. 2.

____. Trade Act of 1970. Amendments 925 and 1009 to H.R. 17550, Social Security Amendments of 1970. Hearings, Parts 1 and 2. Washington, D.C.: U.S. Government Printing Office, 1970.

____. The Trade Reform Act of 1973. Hearings, 93rd Cong., 2d sess., on H.R. 10710. Washington, D.C.: U.S. Government Printing Office, 1974.

U.S. Congress, Senate, Committee on Governmental Affairs. The Buy American Act Amendments of 1977. Hearings before the Subcommittee on Federal Spending Practices and Open Government, 95th Cong., 2d sess. Washington, D.C.: U.S. Government Printing Office, 1978.

____. To Creating a Department of International Trade and Investment. Hearing, 95th Cong., 2d sess. Washington, D.C.: U.S. Government Printing Office, 1978.

U.S. Congress. Senate. Committee on Rules and Administration. Standing Rules of the United States Senate. Washington, D.C.: U.S. Government Printing Office, 1975.

U.S. Council of Economic Advisers. Economic Report of the President, 1974. Washington, D.C.: U.S. Government Printing Office, 1974.

U.S. Council on International Economic Policy. Annual Report 1975. Washington, D.C.: U.S. Government Printing Office, 1975.

U.S. Department of Commerce. "Aspects of International Investment." Survey of Current Business 54, no. 8, Part II (August 1974). Washington, D.C.: U.S. Government Printing Office, 1974.

____. "The International Investment Position of the United States: Developments in 1973." Survey of Current Business, August 1974.

____. Survey of Current Business, June 1971, June 1974, August 1974 (Part 11). Washington, D.C.: U.S. Government Printing Office, 1971 and 1974.

____. U.S. Commodity Exports and Imports as Related to Output: 1971 and 1970. Washington, D.C.: U.S. Government Printing Office, 1974.

____. U.S. General Imports (FT/135). Washington, D.C.: U.S. Government Printing Office, 1974.

U.S. Department of Commerce. Bureau of the Census. Highlights of U.S. Export and Import Trade (FT/990), December 1973 and December 1974. Washington, D.C.: U.S. Government Printing Office, 1974 and 1975.

U.S. Department of Commerce. Office of Business Economics. U.S. Business Investments in Foreign Countries. Washington, D.C.: U.S. Government Printing Office, 1960.

U.S. News and World Report. "No Winners in a Trade War—And One is Getting Started." U.S. News and World Report, September 14, 1970, pp. 46-48.

U.S. Tariff Commission. "Economic Factors Affecting the Use of Items 807.00 and 806.30 of the Tariff Schedules of the United States: Report to the President on Investigation No. 332-61 Under Section 332 of the Tariff Act of 1930," TC Publication 339. Washington, D.C., 1970.

____. Implications of Multinational Firms for World Trade and Investment and for U.S. Trade and Labor. Report to the Committee on Finance of the United States Senate and Its Subcommittee on International Trade, On Investigation No. 332-69, Under Section 332 of the Tariff Act of 1930. Washington, D.C.: U.S. Government Printing Office, 1973.

Vernon, Raymond. "International Investment and International Trade in the Product Cycle." Quarterly Journal of Economics 80 (May 1966): 190-207.

Wall Street Journal. "Did Protectionism Create Hitler?" Wall Street Journal, October 1971, p. 20.

____. "The Folly of Protectionism." Wall Street Journal, March 10, 1970, p. 22.

____. "The Unions Against Their Members." Wall Street Journal, April 14, 1972, p. 14.

Walter, Ingo. "How Trade Policy is Made: A Politico-Economic Decision System." In The United States and International Markets: Commercial Policy Options in an Age of Controls, edited by

Robert G. Hawkins and Ingo Walter. Lexington, Mass.: D. C. Heath, 1972, pp. 17-38.

Washington Post. "The Cost of the Textile Quotas." Washington Post, October 18, 1971, p. A22.

Woodcock, Leonard. "Remarks before the National Foreign Trade Convention." New York, November 14, 1972.

INDEX

Abel, I. W., 20, 153, 154, 155, 162-63, 166

abundance, physical definition of, 53

Adler, F. M., 62, 63, 135, 206

Admiral Corp., 119

AFL-CIO (see American Federation of Labor-Congress of Industrial Organizations)

Agricultural Adjustment Act: of 1933, 28n.; of 1956, 28n.

Agricultural Trade Act of 1978, 41, 42

agriculture, and export market, 60-61

AID, 20, 77

Alliance for Progress, 108

American Economic Review, 210

American Farm Bureau Federation, 60, 60n.

American Federation of Labor-Congress of Industrial Organizations (AFL-CIO), 20, 22, 37, 121, 214, 216, 217, 218, 220, 221; Congressional testimony of, 153, 154, 156, 157, 158, 161, 162, 167-70, 178; and direct investment, 110; on DISC, 38; on employment, 119; Industrial Union Department, 21; and interest group behavior, 9, 12, 205, 207; and legislation, 16; on resource mobility, 114; and tariff schedules, 19; trade posture of, 3, 5n., 6n., 18, 19, 58, 124, 130, 194, 221-22

American Importers Association (AIA), 137

American Selling Price system, 18, 21, 156, 190

Andean code, on direct foreign investment, 129

Anglias, 159

antidumping law, 35

Appropriations Committee, House/Senate, 8, 146 (see also Congress)

Aspin, Les, 211

automobiles, 97, 130, 159, 160; import quotas on, 125; tariffs on, 18

Bailey, Stephen K., 8

balance of payments statistics: basic balance, 72-74; and commodity groupings, 78, 80-81; and consumer goods, specific, 70, 82-83; federal subsidies, and exports, 76-77; and inflation, 175; and institutional setting, 86-91; and insurance/freight costs, 77-78; merchandise trade, 74-75, 79; and unemployment, 84-85, 86

Balassa, Bela, 51

ball-bearings, import quotas on, 130, 139

bancor, proposal for, 89, 89n.

banks, central international, proposal for, 89 (see also Export-Import Bank)

Bauer, Raymond A., 7, 59

Bell, Philip W., 62

Bennett, Senator, 158

Bentsen, Lloyd, 40

direct investment theory, 9, 61,
116-17, 116n., 117n., 135-
36, 204
Domestic International Sales
Corporations (DISCs), 38,
42, 133, 135, 155, 156, 158,
175, 178, 179, 192, 222
Douglas, Paul, 211

East India Company, 93-94
East-West Trade Exchange Act
of 1971, 196n.
Eberle, Ambassador, 162
Economic Adjustment Organization Act (EAOA), 36
Eisenhower, Dwight, 7
Electronics Industries Association (EIA), 173, 194-95
electronics industry: employment in, 120; future trends
in, 174; and import competition, 82; protection of, 139,
206; technology in, 164
Emergency Committee for
American Trade (ECAT),
60n., 129, 131n., 137, 163,
171-72, 173, 176
England (see Great Britain)
"escape clause," and imports,
19, 34
Europe, Western: economic
power in, 128; market in,
88; recovery of, 71, 86, 204
European Coal and Steel Community, 92
European Economic Community
(EEC), 71; emergence of, 1;
GNPs in, 87n., 92-94
European Free Trade Association (EFTA), 1, 92
European Payments Unions, 90
exchange rate: control of, and
depression, 90; and inflation,
209; and interest groups, 8;
and trade distortion, 222

Export, Import Bank, 42;
authority of, 41; extension of,
178; and merchandise trade
figures, 77

factor mobility, international, 55
factor price equalization, theorem,
57, 59
f.a.s. (see free along side ship
formula)
Federal Reserve System, 108,
144n., 145n., 189
ferrochromium, high-carbon,
and import relief, 39
Field, John E., 172, 173
Finance Committee, Senate, 12,
36, 39, 40, 209, 214; hearings,
152, 153, 155, 156, 166; Subcommittee on International
Trade, 156-57, 158, 175; and
taxes, 146, 148, 149; and trade
bills, 2 (see also Congress)
Fisher, Joseph, 211
Food for Peace, 77
footwear industry, and import
competition, 82, 198, 206,
211
Ford, Gerald, 16, 197
Ford II, Henry, 158
Ford Motor Company, 158, 159,
221
Ford-Philco Corporation, 119
foreign direct investment theory,
9, 61-65, 128; factor mobility,
61-62; locale selection, 63;
and taxes, 63-64; and technology, 64
Foreign Earned Income Act of
1978, 27n.
Foreign Relations Committee,
Senate, 134 (see also Congress)
Foreign Trade and Investment
Act of 1972, 2-3, 138n. (see
also Burke-Hartke Bill)